The Great Eskimo
Vocabulary Hoax

Geoffrey K. Pullum

The Great Eskimo Vocabulary Hoax

and Other Irreverent Essays on the Study of Language

The University of Chicago Press
Chicago and London

The University of Chicago Press, Chicago 60637
The University of Chicago Press, Ltd., London
© 1991 by The University of Chicago
All rights reserved. Published 1991
Printed in the United States of America
00 99 98 97 96   5 4 3

Library of Congress Cataloging-in-Publication Data

Pullum, Geoffrey K.
    The great Eskimo vocabulary hoax, and other irreverent essays on
the study of language / Geoffrey K. Pullum.
        p.   cm.
    Collection of 23 essays originally appeared in the journal Natural
language and linguistic theory.
    Includes bibliographical references and index.
    ISBN 0-226-68534-9 (paper)
    1. Linguistics.   2. Language and languages.   I. Title.
P27.P85   1991
410—dc20   90-11286
                                                                CIP

∞ The paper used in this publication meets the minimum requirements of
the American National Standard for Information Sciences—Permanence of
Paper for Printed Library Materials, ANSI Z39.48—1984.

Contents

Foreword

A large proportion of the readers of this book will undoubtedly be subscribers to *Natural Language and Linguistic Theory* who experienced four times a year excitement of a sort that the arrival of a scholarly journal in one's mailbox rarely occasions: amidst the sheaf of paper consisting mostly of book advertisements, announcements of lectures that had already been given, and requests for letters of recommendation, one found an envelope that might contain[1] (and four times a year did contain) a journal which had at its end five or six pages that demanded to be read immediately, even if that meant shortening one's lunch hour or waiting until tomorrow to return those books to the library or spending less time than one had intended in preparing a seminar presentation. While Pullum's TOPIC . . . COMMENT column might not be as relevant to one's research as some of the intriguing-sounding articles that were listed above it in *NLLT*'s table of contents, those articles could wait until the weekend but Pullum's column couldn't. Each Pullum column was an exquisitely crafted piece of criticism, satire, fantasy, and/or reporting, dealing entertainingly and provocatively with important issues relating to the ways in which we linguists practice our profession or to the ways in

1. Kluwer Academic Publishers' switch from opaque cardboard to transparent plastic mailing envelopes eliminated the suspense that accompanied the opening of one of their envelopes: the prospect that it might contain a new issue of *NLLT* and a new Pullum TOPIC . . . COMMENT column spurred my fingers to move with unusual rapidity in opening a cardboard envelope bearing Kluwer's return address. Even if I didn't find *Linguistics and Philosophy* and *The Journal of Philosophical Logic* of great relevance to my research, it would have been worth my while to subscribe to one of them, back in the opaque-envelope days, so as to allow my subscription to *NLLT* to realize its full value as a generator of adrenalin.

which the world beyond our journals, classrooms, and conferences impinges on linguistics and its practicioners.

But the first category of readers of this book already know that. What of the other readers of the book, those who know of Pullum's reputation as the H. L. Mencken, Mike Royko, and Hunter Thompson of linguistics but have not yet read the columns that provide the basis for that reputation? My first inclination, in contemplating linguists who have not yet experienced the delight of reading Pullum's TOPIC . . . COMMENT columns, was to urge them to recreate the experience of the first category of readers by reading only one column every three months or so. To really simulate that experience, one would need a computer program to select dates at roughly three-month intervals (dates on which mail is delivered, if this is to be a realistic computer simulation) but not inform the user until the day selected that he is entitled to read one TOPIC . . . COMMENT column that day; the user should then read only that column and close the book without exceeding one's quarterly dose of TOPIC . . . COMMENT. But recalling the classic potato-chip ad in which Bert Lahr looks longingly at the bag of Jay's Potato Chips—or was it Lay's?—and says "I'll only eat one, I'll only eat one," I have concluded that that advice is impractical. Instead, I merely admonish graduate students not to start reading this book while they are preparing for qualifying exams and not to heed their own protestations of "I'll only read one, I'll only read one."[2] Tenured faculty can probably get away with starting the book at any time, but I urge caution on the part of untenured faculty and those employed in nonacademic positions.

While TOPIC . . . COMMENT was pretty much Pullum's column, Pullum did invite a select group of scholars to contribute to it, and the five who responded to that challenge produced fascinating, well-crafted, and perceptive essays: worthy companions to the 23 Pullum columns collected here, in the way that the Art Institute of Chicago's Braques and Miros are worthy companions to its Picassos. I take pride in Pullum's having invited me to do a TOPIC . . . COMMENT column, and I hang my head in shame at never having produced one. Of several fragmentary manuscripts that are lying around my apartment,

---

2. The presumable inability of most linguists to heed Pullum's admonition to "use this book only in small quantities" lends added importance to his advice to use it "only in well-ventilated spaces."

the only one that might actually have yielded an essay that would not tarnish the proud TOPIC . . . COMMENT rubric is one that begins as follows:

Overture to 'Don Giovanni'	*Traditional*
Symphony number eighty-something in a minor key	*Franz Josef Haydn*
Rhapsody on a theme of Rachmaninov	*Niccolo Paganini*
Stars and Stripes Forever	*Johannes Brahms*

That concert-goers will never see a program such as the above is one of the pleasanter consequences of the fact that concert programs are not written by linguists.

Had I devoted to this fragment the amount of work that Pullum put into each of the 23 essays collected here, I probably could have developed it into an amusing diatribe against the shockingly low standards of scholarship that linguists display in their frequent misattributions, nonattributions, vague attributions, and botched attributions; it wouldn't have risen to the Pullum/Picasso level, but it might have entitled me to fancy myself briefly as a linguistic Kandinsky. In another abortive attempt at a TOPIC . . . COMMENT column, I at least came up with a fitting title for a gallery-mate of the Pullum columns: "If we're so smart, why aren't we rich?" That column was to have dealt with the frequent lament of linguists that our profession does not enjoy the widespread respect that is accorded to many scholarly professions. I would regard that complaint as legitimate if linguists could point to riches such as my aborted title hinted at: published volumes giving full details of thorough, robust[3] analyses of the syntax, the phonology, the morphology, and the lexicon of English, Spanish, Chinese, Japanese, and other languages, volumes that one

---

3. A robust analysis isn't one that everyone necessarily agrees on—it's just one whose proponents aren't forced to revise it at every encounter with a fact that they hadn't yet considered seriously. Pullum provides an ostensive definition of "nonrobust" in "The incident of the node vortex problem" (chapter 23).

could expect to go into a second edition.[4] No matter how much faster a linguist's heart beats at seeing his favorite syntactic theory achieve insights into the distribution of *wanna,* those insights won't earn his school of linguistics any respect among nonlinguists until it has extended them into a body of results whose breadth is commensurate with the grandiosity of its claims of generality.

A few paragraphs earlier, I divided the prospective readers of this book into two classes. Those in the first class, who read the TOPIC . . . COMMENT columns as they came out in *NLLT,* are familiar with Geoffrey Pullum not only as a witty commentator on linguistics but also as the author and co-author of a large body of original, perceptive, well-informed, well-argued, and of course well-written articles and books on syntax, semantics, morphology, and phonology. Some of those in the second class of readers will as yet be as unfamiliar with Pullum the linguist as they are with Pullum the linguistic belletrist. I urge such readers to fill this major gap in their linguistic education as quickly as possible, not only for what they will learn thereby about linguistics but for the pleasure that they will derive from seeing linguistics done well and from sharing with Pullum the pride that he takes in getting the details right. It is this pride in craftsmanship more than anything else that marks the TOPIC . . . COMMENT columns and Pullum's more "serious" publications as being the work of the same author, and it is the lack of such pride in craftsmanship that figures in the greatest number of Pullum's gripes about his fellow linguists. The statement that "God resides in the details" has been attributed to Flaubert, Einstein, Mies van der Rohe, Le Corbusier, and probably many others; those who accept that sort of theology will find in this book a religious experience that goes especially well with a pint of brown ale.

James D. McCawley

4. Hey, there's one that Pullum missed in "Some lists of things about books" (chapter 22)—a list of linguistics books that went into a second edition; how many can you think of?

Chapter One

Prologue: The TOPIC . . . COMMENT column

The essays collected in this book were first published in the journal
Natural Language and Linguistic Theory between 1983 and 1989 in
a section bearing the banner TOPIC . . . COMMENT. The idea of having a section of the journal reserved for informal commentary and
opinion was one that antedated the journal itself; the founding editors, Adrian Akmajian, Frank Heny, and Joan Maling, suggested it
to me late in 1981. It would not be the same kind of carefully refereed, thoughtful and scholarly material they would insist on in the
body of the journal, they stressed; it could be more irreverent, more
casual, more controversial. Their idea was that at first I would write
contributions to it, and then offerings by others would be sought,
and, as other linguists began to relate to the genre, there would start
to be more and more contributions from all sorts of people, and a
general opinion column for the field of linguistics would be born.

It sounded like an interesting thing to try, so early in 1982 I began
work on writing the kind of material that they had suggested to me.
It turned out to be quite difficult. The first column published was
'Watch out for the current' (chapter 2), but it was not the first one
written; the story is told in more detail in 'The final curtain' (chapter 24). I persisted, and from the first issue of the journal in 1983
until the end of 1989, every issue carried a TOPIC . . . COMMENT
column.

At the end of this time, however, there was still no sign of any
great upsurge in demand for access among linguists wanting to write
TOPIC . . . COMMENT columns. In fact, linguists were disdaining the
task in droves. They were lining up behind one another to avoid vol-
unteering their services. Only five linguists other than myself ever
published in the section (though a couple of shorter letters were also
published). It is not clear whether pressure of other commitments, a

disinclination to go in for nonscholarly writing, or fear of the consequences was the cause, but hardly anyone seemed to want to publish
flippant and inconsequential chitchat in a place where other linguists
would see it (as opposed to uttering their views orally over drinks,
which they were prepared to do until the small hours of the morning
even when begged to desist).

The unavailability of contributions was not due to any lack of
efforts to elicit them. I wrote personal letters to numerous people in
1983 and 1984 asking them to submit something, and followed up by
asking them in person when I saw them at conferences. I even published a letter in *NLLT* pleading with people to submit (*NLLT*
3.114–15, 1985). But to no avail. *NLLT* was well provided with
manuscripts of serious research papers, but suitable short columns
for the last half-dozen pages of each issue did not come in (a few that
were submitted were rejected by the editors as too short, too silly, or
most often, too boring). So as it turned out, twenty-three of the
twenty-eight columns published came from my pen.

After five years of publication, in an editorial board meeting at the
New Orleans meeting of the Linguistic Society of America in December 1988, the editors decided that the supply of willing hands to
continue the column in the same format was never going to pick up:
either I would have to keep doing it almost entirely on my own for
life, which didn't seem fair either to me or to the field that would
forever be stuck with two-dozen pages a year of my opinions and literary experiments, or the format would have to be changed. They
opted for the latter course, and decided to start a straight letters-to-
the-editor column under the TOPIC . . . COMMENT banner. It began in
the first issue of 1990 with a grim-jawed, serious letter from the il-
lustrious Noam Chomsky. By the second issue of that year, nobody
having sent in anything printable, the editors had no choice but to put
out the first issue since the foundation of the journal that had no
TOPIC . . . COMMENT section at all.

For my part, I agreed to fade away. Indeed, I actually promised in
print (see chapter 24) that I would "not keep re-surfacing to make yet
one more farewell appearance, like Garrison Keillor or the Rolling
Stones." Naturally, since I am a man of integrity, I will not break
that pledge, unless I get up some morning and decide I really feel
like it.

But there is a difference between a farewell concert tour and a col-
lector's edition album with sleeve notes. This book presents, with no

apologies (but with new partially apologetic introductory and explanatory notes prefaced to each) my complete TOPIC . . . COMMENT columns, reproduced almost exactly as my closest friends and colleagues originally warned me not to publish them. Typographical errors have been corrected, and a little revision has been done where I could not resist gilding the lily. I have also amended the titles of two of the columns to what I would have called them in the first place if my brain had been operating at full wattage. The list in the appendix to this book gives the original titles and exact references.

The reader will find that most of the writing collected here hovers in the region between the distinctly undignified and the downright insulting, with some excursions venturing into the realm of the positively outrageous. But a lot of the time, I hope, the reader will find humor in what I have written. The reader I had in mind was always a reader unable to resist giggling and snorting with suppressed mirth, being frowned at in the library journals area perhaps, or reading passages aloud to people who happened to be next to them on a bus and couldn't get away.

I do not find it incongruous to be attempting to elicit mirth from intellectual issues in an academic context. I have found the profession of academic to be an extraordinarily enjoyable one, and I have had some of the best laughs of my life sitting around with members of the linguistics profession talking shop. Despite their rather arcane field of research, and their ability to remain eminently serious about working on linguistic problems for huge swaths of time, linguists often have a great sense of humor. I only wish that more of the wittiest linguists I have known could have been persuaded to submit TOPIC . . . COMMENT columns. We would be the richer for it.

I should confess to some residual seriousness, though. A lot of the time I did have quite serious ideas in mind as I relaxed by writing my quarterly TOPIC . . . COMMENT column. Although my satires and spoofs may be mainly for entertainment, they are fairly academic entertainment, and for the most part they are intended for participants in the linguistics profession only. Throughout the period I was publishing these pieces, I was also doing serious research, writing, editing, and collaborating (my name appeared on the title page of five books and about fifty articles between 1982 and 1989). Underlying my harangues and jests in the more freewheeling writing collected here are real underlying concerns about the state of the field of linguistics and the profession that sustains it; but instead of making my case solemnly, I tried to write with levity about (or around) what irked me.

I also tried to keep my scholarly work quite distinct from my journalistic writing, and mostly succeeded, except perhaps in the case of the wisecracking in the early sections of 'Assuming some version of X-bar theory' (*CLS 20,* 1985), a paper that originated as a Saturday night talk to the Chicago Linguistic Society. Some of the quips and sarcasm that seemed right for the large audience that well-lubricated Saturday night seem to have survived into what should have been sober print. Mea culpa.

Some readers have asked me what influences might have given rise to the style that became typical for TOPIC . . . COMMENT: the tone of overstated outrage, the random rhetorical sideswipes, the unexpected fact cheek by jowl with the plausible fiction. Looking back on what I wrote, I would say this: study the best works of the authors I have been most entertained by—such writers as Ambrose Bierce, Lewis Carroll, G. K. Chesterton, Paul Feyerabend, Jerry Fodor, Steven Jay Gould, Marvin Harris, Clive James, Garrison Keillor, Stephen Potter, George Bernard Shaw, James Thurber, Calvin Trillin, Mark Twain, and Auberon Waugh—and you will see. . . . Well, you will see that I cannot possibly claim to be the literary heir of any of them, and that they cannot possibly be to blame. I do not know where the style came from; it just grew.

Sadly, I have occasionally run into people who did not perceive that it was a style and an affectation: people who apparently assumed that everything I wrote was dead serious, and who wanted to respond to it in a deadly serious vein. Once (as mentioned and embroidered upon in chapter 8) I found that some of my columns had been picked up and reviewed in an abstracts journal as if they were research papers. Such indications that it is becoming hard to tell fantasies and satires from real life are quite alarming. My Santa Cruz colleague Tom Lehrer says that he was driven out of the satirical songwriting business by this sort of thing; ever since Henry Kissinger was awarded the Nobel Peace Prize, Lehrer has been unable to do satire. He now contents himself with teaching mathematics and musical theater at my university and eschews the craft of the satirist completely.

Regarding the reference points my columns had in the actual world, I have indicated in prefatory notes wherever I can recall a few fragments of reality that I thought at the time my remarks could be connected to. I have also explained some of the in-jokes that seem with hindsight to have needed a little explanation. But the reader is urged to neglect reality most of the time. Read the TOPIC . . . COMMENT columns collected here as spoofs, whimsies, lampoons, parodies, fantasies, pieces of simple innocent silliness or self-parodying mock rage, not as contributions to the field of linguistics expressed in some arcane code. Bits of truth about the field of linguistics were thrown into the mixing bowl for flavor as I wrote these pieces, but the ultimate product was intended as the literary analogue of candy.

Actually, I guess it mostly came out rather too caustic to be analogous to candy, or even extremely strong breath mints. I confess I am quite dissatsified with the intellectual standards that are current in our field, and frequently, optimistic and enthusiastic though I am by nature, I allow my dissatisfactions to become very evident.

Perhaps the writing gathered between these covers should be represented metaphorically not by candy but by paint remover. There is a lot of defensive rhetoric and anti-scientific obfuscation encrusted like old paint on the presentation of current ideas in linguistics; it gets in the way of our seeing what current linguistics theories have to tell us about language. My TOPIC . . . COMMENT columns are intended above all else to make this encrustation smoke and bubble and go soft and gooey so it can be scraped off.

So use this book only in small quantities, and only in well-ventilated spaces. Handle with gloves. Do not spill. If it comes in contact with the skin, rinse immediately with plenty of cold water. If swallowed (and some of it is pretty hard to swallow), contact a physician and induce vomiting.

Part One

Fashions and Tendencies

Chapter Two

Watch out for the current

This was the first published TOPIC . . . COMMENT column. It makes an attempt at futurology, trying to predict, at the inception of *Natural Language and Linguistic Theory*, which way linguistics would be moving during the remainder of the 1980s.

Its predictions have not fared too badly, but it obviously missed a lot. It predicts (from a vantage point in mid-1982) a consolidation of radical lexicalist approaches, and the relatively harmonious relations between LFG, HPSG, and other unification-based versions of syntactic theory confirm some such consolidation; but it does not foresee the amazing battle of the initials that Generalized Phrase Structure Grammar (GPSG) later engendered: HPSG (Head-driven Phrase Structure Grammar) developed (at Hewlett-Packard Laboratories, of course) by about 1985, JPSG (Japanese Phrase Structure Grammar) by Takao Gunji in Japan very soon after, and both KPSG (Korean Phrase Structure Grammar) and LPSG (Linear Phrase Structure Grammar) in Korea by about 1988.

It predicts rapid growth of government-binding (GB) theory, but doesn't foresee the extraordinary proliferation of maximal projections that now litter GB-style tree structures (with eighteen, twenty-one, or even more nodes in the structure of a two-word sentence being commonplace by 1989).

The column opines that the appearance at last of a large number of relational grammar (RG) works will not prevent the failure of RG to become a mainstream paradigm for syntax, the long delay (from 1974 to 1983) during which people waited in vain for details of the framework having "almost certainly sealed its doom" (it was a long time before I was invited to any more relational grammarians' parties, let me tell you); but I seem to have been mistaken: the amount of interesting and original RG research being done at the beginning of the 1990s was still quite substantial, enough to make the biennial conference on grammatical relations worth the trip.

Easy predictions include an increasing consensus about relatively surfacy syntax; increasing cannibalization of RG work by GB researchers (imitation is the sincerest form of flattery); the return of highly abstract phonology and the demise of 'natural phonology'; and the continued rise of interest in learnability issues. But many other significant developments coming down the pike weren't spotted at all— for example, the return of classical generative semantic ideas like lexical decomposition in GB guise, the revival of approaches based on categorial grammars (actually, it's a vival rather than a revival: no one took any notice of categorial grammars thirty years ago), and the rapid pace of tier inflation leading to phonological representation geometries that make fractals look positively unimaginative.

Not a great record of soothsaying; but I am so grateful that I didn't try to do a similar future-peeking piece in the early 1980s about Eastern European politics.

All areas of human culture are subject to the whims of fashion. No one doubts this with respect to clothes, politics, or the visual and performing arts. It is probably true with respect to linguistic change; Paul Postal[1] once claimed that the sole discernible cause of linguistic change, at least in phonology, was the shifting of fashion. Sound change was like the changing styles in automobile design that used to add and subtract fins from one year to the next in the days before the physics of drag coefficients started to dominate the business. He may be wrong, though personally I never encountered an explanation for sound change that was more plausible. Certainly not those push and drag chain models of the forties with their allophones moving around a rectangular space bumping into each other and eating each other up like those little creatures in video games.

Anyway, whether sound change proceeds according to fashions or not, controlled human activities essentially all do.

And science is almost certainly just as prone to follow fashions as any other domain of human endeavor, but to point this out raises a few hackles here and there. Thomas Kuhn, whose book on scientific revolutions[2] is quoted so often by linguists that on the basis of his citation index any Dean would grant him tenure in a linguistics de-

1. Paul M. Postal, *Aspects of phonological theory*, Harper and Row, New York, 1968.

2. Thomas S. Kuhn, *The structure of scientific revolutions*, University of Chicago Press, Chicago, Illinois, 1962.

partment, is quite explicit about this; but he has taken a lot of flak for it. Many philosophers of science have been somewhat aghast at the prospect of irrationality in theory choice. Living as (I assume) they do, in such a measured and calculated way that they use modus tollens to reason their way to the conclusion that it's time for a cup of coffee, they are horrified to think that a nuclear physicist might adopt a theoretical stance just to look avant garde, or (as Paul Feyerabend put it) to impress a lover.[3]

If in Big Science, then surely also in linguistics, that littlest of sciences. The weft and warp of the universe shows through less clearly in our endeavors than it does in relativistic cosmology or particle theory, and it is all the easier for us to be influenced by a current intellectual vogue—or, as so often happens, a slightly out-of-date vogue that was influencing physics several tail-fin changes ago.

Certainly we linguists do not always adopt ideas because the facts have at a certain point forced them upon us, or because the pristine logic of our theory has driven us inexorably toward them. Sometimes we simply allow ourselves to drift a little in the direction of the current as we swim toward the solution to the fundamental problem. And it is quite important that we should. I know of few things more tragic than the lonely figures of linguists pursuing original lines totally unconnected to the rest of the discipline, and hence unevaluated by the discipline's usual standards; carving out a theory that owes nothing to the field, and finding too late that *ipso facto* the field owes nothing to them. Paying no heed whatever to trends in the field that provides one's livelihood constitutes a kind of arrogance that is still just as arrogant when cloaked in the I'm-just-a-humble-seeker-after-truth that the lone rangers of linguistics often affect.

Being in touch with the drift and sway of current ideas just enough to be responsive to them is not weak-mindedness. It is the property Morris Halle was referring to when he once described Noam Chomsky as "plugged in". One can keep a finger on the pulse of fashion without licking its boots.

One clear example of a vogue-driven idea is the notion that explanation is a nobler goal than description. Many linguistics papers

3. I have suppressed a smidgeon of sexism on Feyerabend's part here; what he actually said was that the epistemological anarchist's aims may 'remain stable, or change as a result of argument, or of boredom, or of a conversion experience, or to impress a mistress, and so on' (Paul Feyerabend, *Against method,* NLB (New Left Books), London, 1975, p. 189).

could be written in either description or explanation mode, with the same examples and the same hypotheses. It would be a matter of changing from "The Coindexed Category Constraint conveniently summarizes the facts of interpolated anaphora blockage in a manner suitable for the description of a wide range of languages, possibly all . . ." to "And thus we see that the Coindexed Category Constraint *explains* the facts of interpolated anaphora blockage on universal grounds, and quite possibly the biology of the brain is . . ." etc. etc. What we find the facts to be does not determine our choice. Nor do the broader generalizations we uncover. And the much-documented shift from interest in philosophical grammar to mid-twentieth-century descriptivism surely shows that we are not dealing with an inexorable evolution toward explanatory concerns. Science goes through phases like everything else does.

A very interesting case of shifting intellectual fashions in linguistics is to be found in the issue of 'concreteness' versus 'abstractness' in phonology and syntax. Abstractness in syntactic theorizing is basically measurable in terms of the extent to which we see levels of syntactic description postulated that are significantly different from the level postulated to describe surface order and phrasing. And phonological abstractness is proportional to the extent that we find levels of phonological representation differing greatly from phonetic representations. A genuine pendulum effect has been operating here in American-influenced generative linguistics, with only occasional signs of a firm connection to fundamental underlying ideas. Let me try to give a terse, encyclopedia-style breakdown of major trends, breaking recent history into five-year slabs with no embarrassment at the resulting arbitrariness, and paying attention to dates of influential publications rather than inception of ideas.

1. 1960 to 1965: With phonology somewhat in recession, syntax consolidates its hold on the theoretical part of the field. Syntax is looking fairly concrete, but pushing toward abstractness as the Katz-Postal hypothesis is developed.

2. 1965 to 1970: Syntax heads for even further abstractness as *Aspects* is published and Lakoff, McCawley, Postal, Ross, and others start pushing deep structure back to semantic representation. Generative phonology suddenly blooms in 1968, with *SPE* introducing the most abstract synchronic phonology the world has ever seen.

3. 1970 to 1975: Syntax bifurcates, with the generative seman-

ticists heading for astonishingly abstract analyses (like English, or even all languages, having VSO deep constituent order, or all lexical items being underlying verbs), with a very sharp backlash starting under Chomsky's direction. Phonology heads for much more concrete analyses under the influence of Kiparsky and others; by 1974 a whole Chicago Linguistic Society parasession is devoted to highly concrete "natural phonology", and parochial rule-ordering (a major prop in abstract analyses) is under a concerted attack from the midwest.

4. 1975 to 1980: Generative semantics suffers a complete collapse and disappears under mysterious circumstances,[4] leaving Chomsky alone on the podium for a while, where he is soon joined by Brame, Bresnan, and others who push for a radical, lexically-based concreteness in syntax that goes beyond what even anti-abstractist transformationalists are prepared to accept. Meanwhile a rather slow reassertion of abstractness begins in phonology, with critiques of Koutsoudas' anti-rule-ordering program being published and natural phonology coming under attack. The emergence of syllabic, autosegmental, and metrical approaches assists this by opening up a great deal of experimentation with new and expressive formalisms, but also distracts phonologists away from the issue somewhat.

This four-paragraph reduction of twenty years to trite generalizations will no doubt offend virtually everyone, but let me assume it as a crude summary, and raise the $64,000 question about 1980 to 1985. What is going to be happening in the period that will include the first two volumes of *Natural Language and Linguistic Theory?* Nothing I say at this point should be taken down and used against me. I will not hestitate to use future columns in this series to retract every word. But it seems to me that there are certain things that the truly plugged-in should expect to see.

One is a certain consolidation of the move that has brought concrete approaches to syntax (phrase-structure and lexical-functional) closer and closer to Montague-influenced work in formal semantics. One impressive paper that recently came my way is jointly authored by (no prizes offered) a comparative Germanic grammarian, a mathe-

---

4. For an investigation of the crime and an attempted solution, see Frederick J. Newmeyer, *Linguistic theory in America* (Academic Press, New York, 1980), chapter 5.

matics and semantics whiz, an industrial-sector computational linguist, and a lexicalist syntactic theorist. At four different institutions, widely scattered. That says something about who is talking to whom.

We should also be prepared to see the extremely rapid growth of work based on Chomsky's government-binding ideas lead to many more publications. If I had ten dollars for every revision so far to the definitions of government, proper government, and the binding conditions, I would be a lot closer to owning a Porsche.

Both of the foregoing suggest that syntax is in a concrete mood. Despite Chomsky's decision to hold firm on the existence of transformations (the chief source of the kind of expressive power that can make underlying structures look vastly different from surface ones), and despite the unknown extent of abstractness implicit in the logical form level once it is accepted as syntactic, he has flirted persistently in his last few books with phraseology designed to downplay the issue, and to narrow the gulf between transformational and nontransformational work in syntax, which has meant an apparent decrease in abstractness in comparison with classical TG.

Not that the use of transformations is the hallmark of abstractness in syntax, of course. Essentially the last survivor of the abstract syntax of the seventies is the completely detransformationalized work of Perlmutter, Postal, and others in relational grammar and its formalized cousin arc pair grammar. The next couple of years will see the appearance, at long last, of a series of books containing the original work on relational grammar by Perlmutter and Postal. The public-relations disaster that has kept relational grammar out of the mainstream of linguistics for essentially the whole of the decade in which it would have been welcomed has almost certainly sealed its doom, but nevertheless there are interesting ideas in the books Perlmutter has now sent off to the press. Other frameworks have borrowed more from the wreck of relational work than they sometimes choose to admit, and they will be assisted in their cannibalizing activities by the appearance of the forthcoming *Studies in Relational Grammar,* even if the main function of the volumes is a kind of official crash report.

In phonology, there seems little doubt that abstract analyses are acceptable again. Design a really strong argument for an absolutely neutralized underlying laryngeal and you will be welcomed in polite phonological society. Evidence that even parochial rule-ordering constraints (unceremoniously dumped from syntax by Chomsky and Lasnik in 1977 without even a nod in the direction of the midwest) are needed in phonology will be welcomed with open arms by the *Linguistic Inquiry* squibs columns, and as Richard Coates has recently pointed out,[5] the late-seventies textbooks we all use keep a very low profile on the subject of getting rid of ordering constraints. One article that seems to me to have set the tone for the first half of the eighties is Stephen Anderson's 'Why phonology isn't natural.' Its argument that the mind will not reduce to the tongue has considerable cogency.

An important task for phonologists is to come to some kind of *rapprochement* with an important and highly fashionable metatheoretical concern of the syntactic part of the field, namely the issue of the connection between linguistic theory and language learnability theory. This is addressed by a couple of the papers in *The Logical Problem of Language Acquisition.*[6] There is a strange paradox inherent in the simultaneous renewal of interest in both abstract phonology and Chomsky's "fundamental problem" of how babies learn a linguistic system. Abstractness is a good-guy notion because it backs up the enthusiasm for rationalist philosophy of mind that is still as characteristic of some[7] generative linguists as it ever was: if there's all that intricacy in the system there must be lots of innate structure in the mind to assist with learning it. But of course, the more nonuniversal intricacy linguists find, the harder it is to see how learning can take place at all, and the easier it is for empiricists (boo!) to win points by showing that the fundamental problem submits to solution more easily if syntax is surface-defined and phonology hugs the phonetic ground.

That sort of paradox tends to lead after a while to another shift of fashion, but only people who are properly plugged in will be able to sense when. The point of being plugged in is to get current, but it is important not to forget that the current may be alternating.

5. Richard Coates, "Why Hungarian isn't as extrinsic as Vago thinks' [sic], *Journal of Linguistics*, 18.167–72, 1982; p. 167.

6. C. L. Baker and John J. McCarthy, eds., *The logical problem of language acquisition,* MIT Press, Cambridge, Massachusetts, 1981.

7. Not all, though. Jerrold J. Katz's book *Language and other abstract objects* defines a philosphy (which I have called New York Platonism, since New York area residents Paul M. Postal and Thomas G. Bever and erstwhile New York area resident D. Terence Langendoen are prominent among its other adherents) for those generative grammarians who do *not* believe that a grammar represents an aspect of the structure of the mind/brain.

Chapter Three

The stranger in the bar

I have retitled this because it was first published under the unbelievably boring title 'Linguists and computers'. I don't know what was wrong with me. It's the sort of title Shakespeare might have come up with.

(Now don't just bristle, think it through: Shakespeare was hopeless at titles: name of central character for historical plays and tragedies, stupid cliché or other irrelevant phrase for comedies, and that's basically it. We must face facts: the bard's plays are sublime, but his titles stink.)

The conference I report on in this article took place in February 1983 (the proceedings are available from the Association for Computational Linguistics, now at Bellcore MRE 2A379, 445 South Street, Box 1910, Morristown, New Jersey 07960-1910). I'm not sure if my melodramatic announcement that "a silicon curtain has descended across the profession" was justified (that's a Winston Churchill allusion, let me point out for the extremely young), but linguistics certainly has been changed by the revolution in computational linguistics that has taken place in the 1980s.

The surge of funding from military sources under the Strategic Computing Initiative was yet to come (I wrote more about my horror at military application of computational linguistics in 'Strategic computing and natural language interfaces', *Artificial Intelligence in Society* 1, 1987, 47–58). But by 1989 the surge had diminished considerably, and the military funding agencies had begun to pull back from symbolic computational linguistics, preferring to concentrate on getting some hard progress in the area of speech recognition, where things have been going rather better than might have been expected (speech is a hot area in industry, too).

The day of weapon systems operated by spoken commands (and subsequently toaster ovens operated by spoken commands) cannot be far off now. That doesn't bother me too much; a gun that fires when you shout "*Fire*" at it isn't too much more dangerous than a soldier who fires when you shout "*Fire*"; no, the worry is about so-called intelligent systems. I still experience the same feeling of unease that I described at the end of this column when I reflect on the idea of systems that can understand a spoken command to rain death from the sky but cannot understand anything of what they have done. It's nothing to do with being anti-military; I would feel the same about venomfanged flying dogs being employed to guard junkyards. It's simply that if killing is on the agenda, I guess I want it to be in the hands of creatures like me.

Intelligent killing systems that go out of control have continued to be a standard theme in science fiction. The movie *Robocop* has a scene—described by reviewers as hilarious—in which a robotics company executive is machine-gunned to death in the boardroom by a massive security-maintenance robot with semantic and pragmatic problems. The reader will not be too surprised to learn that I did not laugh at all.

David Lightfoot dedicates his book *The Language Lottery* (MIT Press, 1983) "to anyone who ever met a couple of linguists in a bar and asked them what they did for a living". It's clear that, like me, he has often been asked that question. Doubtless it has often led to his being asked what linguistics is, as well. How should you answer the latter question when you don't have time to write a book in reply, and you don't have any means of forcing the stranger to read your book anyway?

Often I think I ought simply to lie about what I do. Arnold Zwicky never gives his unusual name when reserving a table in a restaurant. He is tired of hearing puzzled hostesses call for Swickley, Stickney, Sickly, Zippy, and so forth in vain efforts to track him down when his table is ready. "Alexander Adams," he tells the reservations desk boldly. No one ever misspells or mispronounces either Alexander or Adams.

But when I am asked my profession, instead of telling strangers that I'm in farm machinery insurance or commodity speculation, I always feel impelled to try and explain the truth, in a quarter of a minute assuming no prerequisite courses.

I have experimented with many ways of outlining what linguistics is without allowing an opening for the Most Dreaded Question for theoretical linguists, "How many languages do you speak?" (since in my case it is so miserably few). One technique has proved to be more effective than any other. It uses an example of an applied linguistics problem, forestalling also the Second Most Dreaded Question, namely, "How does linguistics help anyone feed the chickens?"

What I say is basically this. Suppose you wanted to program a computer to understand plain English, like the HAL 9000 computer[1] in Stanley Kubrick's film *2001: A Space Odyssey.* Linguistics is the subject that figures out what you'd need to know about language in order to do that, for English or for any other language, in a general and theoretically principled way.

Now, of course, nothing in human interaction is foolproof, and there are awkward customers who either see this as much too easy ("Haven't they already done that?") or fail to grasp that the enterprise is not simply one of electronics ("You mean you build computers?"). But David Lightfoot's hard line about X-bar theory in the genes and the chemistry of the mind/brain cannot possibly be foolproof either. I bet there are a few strangers in bars who think Lightfoot is a brain surgeon.

Often, however, the effect of my little explanation is exactly right. It manages to convey the idea of an extremely complex enterprise that involves a whole range of activities from dictionary compilation and grammar writing to psychology and acoustics; an enterprise that could conceivably have a real impact on human lives, but is at present rather a matter of preliminary theoretical investigation of grammar, speech, and meaning. The fellow-passenger or stranger in a bar says it sounds very interesting and falls silent, ruminating on the strange things some people do in order to make a living.

But am I in fact telling anything like the truth to these strangers? Does my description capture at least something of what linguistics is about, or am I offering a perverted caricature of the discipline? Should I be attempting to develop a two-sentence summary of Lightfoot's book instead? I am not going to answer these rhetorical questions. The question of the popularization of the discipline does not occupy the majority of my thought or energy. But it did occur to me on a recent conference trip that it is possible that my cameo summary of linguistics is destined to become truer than I ever intended it to be.

---

1. How many people who were not tipped off by a knowledgeable friend spotted that the initials "H.A.L." are the immediate predecessors in the alphabet of the initials "I.B.M."? Was Arthur C. Clarke surreptitiously publicizing the International Business Machines Corporation with this allusion in his novel, or was it coincidence?

The Association for Computational Linguistics recently held a meeting in Santa Monica under the title "Applied Natural Language Processing." I went out of curiosity, the air fare for the 400-mile trip to Southern California at the moment being less than the cost of a modest dinner for two. The program looked educational, and Martin Kay, one of my favorite public speakers, was giving one of the lunchtime addresses. What I saw in Santa Monica would have seemed quite natural to me if I really believed in my characterization of linguistics. I guess the experience taught me, if nothing else, that I do not really want to believe myself.

A large part of the conference was devoted simply to exhibiting and discussing some of the engineering that has resulted from the science in which we all work. But in fact it astonished me, and even frightened me. I doubt whether most linguists are aware of how much can currently be done in the direction of getting computers to respond to natural language input. Much of the most significant progress toward products has been made extremely recently—in the last two years. It is difficult to take in how fast the technology is progressing, or how much money is going to be made by the companies involved in producing it, or how many diverse sorts of people it is going to put out of work.

One presentation reported on a machine translation system (German to English) that works measurably better than a human on similar material. (The material was not Goethe, of course, but a huge, boring, technical manual on a telephone switching system.) Post-editing the computer's draft translations takes less time than is needed for human drafts. Since many linguists still repeat the story of the failure of machine translation efforts as an awful warning about the over-optimistic fifties, this recent development may come as something of a surprise.

A different machine translation project described at the conference translates between English and Japanese, using techniques derived from Montague grammar.

Another paper reported on a system that accepts instructions in English typed in by geologists and prepares requisitions for geological maps to specifications that are clarified in a dialog with the user if necessary. This system was not only described but demonstrated at the meeting, and subjected to unprepared input from the audience. True, Ivan Sag blew its automatic mind away with one input sentence, and it came back with an embarrassingly stupid response, the exact opposite of what was called for. But on the whole, it acquitted itself rather well.

There was a report on the progress toward producthood of a program (the IBM EPISTLE system) that reads business letters to suggest corrections not only in their spelling and punctuation but also in their grammar.

Yet another presentation included a movie showing the behavior of a computer system that not only accepts English questions as data retrieval requests but also accepts English statements and updates the database consistently in the light of them.

These are not easy things to accomplish. Certainly one must allow for the fact that some systems are being oversold. But with a couple of the systems I have had personal experience, and I can vouch for the fact that they are not fakes or toys. Linguists should make every effort to witness for themselves demonstrations of the kind of programs I am talking about, because it is important that they should neither overestimate nor underestimate the scale and the scope of what is being done.

For one thing, these developments (and the much more far-reaching developments in the computer industry on which they are based) are rapidly changing the character of the linguistic community in a number of places in the United States. The character of the audience at the Santa Monica meeting was as different from that of a NELS conference or a GLOW meeting as one can easily imagine. There were naval officers interested in machine processing of ship-to-shore messages; businessmen who wanted to be in on the ground floor either using or selling natural language software products; intelligence agency representatives with noncommittal "Washington D.C." addresses in the published list of participants; medical professionals interested in natural language access to computerized records and expert systems for medical diagnosis; and linguists with business cards, walking around with badges bearing names of commercial companies, not universities. No jeans; no dittoed handouts; no public wrangles about disputed points of theory. It was business suits; professionally prepared color transparencies; and polite questions about cost-effectiveness, portability, and man-months.

Keep in mind that there is no linguistics teaching or research without money. The Linguistic Society of America, seeing serious dangers ahead for the linguistics profession in America in a time of cutbacks in education, has started a Fund for the Future of Linguistics. Perhaps I witnessed part of that future in Santa Monica. If so, there are major changes in store.

It would be fine if the changes would simultaneously secure the financial future of linguistics, leave its intellectual excitement and freedom untrammeled, and assist us in explaining its nature to the stranger in the bar. But that would be something of a fantasy.

The money will probably come easiest. Research support bodies like the Sloan Foundation and the System Development Foundation have not millions but tens of millions of dollars to hand out for computationally sophisticated and cognitively oriented linguistic research. And their money comes from private industry, which has vastly more where that came from. Linguistic work resulting in natural language processing applications that make computer systems easier to use or more attractive to purchasers could have financial implications counted in hundreds of millions of dollars. Optimists may say that the military funding of linguistics in the sixties had no discernible effect on the kind of work done; the research that went into *Aspects of the Theory of Syntax* was partly supported by military contract money given to MIT, and Stockwell, Schachter and Partee's *The Major Syntactic Structures of English,* was wholly paid for by the US Air Force, yet neither work seems very militaristic. Perhaps, therefore, industrial funding will permit linguistic research to flourish without altering its character. But I wonder. Industry is more powerful than the military, and its leadership is less stupid.

What of the excitement and freedom? One of the key elements of the delight I take in belonging to the linguistics professions is the open-mindedness that pervades it. Ideas are shared and eagerly passed around in xerographed typescripts too new to be in print. Talk is free and frank. First drafts are circulated for feedback. Minds change overnight as a new idea takes hold. Hypotheses are created and defended only to be slashed to ribbons at the next conference. The field is vibrant and alive. Would this innocence survive a seduction by industry? Already I have seen worrying signs that suggest otherwise. No one at Santa Monica was showing more than simplified illustrative examples of their syntactic rules or their inference principles. The systems were black boxes, ready for marketing and not available for internal inspection. One panel chairman told me that part of the reason for the blandness that characterized his session was that two of his panel members had been told by their companies they could not reveal any details of the systems they had been working on.

Try asking around to see if you can get a look at the source code for the parser, or even the grammar, of any interesting natural language system being commercially developed, and you will find that a silicon curtain has descended across the profession. True, it is not totally impermeable. There are industrial research laboratories, particularly in California, that have very much the air of a university about them, and which recognize the value of the free exchange of scientific information. But at Santa Monica one could observe every now and then that conversation would falter on a blush or a mumble, and one could catch a hint that something proprietary had been touched on. There was something faintly chilling about it, as if the shadow of a cloud had passed over the profession.

There were a couple of moments that were much more chilling, however. A couple of the presentations were not just military-funded but openly devoted to practical military systems development. One dealt with techniques for automatic summarizing of natural language intelligence reports of incidents such as airspace violations. Another, quite independently, was concerned with the provision of a natural language system for providing an air force commander with ready access to the locations and ranges of the aircraft with which he could order some target destroyed. I listened with mounting horror to these presentations, and watched the faces of the friendly-looking people who gave them, looking for signs of loathing or at least embarrassment; but there were none. Much of the audience listened peacefully to these talks about how linguistic research could assist the armed forces to watch for aggression and efficiently marshal their counter-attack if they encountered it. But I turned away with a shudder and went to the bar.

My sleep was uneasy that night. I kept imagining a world laid waste by a war that started because of a mistake in the semantic rule for relative clauses that led to a misinterpretation of a missile launch report.

Chapter Four

If it's Tuesday, this must be glossematics

It was a great shock to all those connected with *Natural Language and Linguistic Theory* when, after only two issues had appeared, Adrian Akmajian suddenly died. It was hard to take in. Nearly ten years before, he had been forced to drop out of teaching an introduction to syntax at the 1974 LSA Linguistic Institute at the University of Massachusetts, Amherst, when he was diagnosed with Hodgkin's disease, which dictionaries describe as a "generally fatal" disease. Everyone who knew Adrian had been so glad when modern techniques of treatment drove his Hodgkin's into remission and gave him another decade of life. But when leukemia came to claim him in the summer of 1983, there was to be no similar reprieve.

The editors decided to dedicate an issue of the journal (volume 2, no. 1) to Adrian's memory, including in it a paper that he had nearly finished when he died, 'Sentence types and the form-function fit' (finished and edited for him by Susan Steele), and several pending papers that he had been involved with: one by his friend Ray Jackendoff, one by his student Eloise Jelinek, one by his colleague Peter Culicover, and one by Janet Dean Fodor which he was particularly responsible for in that he persuaded Fodor to write it.

It remained to find something to fill the TOPIC . . . COMMENT section. I reflected a while, and recalled some thoughts that had been stimulated by some perceptive remarks of David Lightfoot's in the *Times Higher Education Supplement* for January 1, 1982, together with some discussions that Adrian and I had had on the topic. The following column emerged from my ruminations. One reader, Andrew Carstairs, later published a letter discussing some of the issues it raised (*NLLT* 3 (1985), 113–14).

The title alludes to a 1960s comedy movie about a whirlwind tour by a party of wacky American tourists, reviewing the majesty of Europe almost as rapidly as some linguistics courses review the various approaches to the study of language. It was called *If It's Tuesday, This*

23

Must Be Belgium. I thought I should mention that, because the movie
was not exactly a cinematic classic, and the likelihood of its being
preserved for future generations is slender. I never even saw it myself.

Adrian Akmajian was an ideal person to share a wilting fifteenth
draft with. He would always find something encouraging to say. He
was unfailingly careful and thoughtful in his comments; tender and
full of tact in the way he would criticize; full of wit, and appreciative
of humor. I recall struggling with early attempts at TOPIC . . . COM-
MENT columns—dozens and dozens of them—after the editors of
this journal had broached the idea of the column and I was struggling
to see if I could realize it. So often my efforts just didn't quite seem
to hit the mark or hold the right tone. I was either too scurrilous or
too boring; either undesirably narrow or utterly vapid. It was never
quite right. There were no models to follow; no one had tried to write
about what was going on in current linguistics in the particular way
that the editors were envisaging. Sometimes, after perhaps thirty
hours spent over several weeks on an attempted column that was going nowhere, I would get despondent, and begin to wonder whether I
was going to be able to do what the editors had in mind. What I
would do at those times would be to dial up Tucson, Arizona, and
talk to Adrian.

I have found it hard to comprehend that I will never be able to call
Arizona and hear his friendly voice again. I find I still try to reword
things the way he would have gently insisted, taking account of objections I feel he would have raised; but his original suggestions and
stimulating ideas are gone forever now.

Looking through my files I found two close-packed pages of sage
and judicious typed commentary that Adrian had sent me on an early
attempt at a column that I finally decided not to use, after about
twenty revisions. The structure of the column was wrong. But the
subject matter of at least one part of it was interesting, and I have
wanted for some time to return to it. It concerned two different views
of how linguistics should be taught. The distinction between the two
had been put into very sharp relief in a letter that David Lightfoot
published in the London *Times Higher Education Supplement* on the
first day of 1982. Lightfoot referred to the belief in "eclecticism and
a belief in the value of surveys" that seems to pervade linguistics

teaching in Britain. The predominant British view, he said (picking up on a characterization given a few weeks earlier in Geoffrey Sampson's review of a book by John Lyons), is that

> Students should be introduced to the study of language by taking a fast Cook's tour of all its aspects, getting to know 'the field'. This is the approach . . . of virtually all linguistic programmes in British universities.

Lightfoot proposed an alternative: to

> train students in one research programme, a programme which tries to develop a detailed answer to one central question about language (e.g., how it is attained by children or how it is used by poets, how can it change, or how does it reflect cultural values?).

Now, Lightfoot was writing at a time when Margaret Thatcher's government had just announced a shocking program of cuts which had panicked departments of linguistics as much as those of any other nonscience subject. Universities in the UK were being instructed to make cuts of around twenty per cent—twice as bad as decimation, which (as so many people forget) etymologically implies the killing of one in ten. Entire programs in linguistics were being closed down (the departments at Birmingham and Liverpool were never again to see the light of day), and here was Lightfoot saying things that might seem to provide justification for such actions.

A phalanx of sixteen Romance linguistics scholars rose as one to respond to Lightfoot in a letter published in *THES* on 15 January 1982. They positively fulminated, accusing him of being interested solely in "amassing disciples" whom he could brainwash into his own narrow theoretical point of view (despite the openness to alternative approaches implied by the parenthesis in the Lightfoot quote above). What were his motives, they must have wondered? He might have the best interests of British linguistics at heart, or he might be after a job. Was there a British linguist whom Lightfoot might want to succeed? Or was there one whom he might wanna succeed? The real issue seemed to get lost. Which is the better way to teach linguistics: the eclectic survey of the field (let us call it *survey-oriented* teaching), or the enlisting of students into the single-minded pursuit of a research goal (call it *investigation-oriented* teaching)?

I am in the position of having been both a student and a teacher of linguistics in both Britain and the United States. I have witnessed and participated in both of the educational styles we are discussing, from both the consumer and the purveyor standpoints. I have a strong preference. But while people's preference in logic textbooks and visual editor programs is universally, in my experience, a preference for the first one they encountered when they were a student, my preference in educational style runs the other way, against the style I first encountered.

My undergraduate study of linguistics was replete with If-It's-Tuesday-This-Must-Be-Glossematics courses. Martinet said this, Hjelmslev said that; Harris wouldn't mix levels but Pike believed in grammatical prerequisites; on the one hand Chomsky but on the other hand Halliday; some people think there are phonological segments, but then again, Firthian prosodies . . . The approach was ponderously eclectic. The feeling hung in the air that to actually believe in some approach was almost disreputable.

This latter was especially so if the position in which one was in danger of investing some belief had any link with generative grammar. Generative grammar is, of course, the program that Lightfoot would like to get his students embroiled in. By the very fact of its determinate theoretical stance, it has been antipathetic from the start toward eclecticism. The extent to which the whole generativist ethos was regarded as a threat in the department where I first studied linguistics can hardly be exaggerated. Naturally, I and many other interested students were perverse enough to see immediately that generativism must be the thing to get into, so to some extent the department's orthodoxy was subverted. And, thank goodness, there were also rebel faculty who took an interest in generative grammar. But they did not define the cultural milieu. They represented the beginnings of a reaction against it. The curriculum, meanwhile, was still definitively in Cook's tour mode.

I did not really experience investigation-oriented teaching until I attended a Linguistic Institute and saw people teaching courses of a type utterly opposed to the If-It's-Tuesday-This-Must-Be-Glossematics type of course. These were Here's-A-Proposal-That-Makes-Sense-To-Me courses. Here were teachers who had made decisions about what counted as research questions in their field, and they were prepared to teach what currently looked to them like solid answers, and stand staunchly against purported counterarguments that might come up. What they taught might turn out to be wrong (and some of it clearly was), but it seemed, for the time being, better than the alternatives, and they had a personal stake in it.

Of course, the classes I met with at the Institute (at the University of Massachusetts, Amherst, in 1974) were at the graduate level. And there are many people, I think, who would maintain that survey-oriented courses are appropriate to introduce undergraduates to the content of the field, while investigation-oriented courses are appropriate at the graduate level, where the instructor's ideas are presented to students whose minds are already trained and whose viewpoint is informed by an acquaintance with the literature. Well, the department in which I was an undergraduate offered the survey type of course to its graduate students as well, so it is not the case that the undergraduate/graduate distinction actually provided a rational basis for the policy that it followed. But the question merits discussion: is linguistics right for an undergraduate curriculum?

I'm biased again, of course. Despite everything, I enjoyed my B.A. degree course. Moreover, I now teach in an undergraduate linguistics program. I believe linguistics is a superb undergraduate-level major. It offers at least a glimpse of scientific modes of thought. But unlike physics and chemistry, it has safe subject matter: the novice can be trusted in the lab with the raw materials immediately, with no experts or technicians to mediate access to them. None of it is toxic or explosive. Moreover, no expensive equipment is required for measuring it or operating on it (setting acoustic phonetics and click experimentation aside).

Yet there is more: language is simultaneously the stuff of art—the fabric of which poetry is wrought—and a puzzle for social and biological science. It spans the alleged gulf between the humanities and the sciences (and in consequence, as Barbara Hall Partee recently pointed out to me, is perhaps the only subject that regularly gets research funding from agencies in the humanities, the social sciences, and the natural sciences). And it is genuinely humanizing, it seems to me. The process of examining analytically the complexities in one's own language and in others seems inherently likely to increase one's sensitivity to ways of expressing thought, and one's awareness of the mystery of human intelligence and its intriguingly diverse channels of expression.

So I certainly do not think that undergraduates should be deprived of the opportunity to major in linguistics. Nor do I agree with the view that undergraduates should be protected from investigation-oriented courses in it. I think it is patronizing, and simply incorrect, to see undergraduates as so docile that to present them with a well-defended point of view is to blight their intellects and render them incapable of perceiving the possibility of alternatives to it.

I have seen syntax, in particular, taught with striking success to undergraduates in a way that could hardly be further removed from the eclectic survey. Syntax can be taught with no textbook, no readings, no exams, and no term paper requirement. The point, under this conception of the task, is not to present knowledge to the students to be absorbed. The main material, the principles governing the construction of sentences in everyday English, is already known to everyone in the room, after all. Teaching the subject consists in getting students to wrestle directly with ways of systematizing those principles, and developing suitable hypotheses to explain known facts and predict others. A quarter of that kind of instruction can produce undergraduates who know about syntax because they've done it rather than because they've heard about it, and who have a long-lasting enthusiasm for the subject.

Of course, there is a difference between an investigation-oriented course that is student-driven, where the instructor merely elicits and guides, and one in which the instructor just presents his own theories and brooks no argument. But in fact the two are much more closely related to each other than either is to the eclectic survey. The difference between "Here's-A-Proposal-That-Makes-Sense-To-Me and Think-Of-A-Proposal-That-Makes-Sense-To-You is not extreme. For one thing, neither could care less what Hjelmslev thought. And for another, the instructor's ideas tend to leak through: students tend to come up with hypotheses and structures similar to those that their instructor believes in, with overwhelmingly greater than chance frequency. So I feel justified in lumping both types together.

In siding with investigation-oriented teaching, I am agreeing with the dominant view in American linguistics education, and the one that is epitomized above all by the practice of the department in which Adrian Akmajian earned his doctorate: the one at MIT. But Adrian, in correspondence with me, argued the other side. In some ways, he felt, American linguistics departments are over-committed to investigation-oriented teaching. The result is students who may be interested in their subject and convinced of the worth of their ideas (or their adviser's ideas), but are narrow in their grasp of linguistics as a whole. In a letter dated April 14, 1982, he wrote:

> Many linguists in this country complain that linguistics departments don't train their students in the Cook's Tours method. These are often 'linguists' outside of linguistics departments (e.g. in anthro, foreign languages, education, etc.) who complain that linguistics departments aren't 'broad' enough or that training isn't 'applied' enough, and so on. Even though the majority of well-known linguistics departments in the U.S. . . . . attempt to provide students with sound training, nevertheless we often hear (at least at non-elite non-private schools) the voices of the tour-guides carping at us.

I can well imagine what is meant by the people Adrian is referring to. Imagine getting your anthropological linguistic training in the late fifties and early sixties, with the familiar old textbooks and their solid-sounding titles (*Phonetics; Phonemics; Morphology; Laboratory Manual for Morphology and Syntax; Workbook in Descriptive Linguistics*), and then encountering someone with a recent degree from a linguistics department, and discovering that they have literally never heard of Kenneth Pike, or Item-and-Arrangement, or *IJAL*, or phonemic overlapping. It must be an unpleasant shock.

Nonetheless, you cannot instill breadth with a teaching method that doesn't work. I just don't think that the right way to teach linguistics is to parade before the neophyte all the different views of linguistic theory people have had through the ages. The right way to do it is . . .

Well, of course I have some ideas about what is the right way, but I feel sure Adrian would have warned me against dogmatically announcing a proposed panacea. We are all striving toward the elusive right way to teach our subject, and it would be arrogant and foolish to pretend there is a simplistic recipe for the perfect course, he would have said. Right again, Adrian.

Chapter Five

The conduct of *Linguistic Inquiry*

Frank Heny thought it was rather risky to do anything in the first year of a new journal that involved criticizing the opposition. Bad luck or bad taste or something, he seemed to think. But by the time a few issues had come out and had been well received, I succeeded in convincing him that *Linguistic Inquiry* was enough of an institution to merit discussion, and he grudgingly agreed to take the risk.

Since what I wrote received not only criticism from defenders of MIT's house journal but also hostile comments from people who thought I had been far too lenient with the journal and its editor, I assume that here we have a rare instance of my having achieved that most boring of properties in a commentary, balance. I can only apologize. Nothing was further from my intentions than to provide a mealy-mouthed, on-the-one-hand-this-but-on-the-other-hand-that assessment.

Perhaps it is not too late for me to atone, by making it clear that I regard *Linguistic Inquiry* as a miserable trash-stuffed rag of a journal through which the pathetic blitherings of an army of knuckle-dragging intellectual toadies are shepherded to prominence by the unprincipled back-room machinations of a pea-brained lackwit of an editor whose fawning subservience to the power clique that controls modern linguistics is matched only by his contempt for civilized standards when dealing with the work of those whose integrity prevents them from prostituting their scholarship by kowtowing to the self-ordained guardians of a baseless pseudo-theoretical hegemony. I can't imagine, frankly, why I still subscribe.

Every linguist has a gripe against *Linguistic Inquiry* (*LI*). No journal but *LI* sparks such controversy. No editor but Samuel Jay Keyser so regularly gets accused by furious authors of being biased both in favor of and against a specific line of work—today, usually the work of Chomsky and his associates, formerly, believe it or not, generative semantics. Often, Keyser has been accused of running a journal that exists solely to publicize MIT—and specifically, Chomskyan, thinking. But not long ago I met a distinguished graduate of MIT's linguistics department who swore angrily that she would never think of submitting another article to *LI*. It would seem that MIT-connected people are not at all sure the journal is sufficiently in their power. Legend has it that once Chomsky referred to it as "Postal's mouthpiece". And another time, someone suggested that the name should be changed to *Cahiers Susumo Kuno*. (Actually, the feelings that Postal and Kuno were dominating *LI* in the early seventies were not groundless: trivia buffs may care to know that in volume 1, contributions by Postal accounted for more than 25% of the number of pages, and in volume 3, Kuno supplied 25% of the full articles published, and nearly 20% of the page count.)

In the eyes of a wide cross-section of the linguistic community, Keyser cannot do a thing right. And this is obviously a major point in his favor. It is easy enough to find a competent editor; pick someone at random off the street, and provided they have the patience of Job, the wisdom of Solomon, the political skill of Machiavelli, an encyclopedic knowledge of all aspects of the field, and the kind of eye that can spot instantly that one of the items in the bibliography to a fifty-page paper fails to get referred to in the text, and, given an editorial assistant as good as *LI*'s Anne Mark, they'll be able to run a half-way decent journal. But without apparently having any of the above qualities, Keyser has managed to make *LI* the one journal that every generative grammarian really wants to be seen in. That is a notable achievement.

Little knots of linguists gather in the bar at LSA meetings to bad-mouth *LI*. They say that Keyser is biased. Closer to the truth, I suspect, is that Keyser is influenced by the environment in which he works, to wit, the Department of Linguistics and Philosophy at MIT. But the people who would accuse Keyser of obediently typesetting any piece of subscripted drivel that emerges from the typewriters of Chomsky's students are forgetting, or never knew, that in the early seventies he rejected Chomsky's own paper 'Conditions on transformations'. The people who used to accuse him of being a pawn in the hands of lexicalism's enemies in the seventies apparently failed to notice that throughout the 1970s he never printed a single article by either George Lakoff or James McCawley. (This was not because they did not submit anything. Both appeared in the squibs columns, and McCawley published a couple of remarks and replies, but neither ever got a full article-length statement of their views past the *LI* referees during the period when their work was at its most influential.)

Keyser does what a good editor should do, which is take the word of his referees. This makes for frustration on the author's part when the referees are clear candidates for a soft office with no windows, but has on the whole made for a pleasing variety in the journal's offerings (when one takes into consideration the fact that it is avowedly and forever devoted to generative grammar). People who want to make out a case that *LI* is prejudiced this way or that never present hard data, and it is easy to see why. Such data will not be easy to amass. The journal has published work by an astonishing range of people, from Hall to Halle, from Jacobson to Jakobson, from Liberman to Lieberman, from . . . (I leave this list of minimal pairs unfinished in the hope that people will take it up as a party game. One thing linguistics needs is some new party games. Phonetic substitution games are too difficult for most American-trained linguists, and one of the only alternatives is the unbelievably boring game suggested by Katz and Fodor in footnote 9 of 'The structure of a semantic theory': include me out.)

The only bias I see in *LI* is toward the work of MIT people. But it is hardly sensible to complain about that. *LI* is almost totally dedicated to generative grammar; generative grammar originated at MIT; MIT is the editorial headquarters of *LI;* and MIT faculty and students probably produce more publications on generative grammar than any other department in the world. What could possibly prevent MIT work from showing up very strongly in the pages of *LI?*

True enough, one can raise questions about whether Jeffrey Gruber's study of Bushman kinship terms (*LI* 4.427–49, 1973) or Mark Aronoff's whimsical paper on the connotations of automobile names (*LI* 12 (1981), 329–47) could possibly have found their way into *LI* if the authors were not MIT graduates. And one could grumble about the fact that *LI*'s announced length limit of 50 manuscript pages is not enforced on everybody alike (someone connected with MIT can get away with a paper of over 80 *printed pages*); but look at, for example, Bresnan's superb paper in *LI* 13 (1982), 343–434, and ask yourself if you wouldn't have allotted it the necessary 90 pages if you had been editor.

People occasionally grumble about the length of time their submission to *LI* has had to wait in review or in press. Time taken for review varies erratically, and there are some well-substantiated stories of six-month waits without a word. But this happens with any refereed journal, generally because some referees are either unbelievably busy or unforgivably lazy. For instance, in 1981 I experienced a six-month wait for comments on a thirty-page paper submitted to *Journal of Linguistics,* edited in England by Erik Fudge. Several inquiries failed to elicit any replies, and finally a single referee's letter appeared, with an apologetic letter saying that although the referee gave a "fairly favourable" judgment, the paper could not be published because of "a 'logjam' in the *Journal* pipeline" which entailed that no new papers could be accepted for a while. That was annoying in a number of ways. For one thing, I have grave doubts about whether to trust a journal editor who thinks you send logs by pipe. Most logs will not fit in most pipes. No wonder Fudge has backlog troubles.

LI is not notably worse, even at its worst, as far as I know. At the end of six months one can generally expect to have heard something, and often it is only two or three months. And if and when publication is declined, it isn't because of something as dubious as an editor-induced pipe blockage, but because the referees say the paper isn't good enough.

Aye, there's the rub. For *LI* referees are not always endowed with the sort of age-tempered wisdom that permits them to see the merits of one's endeavors. In fact, not to put too fine a point on it, sometimes it almost seems as if Keyser has cast one's pearls of wisdom before some swinish graduate from down the hall whose qualifications for the task do not seem to have equipped him or her with the ability to spell Jespersen without an *o* in it.

If you can keep your sense of humor, *LI* referees' reports can be very funny. Many people have shown me gems with a general drift along the lines of "Admittedly *X* did say this; but he could in principle have put things in a different way, so this is not a valid criticism." There are people who carry their *LI* refereeing horror stories around with them like albatrosses and will grasp you by the arm like the ancient mariner and force you to hear them out. I'll tell you a few tales myself.

A little more worrying than tardiness or eccentricity of refereeing is that the publication lag time for *LI* seems to vary according to what flag you fly. One or two people have mentioned to me that they believe their replies to criticism took much longer to get to the proof stage than the original criticism did, which tends to make them bitter and suspicious. It is not that a linguist from Nebraska cannot criticize a hypothesis from Massachusetts. It's just that the Massachusetts paper may seem to get in like greased lightning as compared to the Nebraska one. Because *LI* does not print the date of acceptance with every published paper, like a number of respectable journals do, Keyser has no defense against such charges other than to throw open his files of correspondence for public inspection. We are waiting, Jay; and we have the Freedom of Information Act behind us.

There is one thing that I had begun to think was a serious problem with *LI*. It concerns standards of citation, attribution, and related matters of scholarship. Around 1978 I began to be struck by a series of scholarly and editorial lapses in the pages of *LI* that, even in this imperfect world, made my hair stand on end. Let me cite just half a dozen cases from volumes 9 or 10.

(A) In 9.1, Sag has a squib (*LI* 9.138–41, 1978) about phenomena discussed in detail by Baker in an *LI* paper seven years before (*LI* 2.167–81, 1971) but fails to mention it because he was unaware of it; neither referees nor editors noticed, and Sag was permitted to publish in ignorance of Baker's work. He had to submit another squib on the same subject later (*LI* 11.255–57, 1980) when he found out about it.

(B) In 9.2, Pullum and Zwicky have a squib (*LI* 9.326–27, 1978) which is one of no less than three back-to-back replies to a squib by Oh (*LI* 8.586, 1977). Publishing Oh's squib, which makes a completely erroneous point about the mathematical definition of the notion 'tree,' was a mistake in itself, and printing three replies simultaneously was surely overkill. But what I want to point out is something worse. Pullum and Zwicky happen to state in passing at one point that they "certainly accept that the clause-mate relation has to be both symmetric and transitive" (p. 326). Well, it's symmetric all right, but it is *not* transitive; and this is pointed out in the very next squib, on the very next page, by Cushing (*LI* 9.327–30, 1978), one of the other replies to Oh. (The reason: A could be a clausemate of B, and B of C, but if A happens to dominate C, then A and C are not clausemates, because pairs of clausemates by definition cannot be in the domination relation.) The editors failed to notice this, and Pullum and Zwicky were allowed to publish a squib containing a false statement, instead of being told to fix up their squib in the light of Cushing's correct observation on the next page. Their point could have been made without spreading even a smidgeon of additional confusion on the vexing little topic involved if only the squibs editors had done their homework.

(C) In 10.3, Asakawa argues (*LI* 10 (1979), 505–8) that "The element which is extracted out of NP is adjoined to the node which immediately dominates that NP." But Asakawa is unaware that his proposal has already been published. Schwartz (*Journal of Linguistics* 8 (1972), 35–85) discusses in detail the proposal that extractions should be restricted in exactly this way. But the referees and editors of *LI* were ignorant of Schwartz's work, too, and they let Asakawa proceed without referring to it.

(D) In 10.4, Kaisse presents the ingenious idea that the failure of contraction in pseudoclefts like

(1)   *What he wondered's whether there was any beer.

can be attributed to the inhibiting effect of a deletion site left by a derivation (of the sort attributed to Peters and Back in unpublished work) roughly like (2).

(2) a. what he wondered is   he wondered   whether
       there was any beer
    b. what he wondered is   ∅   whether
       there was any beer

There is an awful flaw in this neat idea (which Kaisse herself pointed out to me, though of course she hadn't seen it at the time when the squib was accepted): the auxiliary fails to contract even when the subject is pseudo-clefted so that the deletion site is not adjacent to it:

(3) a. what is bothering Bob is your attitude is bothering him

b. What is bothering $\left\{\begin{array}{l}\text{Bob is}\\ \text{*Bob's}\end{array}\right\}$ your attitude.

so the deletion site cannot be relevant. And there is another problem: speakers of the dialects that accept *surface* strings like (2a) still don't accept (4).

(4)   *What he wondered's he wondered whether there was any beer.

So again the deletion site makes no difference. How much thinking did the referees do?

(E) In 11.4, Fodor and Fodor discuss (*LI* 11.759–770, 1980) their observation that (5a) has, but (5b) does not have, a reading with wide-scope existential quantification over edibles.

(5) a. Everyone ate something.
    b. Everyone ate.

They make quite a lot of this observation, criticizing Bresnan's theory of lexical rules for failing to predict it. But Fodor and Fodor do not cite Dowty's paper of two years previously (*LI* 9.393–426, 1978), which has a treatment of unspecified object deletion (see Section 5) that makes the right predictions about (5b) by burying the existential quantifier in the lambda-expression that translates *eat*. (Cf. now Dowty's paper in Michael Moortgat, Teun Hoekstra, and Harry van der Hulst, eds., *The Scope of Lexical Rules,* Foris, Dordrecht, 1982.) The Fodors' referees had not read Dowty either, it seems.

I shall not continue with this catalogue of oversights, though there are plenty of other cases I could add. All of them illustrate the same point: *Linguistic Inquiry* has sometimes shown signs of being refereed and edited without proper attention to the literature of linguistic inquiry. Even that portion of the literature appearing in *LI* itself has not always been properly acknowledged.

Of course, citation standards are rather low in general in current linguistics. Too many scholars are basically only bothering to acknowledge their friends and allies. If a classmate and co-thinker independently discovers your idea, you acknowledge that in a footnote. If a generative semanticist discovered it ten years ago but is now seldom heard from, you don't bother (even if you know). But that is not an excuse for *LI*. It ill befits a leading journal to fall into a state of forgetting what has been published in its own pages.

I wish I could say that all we need to do is to adopt the scholarly values and sense of responsibility found in neighboring disciplines, but regrettably that would be no use. Far from being a model for linguists to turn to, the adjacent social and cognitive sciences are noted for their scandalous inattention to their own recent results. It has been determined by experiment that in psychology, referees can typically not tell that a paper has been previously published during the past three years in the journal they are reviewing for. It is also known that papers are more likely to get published if they offer nothing surprising, emanate from a prestigious rather than an unknown institution, use complex and unintelligible language, and so on. For a review of the (extremely depressing) literature on this plus a good bibliography, see J. Scott Armstrong, 'Research on Scientific Journals: Implications for Editors and Authors', *Journal of Forecasting* 1, 83–104, 1982. The results Armstrong surveys are stomach-turning. But they do not offer us an excuse. *LI* will get like the psychology, sociology, and economics journals only if we let it. I hope it will not. My reading of the last three volumes suggests to me that there has been an improvement, and I hope that will continue.

But remember, all that is necessary for the triumph of inadequately scrutinized scholarship is that scholars should sit back and read it uncomplainingly. So don't. And that applies just as directly to *Natural Language and Linguistic Theory,* which even has a 'Letters to the Editor' column in which readers can express their disgust immediately if they begin to detect any sliding of standards similar to that which I have illustrated from *LI.* Use that column. Give a damn. Write to the editor.

Chapter Six

Chomsky on the *Enterprise*

This piece was written faster than any other column I ever did. Basically, I got the idea late one afternoon, went home, ate dinner, and then sat down and put the piece together in a single concentrated spasm.

For some reason, I had been looking through the 1982 book by Riny Huybregts and Henk van Riemsdijk, *Noam Chomsky on the Generative Enterprise*, which consists of a transcription of a long interview with Chomsky about the enterprise of doing generative grammar. I found myself objecting and disagreeing at numerous points, of course, and for some reason this mental participation led to a fantasy about what it would be like to find another voice intruding upon the transcribed three-way conversation—an impeccably logical and polite voice, like . . . And the word "enterprise" must have triggered it, because I thought of the calm and unremittingly serious voice of Spock, the Vulcan science officer of the Starship *Enterprise* in the television science-fiction series *Star Trek*.

The piece almost wrote itself—or rather, Huybregts, van Riemsdijk, and Chomsky wrote most of it for me. I simply chopped out chunks of the book that wandered close to topics on which I had contrary opinions to present, and inserted my contributions as new text in the familiar tones of Science Officer Spock. What remained the next day was to write a letter to Foris of Dordrecht, the publishers of the Huybregts and van Riemsdijk's book, to ask for permission to quote the numerous passages that had to be quoted. Perhaps I wasn't totally candid with them about the nature of my creation (I think they formed the impression that I was doing a review article), but I did explicitly ask permission to reprint the passages in question, and supplied them with the complete text of the passages I wanted to use. I promptly received written permission to quote them.

I worried a bit about whether linguists around the world would understand what I was talking about. What if not all linguists followed television science-fiction programs basically made for children? What if lots of linguists had no idea who I was talking about? My fears were allayed when I flew to Tokyo in December 1984 to give some lectures on generalized phrase structure grammar. The first person who came up to speak to me was a Japanese graduate student who said, "I *loved* the latest TOPIC . . . COMMENT, the one about Spock!" I realized then that I needn't have worried; Spock is better known around the world than almost any non-Vulcan who has ever lived.

Somebody told me that the people at Foris were quite good sports about it when the column came out and they saw how the excerpts they permitted me to quote had been exploited. They saw the humor, and after asking around rather nervously about what other linguists thought of this, they decided just to rest content on the principle that all publicity is good publicity. Here's to them: a toast to the Foris Publishing Company for all they have done for the field by their dedication to linguistics publishing. The literature of linguistics would have been the poorer without them, and the wicked spoof that follows would not have been possible.

Books that have neither authors nor editors are unusual in linguistics, but they do exist. The rare items in the *Annual Linguistic Metatheory Conference* series from Michigan State University, East Lansing, are examples: and *Psychological Mechanisms of Language* (The Royal Society and the British Academy, London, 1981) is another such bibliographical oddity. But there is one very special category of such books, namely those produced through the medium of tape-recorded conversations.

There is one figure in linguistics who converses with such fluency and clarity that several enterprising people have simply gone to his office with a tape recorder and come away with a publishable item. At least two have turned out to be book-length. Some time around 1976, Mitsou Ronat put fresh batteries in her tape recorder, loaded a new tape, got an appointment, and started asking questions. The result, when transcribed (with the English parts of the conversation translated into French), was *Dialogues avec Mitsou Ronat* (Flammarion, Paris, France, 1977; by a strange turn of events this book ended up being retranslated into English by John Viertel, who did not have access to the original tapes; the result was published as *Language and Responsibility,* Pantheon, New York, and Harvester, Sussex, England, 1979).

More recently, Riny Huybregts and Henk van Riemsdijk held a session with the same interviewee, and produced *Noam Chomsky on the Generative Enterprise* (Foris, Dordrecht, 1983) in a similar way (though without the two-way translation and retranslation process).

I think this is an exciting development. I am all in favor of new advances in the communications media. In fact, I am developing a further extension of the technique, one that is entirely new, yet owes something to time-honored genres like interlinear glosses, exegetical marginalia, editorial footnotes, and the mediaeval tradition of plagiarism. What I plan to do is to produce a book in which new contributions to significant debates by people who were unable to participate in the original are grafted in at appropriate points.

My first foray into this field, tentatively entitled *Noam Chomsky on the Enterprise: A Discussion with Spock,* will be appearing shortly, if I can succeed in finding a publisher a little less lily-livered than my first fifteen choices have turned out to be. I want to use this column to give a preview of this important and innovative work.

In the original version of their book, Huybregts and van Riemsdijk distinguish their words from Chomsky's in terms of type fonts and line lengths: Huybregts and van Riemsdijk are italicized and have a longer line length, while Chomsky is in roman with a shorter line length. I reproduce this visual effect in my own version, reproducing Chomsky, Huybregts, and van Riemsdijk verbatim throughout (by kind permission of Foris Publications), and I interpolate the contributions of Science Officer Spock (by kind permission of the Starfleet Command of the United Federation of Planets) in a bolder font (bold enough to boldly go where no man has gone before), with a line length intermediate between the other two.

I hope the following extracts will whet the appetite of all those who enjoy well-informed debate and imaginative fiction. The page numbers I cite are to the Huybregts/van Riemsdijk book, for those scholars who wish to compare the original with my improved four-way discussion of the issues. We join Science Officer Spock and the three terrestrial linguists as they discuss Chomsky's view that linguistics has not had nearly as many revolutions as some people think it has. (I think Chomsky is quite right, incidentally. I comment on the obsession some linguists have with revolution-watching in chapter 15, "The revenge of the methodological moaners". Huybregts and van Riemsdijk speak first.

Page 41:

*Don't you think that the situation has begun to change since your
'Conditions on Transformations'?*

My own personal feeling is that this is the first work that I
have done that may lead to the possibility of a conceptual
revolution, if you like. Most of what preceded seems to me
pretty much common sense, though I did find it hard and exciting at the time. But I am very hesitant because there are a
lot of problems with it. It also has to be emphasized, as you
know very well, that this framework is only taken seriously
by a tiny minority in the field, certainly in the United States.

**Your remarks are not supported by factual observations,
Professor. Computer data indicate that approximately 81.39
percent of the graduate students doing syntax in the United
States (as opposed to 0.00012 percent on the planet Vulcan)
are followers of your work. But forgive me, I am interrupt-
ing you.**

For example, I rarely give a talk in a linguistics department
on any work of the past ten or fifteen years.

**Professor Chomsky, might this not have something to do
with the fact that your lecture schedule is booked up in
advance by approximately 17.628 earth months, and linguistics department colloquia are generally planned by an
overworked teacher or student no more than three months
ahead? In any case, it does not seem logical for you to claim
that you would like to give talks at linguistics departments
but that they do not wish to invite you, since the record
shows you have spoken about your work at many of the
most important campuses in the United States.**

If I talk about such things it is in philosophy departments or
to literary people, but those are not technical talks.

**You present the material of 'Conditions on Transforma-
tions' to audiences consisting of specialists in philosophy
and literature?**

A lot of this material can be presented in a fairly informal
and accessible fashion, and often I do. But I rarely go into

technical details with linguists, because there are very few
who are interested.

**I am loath to contradict you on an empirical point, Pro-
fessor, but records made of the conversations of linguists
during the seventies indicate a great deal of desire to learn
the technical details of the proposals you loosely adumbrate
in your publications of the period—a desire that seems
largely to have been left unfulfilled. Dr. van Riemsdijk,
please stop kicking my ankle.**

                    *   *   *

[We now move ahead now to a part of the conversation where
Chomsky is talking about a lack of interest in his work that he per-
ceives within the United States but not in Europe (pages 46 ff.).]

It seems to me that there has been something strange happening in the United States which has aborted potentially con-
structive and creative work in the field . . .

*One of the differences between Europe and North America is that in
Europe we have GLOW. Is that symptomatic of the difference you
have in mind?*

I think what GLOW is doing is exactly right. GLOW has succeeded in bringing together the people who are doing the
most active and exciting work in the field. It is a stimulating
group with the right kind of internal contacts, lively meetings, and so on. That is what a field ought to have.

**Computer records indicate that Dr. Huybregts and Dr. van
Riemsdijk have been very active in founding the GLOW
organization. Can you be sure your evaluation of it in the
present company is entirely founded on objectively verifi-
able facts?**

These things develop out of an objective need and they can't
go further than the objective situation allows them to go.

**But is the objective situation very different in the United
States?**

I would like to see an equivalent of GLOW in the United
States, but I don't think the field is ready for it now,
unfortunately.

But data indicate, Professor, that NELS is an exact equivalent of GLOW in the North-Eastern United States, being dominated by your influence and the work of your students and advocates, and having been so dominated for some time, perhaps since its foundation. Do you not maintain a permanent domicile within the North-Eastern United States? Dr Huybregts, I fail to see why you should be emulating Dr van Riemsdijk in kicking my lower leg under the table.

*   *   *

[Now to page 64, where an exciting discussion of mathematical linguistics gets under way, and Spock really finds his interest becoming aroused. Chomsky is speaking about his foundational work on what is now called the "Chomsky hierarchy".]

By the late 50s I did some work which produced some results in mathematical linguistics that I think may be of some linguistic interest, that is, the work on the relationship between push-down storage automata. What that in effect shows is that anything you can do with a context-free grammar, which is, if you are interested in just covering data, virtually anything, you can also do with a left-to-right automaton with a pushdown memory . . .

Professor Chomsky, I feel obliged to point out that it is *not* possible to do "virtually anything" with a context-free grammar, such simple operations as phrasal reduplication and trilateral string-length equivalence checking being entirely beyond the power of such a grammar. Moreover, it was in part your own mathematical work that clearly established this within Earth's scientific community.

That is not very interesting. It does not answer any of the real questions at all, because neither of these two strongly equivalent systems offers any hope, as far as I could see then or now, for dealing with the real problems that have to be accounted for . . .

Still there are people who seem to be attracted to the idea that context-free grammars suffice to deal with the properties of natural language, both along the dimension of weak, and along that of strong, generative capacity. Gazdar, for example, in some of his recent papers expresses this line of thought.

> I have not read Gazdar's dissertation, so maybe I do not quite understand what he is doing.

Illogical, Professor. Gazdar's dissertation was about the pragmatics of presupposition, and has nothing to do with the work on syntax that your interlocutors are discussing with you. What is your opinion of his work on context-free grammars?

> What I have seen of his work on context-free grammars seems to me to be based on a misunderstanding. People often say, I have noticed this in recent papers, that if you can get down to one transformation, say 'move alpha,' then an even better theory would be to get down to no transformation at all. Superficially, that sounds right, but it is completely wrong.

It seems logical to me, Professor. Can you clarify your objection?

> It is only right if other things remain constant, and in fact in Gazdar's theory other things definitely do not remain constant. He vastly increases the number of possible grammars up to a class of grammars that generate context-free languages, which is a radical enrichment of the theory hence a huge step backwards.

Professor, while I hesitate to resort to the *ad hominem*, I must point out that Gazdar cannot have increased the class of grammars to anything that goes beyond what you allow in the base component, because you assume the base is a context-free grammar. Thus whatever he can describe, you can in principle describe using only a base component over some finite nonterminal alphabet. He is simply employing the full flexibility inherent in Type 2 rewriting systems. Is this not in fact what you yourself did in your master's thesis?

> His theory does not seem radically different from what was in my *Morphophonemics of Modern Hebrew* back in the late 40s. That was a phrase structure grammar with a lot of indices, which you could recode as a context-free grammar if

you wanted to. What is sometimes not recognized is that such devices vastly increase the class of grammars available.

It is not recognized because it is not true, Professor. Such systems remain within the bounds of whatever class of grammars corresponds to the class of base components of transformational grammars, which is normally taken to be a class with the generative capacity of context-free grammars.

They may have the weak generative capacity of context-free grammars, but that is a fact of almost null significance . . .

Null significance only if one is unconcerned with matters of truth and logic, Professor.

If you allow yourself the class of context-free grammars, including those coded with indices, then that is just a huge mass of possible systems as compared with for example X-bar theory with 'move alpha' added to it.

Illogical, Professor. There is an infinite class of equivalent X-bar phrase structure grammars corresponding to any context-free grammar. The proof is trivial. I will merely sketch it.[1] For any context-free grammar G there is an algorithm for constructing an equivalent Greibach normal form grammar (in which every right hand side of a rule begins with a terminal symbol). Assume a GNF grammar G for a language L. For each rule $R = A \rightarrow aB \ldots Z$ in G, replace R by $A'' \rightarrow A'$, $A' \rightarrow AB \ldots Z$, $A \rightarrow a$ where A'' and A' are new nonterminals (of bar level 2 and 1 respectively), and replace A by A'' in each rule that has A in its right hand side. The result is an X-bar grammar for L that obeys the strict endocentricity and uniform (2-bar) level conditions. Since any GNF grammar for L can be converted into a larger strongly equivalent grammar in various simple ways, this shows that infinitely many X-bar grammars for L can be constructed. To evade this proof, a stipulated finite upper bound on the number of distinct syntactic categories in lin-

1. Spock's proof sketch has subsequently been worked over in considerably more detail by András Kornai and Geoffrey K. Pullum, 'The X-bar theory of phrase structure', *Language* 66.24–50, 1990. Spock does seem to be right.

guistic theory would minimally be necessary. Your work contains no suggestion that any such stipulation should be made; you have normally eschewed such numerical stipulations as *ad hoc*. For example, in the case of the restriction on human (though not Vulcan) brains to a small, finite number of center-embeddings, you have denied that a numerical restriction in the grammar is called for. When 'move alpha' is added to the theory, the number of grammars is either exactly the same (if there are no variable parameters that have to do with the range of alpha), or, if there are possible conditions on alpha, as you have occasionally suggested, the number of grammars will be greater. But it cannot possibly be less. Logic dictates, therefore, that either Gazdar is working with a class of grammars of the same size as your own, or he is working with a smaller class. Thus I find it hard to appreciate the sense of your remark about a "huge mass" of possible grammars.

> [T]heories of the sort we have been considering for the past 10 years or so allow only a finite number of core grammars anyway (apart from the lexicon), so that all these questions dissolve.

I have just observed, Professor Chomsky, that the class of X-bar base components is infinite, and the total class of transformational grammars under the terms of your theory is either similar or more inclusive. There is no logical construal of your comment about theories that allow only a finite class of systems.[2]

It has been a pleasure making your acquaintance, gentlemen, but now I have some pressing duties aboard my ship. Mr Scott: kindly beam our visitors back to Massachusetts Avenue.

2. The point that Spock makes here is examined in greater detail in Geoffrey K. Pullum, 'How many possible human languages are there?', *Linguistic Inquiry* 14.447–467, 1983. Again, I have to say that Commander Spock appears to be ineluctably correct.

Chapter Seven

Formal linguistics meets the Boojum

First, for those who have never heard of Boojum, or even a Snark, those from whom the phrase 'They pursued it with forks and hope' elicits nothing but a blank stare, let me recommend Martin Gardner's *The Annotated Snark* (Bramhall House, 1962), an annotated edition of Lewis Carroll's poem *The Hunting of the Snark*.

With that out of the way, little remains except for me to say that as I reflected on the state of linguistics in the late 1980s one day, it occurred to me that there is virtually no one left doing real generative grammar, only (a) people who think they are doing it but clearly aren't, and (b) people who used to do it but now do something else. This was no doubt an oversimplification of an exaggeration, or perhaps an exaggeration of an oversimplification, but no matter: rather than do any serious analysis of the question, I decided to exorcize the topic (which I found rather depressing, since I have enjoyed participating in the work of generative grammar) by writing a TOPIC . . . COMMENT column about the disappearance of generative grammatical study as a subfield of linguistics, and play it for laughs.

I hope my concern about the recession of interest in formalized linguistic theories doesn't make this piece too depressing. There are some serious charges in the middle, with quotations and references and all that; poor Noam Chomsky gets hammered again (unavoidable, I'm afraid; as the single most influential figure in linguistics in this century, perhaps in all history, and now as the major anti-formal influence in the field, he cannot but loom large).

The piece isn't ultimately serious, though. It gets crazy at the end, as the reader of TOPIC . . . COMMENT should expect. What the reader should *not* expect is that anyone should take the piece as stone-cold serious and write a serious response to it. But unfortunately, this has actually happened with the appearance of Noam Chomsky's 'On formalization and formal linguistics' (*Natural Language and Linguistic Theory* 8.143−47, 1990).

I will bite my tongue and say nothing here in rebuttal of Chomsky's remarks. But I cannot resist pointing out that the reader who takes the trouble to examine the supposed definition of dominance Chomsky quotes on his page 146, which purports to come from his book *Barriers* (MIT Press, 1986; p. 7), will be startled to discover that *the quoted definition and the original definition are not the same.*
   "For the Snark *was* a Boojum, you see."

I try not to take things too seriously. I am normally able to laugh at things that would be prime candidates for the weeping, wailing, and gnashing of teeth department if my sense of the ridiculous were suddenly amputated. But there is one thing that oppresses my soul in the current linguistics scene; one stomach-gnawing phobia that causes me to wake up and go downstairs and pad about in the small hours of the morning. I want to share it with you. Perhaps the sharing will exorcise the fear—though this is relatively unlikely, because there is so much good evidence that I am right to be afraid.

My fear is that formal linguistics in the true sense will disappear from our profession completely, in the USA and probably the entire world, hence the whole solar system and perhaps the cosmos. Not just recede from some position of dominance in the wider field (it has none), but actually disappear—conferences, journals, intellectual community and all.

The Baker in Lewis Carroll's *The Hunting of the Snark* feared that if he ever met a Boojum he would just "softly and suddenly vanish away, and never be met with again," and attentive Lewis Carroll readers will recall that despite the confidence-inspiring leadership of the Bellman (the Chomsky figure in the poem, I always feel), the Baker's fears were not the least bit unjustified. Nor are mine, I believe.

Of course, one thing there is no danger of is the disappearance of the *word* 'formal'. Part of the problem is that a word can survive the erosion and eventual loss of its referent; think of the word 'equal' in Orwell's *Animal Farm,* or the word 'defense' since 1945. Just because there is a West Coast Conference on Formal Linguistics each year does not guarantee that formal work will survive, any more than the existence of Democratic People's Republics guarantees that democracy will survive.

I do recognize that to take the notion 'formal' in linguistics as rigidly as it is standardly taken in mathematics and logic would be to risk eliminating formal linguistics immediately, since no work yet done would count as instantiating it. The criteria for formal theories set out in logic books are stringent, and doubtless, nothing in linguistics meets them at the level of detail. But one can readily see which work in linguistics is making a concerted *effort* to meet them, as opposed to just tossing them aside. That will be sufficient to satisfy me that a given line of work can properly be called formal. Call me a softy, but I give marks for effort.

The formal linguistics I am referring to has languages and grammars as its objects of investigation, and its conduct involves the precise definition and testing of grammars and classes of grammars. The following three conditions (paraphrased from Robert R. Stoll, *Sets, Logic, and Axiomatic Theories,* W. H. Freeman, San Francisco, 1961, chapter 3) are non-negotiable, at least as statements of intent, for formal theories of grammar in the sense I intend.

(I) The notion 'structural representation' must be effective. That is, there must be an algorithm for determining whether some arbitrary string, graph, or diagram counts as a structural representation according to the theory.

(II) The notion of 'rule' (or 'principle' or 'law' or 'condition' or 'constraint' or 'filter' or whatever) must be effective. That is, there must be an algorithm for determing whether some arbitrary string, graph, or diagram is a rule (or 'principle' or 'law' . . .) according to the theory.

(III) The notion 'generates' (or 'admits' or 'licenses' or whatever) must be effective. That is, there must be an algorithm for determining whether some arbitrary structural representation is generated (or admitted or licensed . . .) by a given set of rules (or 'principles' or 'laws' . . .).

The extent to which most of today's "generative grammar" enthusiasts have abandoned any aspiration to a formal orientation in the above sense can only be described as utter. Consider the state of phonology, for example. Even the best friends of the nonlinear phonology that has driven the relatively formal pre-1977-style segmental phonology into the wilderness (and I am an affectionate acquaintance) will admit that it isn't trying to meet the conditions set out above for formal theories. True, a very significant outpouring of new ideas and new diagrammatic ways of attempting to express them has sprung up over the past decade; but it is quite clear that at the moment no one can say even in rough outline what a phonological representation comprises, using some exactly specified theoretical language. Nor is there much sign of published work that even addresses the issues involved in a serious way. Drifting this way and that in a sea of competing proposals for intuitively evaluated graphic representation does not constitute formal linguistic research, not even if interesting hunches about phonology are being tossed around in the process.

Yet phonologists have good authority for heading in their present direction—the best authority, since Chomsky, still the most influential linguist in the world, has turned his face more and more sternly against formal work over the years, finally reaching the point of openly mocking it and counter-advocating it.

This latter assertion must be documented, because many will insist it is not so. After all, it was Chomsky who in 1957 issued what is still the finest and most cogent defense of the formalist position that linguistics has ever had:

> Precisely constructed models for linguistic structure can play an important role, both negative and positive, in the process of discovery itself. By pushing a precise but inadequate formulation to an unacceptable conclusion, we can often expose the exact source of this inadequacy and, consequently, gain a deeper understanding of the linguistic data. More positively, a formalized theory may automatically provide solutions for many problems other than those for which it was explicitly designed. Obscure and intuition-bound notions can neither lead to absurd conclusions nor provide new and correct ones, and hence they fail to be useful in two important respects. I think that some of those linguists who have questioned the value of precise and technical development of linguistic theory have failed to recognize the productive potential in the method of rigorously stating a proposed theory and applying it strictly to linguistic material with no attempt to avoid unacceptable conclusions by *ad hoc* adjustments or loose formulation. [Noam Chomsky, *Syntactic Structures,* Mouton, The Hague, 1957, p. 5.]

Never was it better put, before or since. And as late as 1976, Chomsky would still speak in broadly approving terms of work that took seriously his 1957 recommendation; for example (from a January 1976 conversation later transcribed to make a book—cf. chapter 6):

> I hope these studies [of formal properties of grammars and generative power] will continue to be pursued, as well as the mathematical investigation of transformational grammars. There has been some interesting recent work by Stanley Peters and Robert Ritchie

on this latter topic. [*Language and Responsibility,* Pantheon, New York, 1979, p. 127.]

Peters and Ritchie's work gets the "interesting" accolade here. But by two or three years later, in 1978 and 1979 lectures, that "interesting" work, with its important consequences for generative grammatical theories, was downgraded to "seriously misinterpreted" (*Rules and Representations,* Basil Blackwell, Oxford, 1980, p. 122) and had permanently lost its status as "interesting".

By about 1979, a rhetorical program to sap the strength of Peters/Ritchie-style arguments had been put into effect: Chomsky came up with his zany "conclusion that only a finite number of core grammars are available in principle," which he claimed "has consequences for the mathematical investigation of generative power and learnability," namely that it "trivializes these investigations" (*Lectures on Government and Binding,* Foris, Dordrecht, 1981, p. 11).

At around the same time, Chomsky began an attack on the very idea of languages as formally specifiable objects, putting forth the view that grammars might "characterize languages that are not recursive or even not recursively enumerable, or even . . . not generate languages at all without supplementation from other faculties of mind." (No sense was ever supplied to the notion of a grammar that is discovered and tested through language study but which does not characterize any language.)

And from this total change of direction, "nothing of much import would necessarily follow" (ibid., p. 13), according to Chomsky. Nothing of much import? Only the defining idealization of formal linguistics: the idea that languages are abstractly definable and can be studied in isolation from biological or biographical facts about their speakers. It may be a methodological fiction (like the idea that economic systems can be studied in isolation from the sometimes irrational spending behavior of actual people in actual shopping malls), but there is no formal linguistics without it.

Since 1979, Chomsky has steadily escalated the scorn level of his opposition to formal linguistics. In taped conversations from 1980 (fortunately, Chomsky has left almost as many taped conversations around as Nixon did) we find him being yet more dismissive about mathematical studies of generative capacity (for example: "the notion of weak generative capacity . . . has almost no linguistic significance" [*Noam Chomsky on the Generative Enterprise,* by R.

Huybregts and H. van Riemsdijk, Foris, Dordrecht, 1982, p. 73]),
and pooh-poohing the idea of making theories formally precise ("I
do not see any point in formalizing for the sake of formalizing. You
can always do that"; ibid., p. 101), and speaking dismissively of
learnability research ("it is hard to imagine many mathematical
problems about the acquisition of systems of a finite class"; ibid.,
p. 112).

By March 1981, speaking at the Royal Society in London, Chomsky was making similar points even more stridently. He asserted that
in the light of his recent work, "most of the results of mathematical
linguistics, which in any event have been seriously misinterpreted,
become empirically virtually or completely empty" (*Philosophical
Transactions of the Royal Society of London,* series B, 1981, p. 233).
In a written reply to a question submitted later, he spoke of "the
meaninglessness of the question of generative capacity" (p. 277),
described mathematical linguistics as "marginalized" (p. 280), and
dismissed a point about parsability with a reductio to a silly view
described as "no more serious than most of what appears in the literature with regard to the empirical significance of results in mathematical linguistics" (p. 278).

Five years later, worse than ever, we find Chomsky going so far as
to say (about X-bar systems) that "there is no point in specifying one
or another of the possible options in detail; in particular, further formalization is pointless, since there are no theorems of any interest to
be proved or hidden assumptions to be teased out in these systems"
(*Barriers,* MIT Press, Cambridge, 1986, p. 91, footnote 3).

Chomsky flatly rejects his 1957 position, in other words. He *knows
in advance* that there cannot be any point in formalizing his ideas.
Forgotten are his claims of three decades before that "a formalized
theory may automatically provide solutions for many problems other
than those for which it was explicitly designed." One is reminded of
the anonymous premature epitaph once constructed for the British
prime minister Lloyd George:

> Count not his broken pledges as a crime:
> He MEANT them, *HOW* he meant them—at the time.

Chomsky only meant his words how he meant them, it would seem.
His contemporary work pays them not the slightest heed. Consider
this total baffler, for example (from *Barriers,* p. 7):

(12)
α is dominated by β only if it is dominated by every segment of β.

That's right, in addition to an unresolved anaphoric *it* (for which I will assume subject control), this mumbo jumbo, apparently intended as a new definition of dominance, refers to dominance on *both sides,* the definiendum occurring in the definiens! It is as if one said in a work on number theory that one was going to assume "*x* is a prime factor of *y* only if *x* is a prime factor of every factor of *y*." What does it *mean?* Only someone fully content to dismiss formalization as pointless could be so cavalier as to redefine something as fundamental as dominance without bothering to make the redefinition coherent.

To give Chomsky his due, one must note that he is completely consistent in his abandonment of formality and explicitness. He even makes it clear that he knows the passage in question may not be coherent as it stands; his nearby footnote 10 says defensively, "Formalization of this idea is fairly straightforward, requiring introduction of the notion of occurrence of a category." Maybe that means something, maybe it doesn't; but who cares? Remember, he has already warned the over-eager reader, seven footnotes earlier, that "further formalization is pointless." So you can just put that pencil down, understand?

The conclusion I draw from the casually bungled definitions in *Barriers* (and the crucial definitions in nearly all current work by Chomsky's co-enthusiasts) is that those syntacticians who are close followers of MIT work are not likely to be the ones who will keep formal linguistics alive. Government-binding syntax (or principles-and-parameters syntax; who cares, it's only words) no longer makes any pretense at being formally intelligible. It is set to develop into a gentle, vague, cuddly sort of linguistics that will sit very well with the opponents of generative grammar if they compromise just enough to learn a little easy descriptive vocabulary and some casually deployed and loosely understood labelled bracketing for which no one will be held accountable.

It is ironic that the people doing GB work are sometimes opposed for being 'formalist' or 'generativist' when in truth they are nothing of the sort. Those linguists who decided long ago that generative grammar was something they were opposed to should look again;

they will find that what they disliked, including not only the algebraic tools but even the conceptual separation of languages from
people, has dissolved away.

There are many separate subcommunities, of course, among these
opponents—the members of the linguistic profession who would
typically reject labels like 'generative' or 'formal' as applied to their
own work. There are anthropological linguists and articulatory phoneticians and correlational sociolinguists and acquisition specialists
and conversational analysts and lexical semanticists and classical
philologists and literary stylisticians and language planners and
worldspeak proponents and TESOL practitioners and all manner of
worthy people. But a particularly relevant subgroup among them
consists of those syntacticians who are referred to by cruel people at
UCLA as the Fuzzies. (This is a wholly unfair designation, which I
utterly condemn, but will continue to use out of laziness and a certain
lack of moral fiber. It may in fact be kinder than some other names in
use. I recently learned that some Northern California linguists call
them 'Flat-Earth Functionalists'.)

The Fuzzies believe that the important directions in grammatical
research at the moment are things like cohesion and information
structuring in discourse, the different flows of information in written
and spoken language, the use of different sentence types in different
situational contexts, the influence of the communicative function of
language on sentence structure, and stuff like that.

I have no antipathy toward such work; it can be mildly interesting
(not that a slow Sunday at a BLS meeting may not sometimes be a bit
yawn-inducing). But it is not giving rise to any formal linguistics,
and it is not likely to. How passives are structured into phrases or
grammatical relation networks and associated with denotational
meaning in a language is something I think there can be a formal
account of, but the same is not true of how much more likely it is that
a passive rather than an active will occur in a particular discourse
context given a certain degree of agency of the predicate, a certain
text frequency of the verb, and a given level of author's empathy with
the protagonist.

What no one seems to have fully appreciated is that *current MIT
syntax will blend very nicely with the work of the Fuzzies.* And the
resultant amalgam will be unstoppable. Students of the early 1990s, I
predict, will write dissertations on such topics as how point of view
of participants affects relative strength of barriers, and their mixed

GB/Fuzzy thesis committees will be delighted. An invincible coalition will have emerged: the anti-formalists in pursuit of the unformalizable.

It will be the death knell for formal linguistics *sensu stricto*. I see the few formal linguists who survive, slightly crazed as a result of isolation and inbreeding, taking to the hills in places like Montana and northern Idaho, like the groups of white racist loonies who fondly imagine they are the last hope of the United States. Occasionally one will read of a heavily armed FBI team shooting it out in a siege of a fortified formalist farmhouse, and mainstream linguists, pausing amid their work of unifying θ-roles with cognitive stereotypes, will say: "Are those crazies still out there?"

Perhaps sometimes a lonely old madman with stringy gray hair and wild eyes will be found seizing people by the arm at an LSA meeting and haranguing them about precise definitions of formal underpinnings, until he is taken away by hotel security people.

Soon there will be no one left in linguistics who knows what an ordered pair is, or when you spell *if* with a double *f,* and no one will have any idea what the consequences of their theories or the denotations of their diagrams are, or what it means to have an interpretation for a notation . . . The whole revolution in linguistics that Bloch and Harris prepared us for and that *Syntactic Structures* ushered in "will softly and suddenly vanish away."

> *'It is this, it is this—' 'We have had that before!'*
> *The Bellman indignantly said.*
> *And the Baker replied, 'Let me say it once more.*
> *It is this, it is this that I dread!'*

Part Two

Publication and Damnation

Chapter Eight

Stalking the perfect journal

This is the first of two columns on the same subject which actually had some influence on developments that, by a very tiny increment, made the world a better place. As the sequel (chapter 11) documents, some journal publishers actually took note of the recommendations it made, and altered some aspects of the appearance and organization of their organs.

The subject is the myriad frustrations of being a scholar and doing library research. It is a little bit dry, but there is a lemon-twist of bitterness in it that (I hope) keeps it somewhat more entertaining than an article on library science would normally be.

My title is, of course, irrelevantly, a nod to Gary Trudeau's cartoon strip collection entitled *Stalking the Perfect Tan*. It occurs to me in retrospect that many of my TOPIC . . . COMMENT columns were titled using Trudeau's normal strategy of plucking an unlikely but memorable line out of the text; *Stalking the Perfect Tan* happens to be a Trudeau title that was not derived in this way, but the majority were (*Wouldn't a Gremlin Have Been More Sensible?*; *But the Pension Fund Was Just Sitting There; Give Those Nymphs Some Hooters;* and so on). I apologize to the tidy-minded for this navel-contemplative digression on the inner workings of the kinds of plagiarism that I employ when creative genius eludes me.

At one point in this column I mention DEC-20s. This will puzzle younger readers, who will never have heard of such a thing. A DEC-20 was a thing like a computer only bigger and noisier. Old people remember them. They are not used any more. I'm sorry I brought the subject up.

Some linguists get by without using libraries much. If you are working in rural New Guinea or Brazil on a language not relatable genetically to any other, there might not be very much a library could

help you with (even if you could get to one). If your work is so profoundly in advance of the rest of the field that there is no point in
your consulting work other than your own, there may again be no
need for you to have access to a library; doubtless your sole need will
be for the soft crayons provided for you by your institution. But the
broad mass of the linguistic public will have worked in libraries, and
will know the experience of searching musty stacks for books and
journals. Often they will have asked themselves questions such as
these:

• Why do philosophy-related journals get stolen so much?
• Why do book reviews so often have the author's name at the end
  instead of the beginning, so when you start to browse you don't
  know who you're reading?
• Who on earth reads *Semiotika?*
• What ever happened to *Word?*
• Why was the spine of *Language* vol. 51, no. 4 (December 1975)
  printed upside down, i.e. from top to bottom, unlike every other
  issue in the last decade?
• Why is *IJAL* shrinking vertically (10″ high in 1973; 9.5″ from 1973
  to 1981; now 9″ high and falling)?

The world is full of such puzzles. I do not seriously expect to have
answers to all of them. But I do have a few basic expectations about
what a journal in my field should provide for me, and I find that each
one provides only a randomly selected proper subset of them. I devote this column to a few suggestions that I feel are reasonable
enough that the perfect journal would follow all of them. In all
cases, I think, following them would serve the linguistic public a
little better and make the researcher's life a little easier. The first nine
are rather straightforward matters of publishing form rather than editorial policy or scholarly substance.

1. *Dates of receipt and revision printed along with each article
   published*

It's often very important to know just when an article first hit the editor's in-tray and when it returned from revision after being refereed.
It could make all the difference. Did so-and-so and whatsisname submit your idea for publication before you even thought of it? That
might call for a note of acknowledgment and congratulation. Or did
you write it down in a letter to a close colleague of theirs about three
months before they published it without acknowledgment? That might
call for something else.

2. *Month of publication printed in each issue*

It doesn't matter whether the journal has a regular schedule like *Language* (March, June, September, December) or an irregular one like the increasing number of journals that aren't quite sure how many issues they are going to get out in a year; we would still be aided by being able to read off the front cover of an issue the month in which it hit the racks.

3. *Author's full mailing address published with every article*

Linguistic Inquiry has this, but hardly any other linguistics journal does. It's extremely useful. Who can remember the zip code for Storrs, Connecticut? And who has a copy of the LSA's guide to *Linguistics Programs in the USA and Canada* that hasn't been borrowed by a colleague just when you need it? So you turn to whatever article by Howard Lasnik comes to your mind, and there's the address of the University of Connecticut. I must have used *LI* as a directory a hundred times that way

4. *Contents list on cover*

This is too obvious. But, for instance, some old issues of *Linguistic Analysis* have it, and some don't!

5. *Page numbers on spine of each issue*

When there are four or more issues per year, and you know you want the paper that took up pages 287–314, you don't know which issue to take down from the shelf. Many journals print this on the spine of each issue, but *Linguistic Inquiry,* for example, doesn't.

6. *First/last page numbers printed on first page of each article*

If I had a dollar for each time I have had to scan to the end of an article to see whether it ended on an odd (right) page and left the following even (left) page blank or ran through to the even page so that the next article started on the immediately following page, I could subscribe to another journal. The problem is that there is no function from contents pages to first/last page numbers of individual articles until you know the policy of a given journal. *Language* never leaves blank pages, and starts articles on left pages if need be. *Linguistic Inquiry* doesn't; page 468 of volume 14, number 3, for example, is completely blank. It is sometimes possible to establish from a contents page that a journal does not leave blank even pages, of course: if any article in any issue begins on an even-numbered page according to the contents page, then there will be no blank pages, and you can read off the first/last page numbers of all articles from the contents list. But if all articles in an issue begin on odd-

numbered pages, you cannot establish what policy you are con-
fronted with, and you have to check to see whether you are dealing
with pp. 447–67 or pp. 447–68. All of this pain is avoided if, right
on the first page of every article (and thus on the front of every offprint of it), the reference details, including page numbers, are given.

7. *Footnotes on the page*[1]

How do publishers think you're supposed to read authors who put
lengthy but crucial digressions and important polemical criticisms
into footnotes, when they put the footnotes forty pages away at the
end of the article? You can't hold a volume open at two places simultaneously and still hold your cup of coffee, that's the main problem.
Notes at the end of the article drive me crazy. Some penny-pinching
publishers even put the footnotes at the end in *books*. The worst of
them put the footnotes at the end of the whole thing in a set of clumps
corresponding to chapter numbers (Notes to Chapter IV, etc.), and
then don't provide in the running head any information as to the number of the chapter you're in. So the procedure is this:

 (1) Memorize footnote number.
 (2) Hold current reading page and look forward to end of book to
     find notes section.
 (3) Look through footnote section to find heading for notes to ap-
     propriate chapter.
 (4) You will now find you have forgotten what chapter you were
     in. Hold first page of notes section and look back to held
     reading page.
 (5) You will now find that the running head within the chapter
     you were in does not reveal the chapter number, but only the
     title and author of the book. Leaf back from current reading
     page to beginning of chapter, attempting to hold beginning of
     notes section and current reading page with two unused
     fingers.
 (6) On arriving at beginning of chapter, memorize its number.
 (7) Still holding current reading page, go forward again to begin-
     ning of notes section.
 (8) Leaf forward through notes section to find notes for relevant
     chapter.
 (9) You will now find that you have forgotten the footnote num-
     ber you memorized in step (1). Go back to current reading
     page, holding current notes page.
(10) Memorize footnote number again.

1. Like this.

(11) Go forward again to current notes page and read footnote.
(12) Go back to current reading page and recommence reading text.

The note, when you get there, will of course just say something like: 'As has often been noted; cf. Quarmby, *op. cit.*' But where was Quarmby's op. last cit.? Was it even in this chapter?

If my widely known patience and tolerance ever gives out and I commit violence on a fellow human being, it will definitely be committed on a publisher who cuts costs by having the printer put the notes at the end of the chapter or article. Sure, it is expensive to do otherwise. Regardless of whether the computation is done by a DEC-20 or by a little old man with a wooden mallet and a tray of lead type, it is computationally very expensive to figure out how to skip just enough lines of text on a given page to allow room for the footnotes whose numbers will fall on that page given the skipping you just did. I fully appreciate that. But some things are worth what you pay for them.

8. *Announcements of articles to appear in forthcoming issues*

It's nice to be able to see into the future. And one gets so few chances to do so. The favored few who are on the personal mailing lists of the right authors get papers in advance; there is no reason why the rest of the humble reading public should not know at least the titles of the papers they will be reading in three months' time.

9. *Style sheet printed in each issue*

Often, when you first consider submitting an article to a journal, you have only a particular issue of the journal to go by as regards style details for submitted manuscripts. If the inside cover provides you with even just superficial details of how your article should look, how the references should be formatted, how many copies you send, and so on, it would be a great help. The rather demanding style sheet for *Language* (bold face is only admissible "for certain forms in Oscan and Umbrian, and when necessary to distinguish Gaulish", it states sternly) is found only in certain issues of the *LSA Bulletin*. This comes to all subscribers to the journal (i.e., members of the LSA), to be sure. But try this experiment: hold your breath, and don't take in any oxygen until you have the right issue of the Bulletin open in front of you, starting now. I don't know your office, but if you succeed in this experiment as opposed to collapsing with anoxia, I salute you. You are extremely well organized, and probably keep your underwear in alphabetical order.

I have conducted[2] a survey of seven well-known journals to see how well they do on this list of basic formal and production-level desiderata for the perfect journal. The league table at the time the survey was done looked like this:

1st (tied):   *Linguistic Analysis*
              Natural Language and Linguistic Theory
3rd: *Journal of Linguistics*
4th (tied):   *Language*
              Linguistics and Philosophy
6th (tied):   *Linguistic Inquiry*
              Linguistic Review

The full details are shown in Table 1.

The perfect journal, I submit, would have pluses all the way down. But there is no such journal in sight.

Let us now turn to matters that bear more on content and substance, and have more to do with the editor than the publisher.

10. *Squibs, notes, discussion*

Does the journal publish short notes or squibs, presenting briefly statable observations or critical comments? Such a forum is a very important one when a field is faced with an explosively growing literature. And I would personally like to see *short* squibs. The squibs in *Linguistic Inquiry* have developed over the years into rather polished little papers that often extend over half a dozen pages. Gone are the brief notes reporting a sudden brainwave, a recent goof, or a new and baffling isolated fact (the "mystery squibs" of yore).

11. *Blind refereeing*

Do referees receive papers for review with the name and affiliation of the author at the top, so that all available prejudices against either can be brought to bear, or is the paper stripped of identifying marks before being passed out for review? (Don't ever think it couldn't make a difference to what gets published!) There are plenty of difficulties, of course, especially with authors who eschew the decent obscurity of the agentless passive, and say brash things like "As I have argued in my recent book . . ."; but we could try.

---

2. Well, I say "I"; this is the kind of mendacity you typically get among people who have research assistants working for them. Let's be honest, for once: it was Holly Hoods who went over to the library and looked these facts up. Thus the denotation of my use of "I" here would actually be better borne if I had put "she". I didn't even move out of my swivel chair in the TOPIC . . . COMMENT office. I should be ashamed of myself. Thanks, Holly.

Table 1: Some journal policies as of early 1984

	NLLT	L&P	JL	LR	LI	LA	Lg.
1. date of receipt	+		+			+	+
2. publication month		+	+	+		+	+
3. authors' addresses	+				+		
4. contents on cover	+	+	+		+	+	+
5. page numbers on spine	+	+	+			+	+
6. first/last page nos.	+	+	+	+		+	
7. footnotes on page	+		+		+	+	+
8. forthcoming papers	+	+					
9. style sheet each issue				+		+	

12. *Heterogeneity of editorial influence*

Does the journal split the editorial duties between the members of an active board that is geographically and doctrinally diverse? Some journals (I name no names) are clearly one-person platforms, with an editorial board whose main purpose is to fill the inside front cover with faraway places and strange-sounding names. Others genuinely parcel out the duties to a group of scholars with distinct areas of expertise, rather than to a knot of cronies.

Finally, let me introduce a criterion that no linguistics journal in existence satisfies. Some will say, in fact, that there is no realistic hope of ever implementing it:

13. *Publication of names of accepting referees*

What I am suggesting is that with each article published there should appear the names of the referees whose judgments determined that it should be accepted. With rejected articles, of course, the names of the referees should remain forever secret; but when referees decide to recommend the publication of a paper, and it does consequently get published, they should be required to agree to have it publicly announced that they endorsed the work.

What would be the advantages? First, more thorough and thought-ful refereeing. A small part of one's reputation would be on the line when one submitted a favorable judgment on someone's linguistic work, and one would be that much more careful.

Second, a very limited way of recognizing the contribution of those hard-working people who do more than their fair share of the thankless work of refereeing. There are many who avoid the chore by the simple expedient of proving to editor after editor that they are lazy, slapdash, or unreliable. (How I wish I could believe that none of those adjectives could ever have been levelled at me.) There are others who spend long hours of what could have been their research or leisure time writing lengthy and detailed comments on papers that are enormously improved before publication as a result, yet few lin-guists ever learn of their service.

And third, a public check on editorial policy. Sometimes one finds oneself suspecting that a certain paper has made it into print on the judgment of referees who were not only partisan supporters of the author's theoretical viewpoint but members of the same class in graduate school. It would be nice to know. And an interesting picture would be built up over time of the referee selection policy of the edi-tor of the journal.

There is no trace of a journal that comes up shining by all thirteen of the criteria I have discussed. It would be pleasing to think that I could exert enough influence on the people who have created *Natural Language and Linguistic Theory* to cause them to go for the whole baker's dozen, but there is little hope.

Chapter Nine

Punctuation and human freedom

Not just a howl of anger directed at copy-editors, but, well, mostly just a howl of anger directed at copy-editors, I must admit. The theme of this piece is bound up with the difference between rules in spoken and written language, take-out food laws on Fire Island, illegal sexual behaviors in Indiana, Shakespeare's *Richard III*, the Grand Teton mountains in Wyoming, Spielberg's comic horror movie *Gremlins*, the LSA style sheet, the Xerox Corporation . . . I guess it wanders a bit, actually.

I did get some correspondence from worried copy-editors who thought I might be angry with them, and I noticed that for a few months I was being treated very gently by the editorial staffs of all the publishers I dealt with, the way one treats someone who has recently been released from an institution for the criminally insane. But soon, after six months or so, they were all back to their old ways, moving my quote marks around, changing my *which* to *that* and my *that* to *which*, capitalizing 'north' if I had not done so and decapitalizing it otherwise, removing hyphens I wanted and putting in others that I didn't.

Cathie Ringen's T-shirt was misquoted when this column was originally published; I said 'University of Iowa, Idaho City, Illinois'; it really says Ohio, not Illinois—but the point is clear either way: people confuse the names of noncoastal states with 'I' in their names. The T-shirt really does exist; Bill Ladusaw has one as well. But the Campaign for Typographical Freedom does not, so please stop sending money.

Geoffrey Nunberg tells me that the article he published in the December 1983 number of *Atlantic* attracted the biggest mailbag that any single article in the magazine has ever elicited. The topic of the article was grammar. Yes, plain old English grammar, such as people (quite wrongly) claim is not taught in the schools any more. It is the most incendiary subject in America today. In the wake of the publication of Nunberg's article (entitled 'The grammar wars'), Nunberg was flown to Boston for a startlingly high fee to be consulted by Houghton-Mifflin about a dictionary they are working on, and was subsequently sent on a tour of radio and TV stations by the same publishers to sit on panels and to guest on chat shows. Lines to the stations jammed and the call-in switchboards lit up like airport runways.

Nunberg feels he knows why. Take a much less incendiary subject like civil strife and governmental misdeeds in Guatemala, and a talk-show guest who purports to be an expert on the subject will be taken as an expert; a few callers who either wish to be further enlightened by competent authority or who themselves have a claim to be called expert in the internal affairs of Guatemala will call in, but otherwise the expert will have the run of the airwaves. Like the mythical Mr. Science invented by the Duck's Breath Mystery Theater radio satire group, "He knows more than you do." But there is no general public recognition of experts on language. Everyone feels entitled to an opinion. Indeed, an astonishing range of people with absolutely no qualifications for the job are prepared to set themselves up as primary fountainheads of grammatical dogma.

How could we linguists have allowed this to happen? The situation bespeaks some real blunders in the public relations handling of our profession. We *are* experts, and it is demeaning that pontificating fools like John Simon, William Safire, Edwin Newman, and the other grammar columnists of the American press (to all of whom Nunberg is much too polite in his otherwise excellent article) should be telling the public where they can and can't use plural agreement. If anyone is going to tell them, it should be *our* job. Moreover, as experts, we linguists deserve certain courtesies, like high rates of pay, and blind trust in our competence on the part of John Q. Public. If auto mechanics, dentists, and Guatemala-watchers merit these things, I see no reason why someone who has sweated through the long agony of producing a doctoral dissertation on linguistics doesn't deserve them.

Depressingly, the lack of firm authority vested in the linguistics profession is likely to hamper (though not too much, I hope) the progress of campaign to change society that has latterly been taking up a large proportion of my political energies. The issue it is devoted to may initially seem a small one, but as Otto Jespersen once said, the world is made up of little things; what is important is to see them largely. I shall argue that an important human freedom is at stake.

I want you first to consider the string 'the string' and the string 'the string.', noting that it takes ten keystrokes to type the string in the first set of quotes, and eleven to type the string in the second pair. Imagine you wanted to quote me on the latter point. You might want to say (1).

(1) Pullum notes that it takes eleven keystrokes to type the string 'the string.'

No problem there; (1) is true (and grammatical, if we add a final period). But now suppose you want to say this:

(2) Pullum notes that it takes ten keystrokes to type the string 'the string'.

You won't be able to publish it. Your copy-editor will change it before the first proof stage to (3), which is false (though regarded by copy-editors as grammatical):

(3) Pullum notes that it takes ten keystrokes to type the string 'the string.'

Why? Because the copy-editor will insist that when a sentence ends with a quotation, the closing quotation mark must follow the punctuation mark.

I say this must stop. Linguists have a duty to the public to use their expertise in arguing for changes to the fabric of society when its interests are threatened. And we have such a situation here.

First, let me establish that we are definitely talking about the fabric of society and not the biological endowment of the species in the present case. There are many crucial differences between the conventions of punctuation for printed English and the grammatical rules of the spoken (or informally written) language. Punctuation rules are everything we teach our first-quarter undergraduates that the grammatical rules of the language are not:

• Their general character is due to invention; it has not evolved along with the species—many advanced cultures show no signs of the superstitious awe with which we regard copy-editors.

• The rules constitute a learned, culturally imposed system; they are not effortlessly attained through casual exposure at an early age according to a biologically determined maturation schedule.

• Mastery of the rules is not common to essentially every non-handicapped member of a linguistically defined community; some people who ought to know them never get an adequate grasp of them, and I can show you term papers to prove it.

• Prescriptivism with regard to punctuation principles is right: there is a correct way to do things, as defined in standard books, and doing things a different way is simply mistaken.

Many of the rules are very sensible and proper; like the more reasonable laws of our national and local communities, they deserve our compliance and support; for example, the rule that a sentence does not begin with a numeral, a formula of any kind, a foreign symbol that does not have an upper-case correspondent, or a parenthesis that encloses only a proper substring of the sentence. This seems as sensible as a law against driving in New York state with a live moose on one's fender.

But in certain seaside towns on the East Coast of the United States, actions such as being barefoot at the beach in the evening have been made criminal offenses for various reasons (e.g. in order to protect the city against lawsuits brought by the unshod), and the legislation is used for harassing young people. (In the summer of 1984 a young man was arrested on Fire Island, NY, for eating pizza in the street outside a pizzeria.) Masturbation has carried a life imprisonment penalty in Indiana throughout most of this century (I have not found it possible to determine whether this penalty has been repealed because the process of inquiring on the topic at libraries and police stations has proved too embarrassing). Sometimes laws are intolerable, and need to be changed—by organized legal protest if possible, but otherwise by actual resistance and civil disobedience. I believe we must take the issue of transposing quotes and periods to the streets if need be.

No copy-editor should have the right to switch the order of two punctuation marks when it can change truth conditions, as (1)–(3) show that it can. And the cases when such transposition could reasonably be interpreted as changing truth conditions are commoner than you would think. Consider the following:

(4) Shakespeare's *King Richard III* contains the line "Now is the winter of our discontent."

This is false whether or not one adds a final period outside the quotation marks (though I believe many people have the impression that it is true). However, (5) is true:

(5) Shakespeare's *King Richard III* contains the line "Now is the winter of our discontent".

This is the first of two lines in the play which together make up the sentence "Now is the winter of our discontent made glorious summer by this sun of York." In this sentence, "Now is the winter of our discontent" is not even a constituent, of course. But the period-before-quotes convention would make it look as if it were.

This issue arises, though less strikingly, in a large percentage of the cases in which words are directly quoted from print. We do not have to put up with this. I say we should change this rule, and we should start now the campaign of direct action it will take. To begin with, we should each work on the copy-editors we are currently having dealings with. I will be sending back today the typescript of an article in which the copy-editor has transposed some of my quotation marks. I am going to object, and insist on keeping the logically correct sequence; I will stand my ground at proofreading time, and I will not submit.

Those of you who wish to make similar protests to copy-editors will find it useful to know that section 5.10 of the thirteenth edition of the *Chicago Manual of Style*, the copy-editor's *grimoire*, actually sanctions the logically correct placement in the case of single quotes around 'special terms'. Even more significantly, William George of Reidel's editorial department has pointed out to me that the 1983 edition of *Hart's Rules for Compositors and Readers* (Oxford University Press), pp. 45–48, explicitly endorses the principle of punctuating "*according to the sense*". What a fine example of British level-headedness, and what an important ally to my cause. These precedents can be used in our struggle as the thin end of the wedge. I have also noticed that many copy-editors will already concede the point for semi-colons; that is, a typescript containing (6a) is not corrected to (6b).

(6) a. Bolinger never said "Accent is predictable"; he said "Accent is predictable– if you're a mind-reader."

b. Bolinger never said "Accent is predictable;" he said "Accent is predictable—if you're a mind-reader."

This is clearly a glimmering of good sense, and a weakening of the blind stupidity of the standard policy. I believe we can win the battle to change the policy once and for all, even for commas and periods.

And I have broader plans for the campaign, soon to be formally registered as a national organization, the Campaign for Typographical Freedom. In a few months (watch the national press), a huge rally will take place at the Lincoln Memorial in Washington D.C. There will also be an international day of protest on which demonstrations will be organized in all the great publishing cities of the world—London, Paris, Rome, New York, San Francisco, Cambridge (the real one), Cambridge (the substandard imitation in Massachusetts), Oxford, and yes, Dordrecht too. I will also be publishing the home addresses of a number of top copy-editors to be used in postcard intimidation work.

Response so far has been gratifyingly enthusiastic. Even I, with my fingers on the very pulse of the linguistic community, could not have foreseen the extent of the upwelling of popular support for the campaign that has already begun in response to private circulation of a dittoed manifesto last year. Direct action has already begun. In one month alone, *Linguistic Inquiry* copy-editing supremo (suprema?) Anne Mark received over eighty thousand postcards at her home in Reading, Massachusetts, essentially all of them supportive of the campaign. (One was from a linguist vacationing in Wyoming who had apparently misunderstood the point of the postcard campaign and merely reported that he was "having a great time" touring the Grand Tetons with his family.)

Checks and money orders have poured in to provide a solid financial base of support for the Campaign for Typographical Freedom. I want to assure the linguists who have so generously made these fully tax-deductible contributions to campaign funds that the resources they have provided are being responsibly administered by the volunteer staff here at the TOPIC . . . COMMENT office. The rapid upsurge in the activities of the campaign has necessitated my doing quite a bit of travelling, and the Executive Committee has decided that it was appropriate for a new Toyota Supra to be purchased in order that I should be able to meet my travel commitments in a timely manner. A certain amount of entertaining has also proved necessary in the pursuit of further fund-raising objectives, and to this end the poolside facilities at my residence have been improved (by the addition of a pool).

But the most striking thing about the developments so far has been the emergence of a clear focus for the anger and resentment (quite justified in my opinion) against one thing above all others, namely, cruel bibliographic practices. The editorial staff of the New York office of Academic Press, Inc., has been much cited as an example of what we have to fight against, but in fact MIT Press policies are very similar. Let me list a few examples of the kind of brutal and unreasoning policies that are imposed on the bibliographies that linguists so carefully and thoughtfully prepare. (The catalog that follows is not for the squeamish; those who felt a bit faint while watching

Gremlins might care to abandon this column and turn to something less upsetting.)

GRATUITOUS CAPITALIZATION

The harsh yoke of (e.g.) Academic Press and MIT Press copy-editing practices imposes on authors pointless and information-destructive capitalization of 'significant' words (roughly, words that belong to the categories, N, A, or V) in titles. (I even use this convention when mentioning titles in the text of the present book, so entrenched is it in normal literate expectations; but I don't use it in bibliographies.)

Language avoids gratuitous capitalization; it follows the French style in abjuring the practice completely. Notice that from the *Language* format it is possible immediately to predict what the Academic Press format would be, should one wish to, but the converse is not true, because gratuitous capitalization destroys distinctions: consider the contrast between the words *Xerox* (the name of a corporation) and *xerox* (a verb that the Xerox Corporation has tried desperately to eliminate, and forbids its staff to use), or between *french toast* (an American breakfast favorite) and *French toast* (toast from France), or between *big Ben* (of the Cartwright family from TV's *Bonanza*) and *Big Ben* (the bell in the Westminster clock tower that is popularly known by the same name), or (for a more pertinent linguistic example) between *case* and *Case*. (What would a paper listed as 'The Case for Case' mean by its title? In today's linguistics there are four possibilities.)

Suppose one encountered in an Academic Press bibliography a critical review of Fillmore's 1968 ideas in a GB context entitled 'The Case Against the Case for Case'. What words are actually in that title? What does it look like without the gratuitous capitalization? The combination of Chomsky's perverse terminologizing ('Case' vs. 'case', 'SUBJECT' vs. 'subject', 'PRO' vs. 'pro', etc.) and the gratuitous capitalization convention would leave us sorting among no less than eight possibilities for how to uncapitalize that title.

REDUNDANCY IN PLACE NAMES

Many publishers insist on state names spelled out in full after every city name in a place of publication. Thus one often has to endure several repetitions of a phrase as long as "*Papers from the Nineteenth Regional Meeting, Chicago Linguistic Society*, Chicago Linguistic Society, University of Chicago, Chicago, Illinois" peppering one's bibliography. The place name "Chicago" itself is redundant here, but they insist on it, and will also insist that "Illinois" be added—in full, the MIT Press requires, not with the official U.S. Postal Service abbreviation "IL"—even though in the entire world there is no place called Chicago other than the city at the southern end of Lake Michigan, and people who cannot place Chicago on a map cannot place Illinois either. (Catherine Ringen has a T-shirt with a slogan making fun of people who cannot place any of those mid-western states with names that begin with *I;* it says: "UNIVERSITY OF IOWA, IDAHO CITY, ILLINOIS". I don't know why I mentioned that.)

REDUCTION OF NAMES TO INITIALS

For utterly mysterious reasons, although they are prepared to waste thousands of characters on redundant names in some contexts, Academic Press and MIT Press generally refuse to permit mention of first names of authors even when they expressly use their first names and suppress some of their initials. Thus they will accept "Chomsky, N." or "Chomsky, N. A." or "Chomsky, A. N." (is it Noam Avram or Avram Noam, incidentally?), but that is not how Chomsky styles himself; he publishes as Noam Chomsky, so it should be "Chomsky, Noam." But no; Academic Press changes known names to obscure initials, thus running the risk of mixing up such pairs as Arnold Zwicky and Ann Zwicky, Neil Smith (London) and Norval Smith (Amsterdam), etc.

And if you thought that use of middle initials would always sort things out, think again: there are pairs such as Jen Cole (from Stanford) and Jennifer Cole (from MIT); John M. Anderson (Edinburgh) and James M. Anderson (Calgary); W. Sidney Allen (the eminent Cambridge classicist and Caucasologist) and W. Stannard Allen (the applied linguist); and so on.

Academic Press will even invade the sanctity of text with its policy on not mentioning first names; Arnold Zwicky and Jerry Sadock (should I be saying A. M. and J. M.?) still positively fume with anger at the way Academic Press, back in 1975 (yes, after fifteen years they still bear a grudge), changed the acknowledgment "is due to Dennis Stampe" (crediting the philosopher of language at the University of Wisconsin–Madison) to "is due to Stampe" (ambiguous, but likely to be read as crediting Dennis Stampe's brother, David

Stampe, then a colleague of Zwicky's at the Ohio State University) in footnote 6 of "Ambiguity tests and how to fail them" (*Syntax and Semantics 4*).

REDUNDANT EDITORS' NAMES

Having saved characters at the cost of introducing ambiguity by suppressing authors' first names, Academic Press then proceeds to waste characters by enforcing a policy of requiring all the editors to be listed whenever a Chicago Linguistic Society or Berkeley Linguistics Society volume is cited, as if the author of the phrase 'et al.' had never lived. Thus what could have been *Papers from the sixth regional meeting, Chicago Linguistic Society,* or even just *CLS 6* with an appropriate abbreviation explanation at the top, becomes, almost unbelievably (but see e.g. *Syntax and Semantics 4*, 1975, page 34):

M. A. Campbell, J. Lindholm, A. Davison, W. Fisher, L. Furbee, J. Lovins, E. Maxwell, J. Reighard, and S. Straight (Eds.), *Papers from the sixth regional meeting, Chicago Linguistic Society.*

These unwarranted infringements on our freedom of expression must be stopped. And if we are united in our dedication to the cause, I believe they can be. We are experts. We know more than they do. We cannot be defeated. Send checks and money orders to the Campaign for Typographical Freedom, c/o:

Geoffrey K. Pullum
Cowell College
University of California
Santa Cruz, CA 95064
U.S.A.

Chapter Ten

A guest of the State

One of my own personal favorites out of all the TOPIC . . . COMMENT columns, 'A guest of the State' is essentially straight fiction. When it was published, the TOPIC . . . COMMENT section of the last two issues of *Natural Language and Linguistic Theory,* since the late summer of 1985, had been written by other hands than mine (Tom Wasow and Arnold Zwicky), a lot of people had assumed that I had given up TOPIC . . . COMMENT permanently and moved on to other things.

But no one had any further columns to offer, so an excuse for a comeback after an unexplained six-month absence seemed in order. From there, the idea of building a review of recent journal articles into the story of my incarceration in a correctional institution, and the self-referential conclusion, grew naturally. If 'naturally' is the right word to use about the genesis of this rather bizarre mélange of fact and fiction, that is. In case you were wondering, Arthur Danner really is the district attorney of the county in which I live, and there really is a bare-breasted woman on the cover of Stephen Anderson's book; but on the other hand, I made up the bit about the *Barriers* study group in D block.

For those who have asked me about my conversation with Leroy, which struck some readers as a little cryptic, BEV stands for Black English Vernacular and RP is Daniel Jones' abbreviation for the Received Pronunciation of standard educated Southern British English (i.e., English pronounced in the kind of way one should speak it if one wishes to be received in polite company among the upper crust of English society). Leroy is transcribed here in strict (but fairly broad) IPA transcription; it was 1979 IPA in the original, but has been updated here to 1990 IPA (in the light of the report of the August 1989 Kiel Convention of the International Phonetic Association).

Leroy was pardoned and released unconditionally in January 1987 after the patrolmen who had testified against him were themselves implicated in a bank robbery carried out by a group of white racist fanatics from northern Idaho. (One of the patrolmen, in an amusing and ironic coincidence, now occupies Leroy's former bunk.)

I immediately offered Leroy a job as my executive assistant at the TOPIC . . . COMMENT office. He proved invaluable in that role, and continues to this day as my personal amanuensis and bodyguard.

Embezzle is an ugly word. How anyone could have misconstrued so badly my honest efforts at good stewardship of the Campaign for Typographical Rights' funds is a mystery to me. Watching stern-faced men in suits carrying boxes of records from my home and checking things off on clip-boards, and police officers in dark glasses leaning against their cars with their hands resting lightly on leather-holstered hardware, I found myself at a loss for the witty conversation that is my normal fare. And during the months of courtroom delaying tactics and unsuccessful motions that followed, my life began to take on something of a dream-like character.

Reality returned one morning as the sunlight streamed through the high windows of the courtroom and a wedge-nosed judge read out harsh words about my "lust for fast cars and fine living" having led to "knowing and deliberate diversion of donated funds" contributed by well-meaning linguists from across the world to my campaign to free scholars from the tyranny of copy-editors.

The eyes of everyone in the courtroom turned toward me with each falling intonation in the judge's sonorous delivery, and I knew what it is that leads accused persons to be reported by journalists as "expressionless". Neither laughing out loud nor weeping pathetically seems appropriate as the judge's carefully phrased monologue is presented; the decision must be listened to with care, addressed with intellectual seriousness. One's face naturally falls into some posture that is neither amused nor forlorn.

For a moment I was actually in that position—so often seen in movies—of having been asked whether I had anything to say before sentence was pronounced. I noticed my attorney's eyes on me as she mouthed the word "No", and shook her head slowly from side to side. She was apparently fearful that I would launch into a polemical critique of the judge's decision, calling his analysis "arcane and inelegant" and implying scornfully that perhaps the difference between his I.Q. and his waist measurement was not very great. I just do not

know where people get this idea that I am likely to lash out without
warning in outbursts of rhetoric and abuse.

The language centers of my brain transmitted to the articulatory
organs an instruction to say "No, your Honor", but the organs in
question turned out to be somewhat dry, and produced a quiet "Ngar-
yuaghna", which, contextual disambiguation being as powerful a
force as it is, was accepted without hestitation as a natural language
utterance.

My lawyer had nothing to add to this inarticulate contribution. She
had made strenuous efforts to obtain statements from notable linguists saying that clemency was in order on the grounds of the importance of my work at the TOPIC . . . COMMENT office. This seemed not
to have met with the response she was hoping for. "Puerile and offensive," wrote one linguistic notable, "with no redeeming social
value or scholarly worth." Another reply said: "The facetious ram-
blings of the TOPIC . . . COMMENT column, like termites chewing on
the very foundations of our discipline, are an insult to decent linguists everywhere. The editors of the journal in which this balder-
dash is permitted to appear deserve the severest censure." After a
day's work reviewing the response to her appeal for friendly wit-
nesses, my attorney had dumped the whole pile of mail in the trash,
put her head in her hands, and muttered something I didn't catch
about throwing away keys.

The judge proceeded to announce in measured tones the exact
number of months during which I was to be a guest of the State. I
remember thinking that this, at last, would force others to write
TOPIC . . . COMMENT columns for a while, if there were to be anything but blank pages at the end of the next few issues of *NLLT*. As
I was led away I noticed district attorney Arthur Danner being con-
gratulated by a number of linguists, psychologists, philosophers, and
anthropologists who had been observing the trial from the public
seating area.

*   *   *

Being inducted into a correctional facility is exactly as boring, demeaning, and unsettling as treatments in the movies make out. The
guards did not actually shout at me. On the other hand, they didn't
exactly use indirect speech acts either. There was a lot of unnecessary undressing and showering and being hustled from room to
room. Personal possessions of a quite innocuous nature were taken
away and placed in boxes. Scrubbed and glowering men were marched

through noisy galleries to designated cells. I calmed myself by reciting the *Language* style sheet from memory under my breath, and tried to adopt the body language that I felt an ideal prisoner would have: tractable without being craven, respectful of authority without being totally servile. The way a dissertation-year graduate student acts at an LSA annual meeting, in fact.

Over the next few days I soon discovered that none of this had worked. Guards sought out opportunities to snarl into my face that although I thought I was somethin' real special I was darn well in jail now and not in goddam school did I understand that. My studied attempts to answer this in a respectful but not totally servile way were unfailingly taken to be clear evidence of me being a wise guy and thinking I was better than them. I never did strike the right attitude. I came to believe that there probably wasn't one.

Meanwhile, my fellow guests in the establishment in question tended to view me, rather extraordinarily, as a wise-ass intellectual snob who was extracting special favors from the screws through toadying to them. No conceivable justification for this was ever offered. The judgment was simply hurled at me by men who made it perfectly clear by the look in their yellowish eyes that any counterarguments would be met by rhetorical techniques that involved removal of the interlocutor's arms and legs.

As the weeks passed, I learned about the structure of the place, and the trapped miniature of society that it contained. Only two things relieved what would otherwise have been a fairly bleak social and intellectual landscape. One was my cell-mate, who by some extraordinary piece of luck was the only sane and sociable being whose presence I ever detected within the walls of the institution, and who became a friend I will always treasure. Leroy was serving his time for a violent attack on two police officers. With the extraordinary agility and resilience of the young, he had managed to break the knuckles of a patrolman by butting him in the fist with the side of his head while lying face down on the ground with a foot on his neck. Leroy and I were surprised to find that we had both had the same defense attorney. We chatted bilingually through many a long evening, he in BEV, I in RP, about whether we could have chosen our counsel more wisely.

One other thing lightened the burden of being in an institution where almost everyone seemed to have an innate hatred of me. (I assume it was innate; it seems rational to conclude this from the fact that it was internalized so rapidly on the basis of such meagre and degenerate evidence.) The quality of my life was enhanced enormously by my being assigned to what was from my perspective the best job in the prison: I became prison librarian.

I was really surprised to find that the linguistics section of the prison library was so good. I was struck by both the depth and the breadth of the collection. There was much of Labov, Shuy, and other urban sociolinguists, of course, together with ample materials on basic articulatory phonetics. Many inmates, confidence tricksters especially, had found it fascinating that there was such a wealth of material available on how to represent oneself as belonging to a different social class from the one into which one had been unceremoniously dumped at birth. There were many books on the two main languages of the prison population, Chicano and BEV, though rather fewer on Standard English, a language in which most library users had virtually no interest, though they understood it passively.

I initially expected the holdings in theoretical linguistics to be poorer, but I couldn't have been more wrong. They were rich, and showed many signs of constant use (the cover on the hardback copy of *Aspects* was nearly off, and several gathers were loose; I spent a quiet hour repairing it with the heavy-duty thread used for sewing mailbags). Even quite recent books were in evidence. Stephen Anderson's *Phonology in the Twentieth Century* had arrived, for example—though the prison governor, shocked to see that Anderson had persuaded the University of Chicago Press to put a picture of a bare-breasted woman on the front cover, had insisted that this be removed.

I found there was a great demand for long, difficult, technical books that would absorb substantial amounts of time in hard, mind-stretching study. The tale was well told by the worn bindings of books like *The Sound Pattern of English, Formal Philosophy, Arc Pair Grammar, The Mental Representation of Grammatical Relations, Situations and Attitudes,* the *Interlisp-D* manual.

The library had many semi-published conference and working-paper volumes, and even some recent unpublished works. I never actually saw a copy of *Barriers* (which was circulating in manuscript form at this time; by the way, why do the metaphors in Chomsky's technical coinages always reek of authoritarianism and restrictions on freedom?), but I heard that it was available; one of the lifers had managed to get it smuggled in, and a reading group had been formed in D block to go through it in weekly meetings after exercise period. I did not try to join; I heard that the GB guys in D block were a very hard bunch, and that one young punk who had spoken up for base generation of empty categories at one of their meetings had been found the next day head down in a dumpster.

The large array of periodicals spanned all areas of the language sciences. I spent a lot of time reading, when not dealing with cataloguing, reference inquiries, or knife fights. I actually read more than my busy life of teaching, administration, and campaign-fund management back in Santa Cruz had permitted. There were many treats in store.

Richard Larson had discovered generalized phrase structure grammar, I learned, and had published a feature instantiation analysis of the phrase structure distribution of bare NP adverbs (though to make it possible to publish the work in *Linguistic Inquiry* (16.595–621, 1985) he had, quite reasonably, suppressed any reference to the GPSG literature, and announced the analysis as belonging to the GB framework; no one had noticed).

In the same issue of *LI*, I found my old friend Michael Brody from University College London arguing (see esp. pp. 529 and 525) that the governing category for x is the minimal category with a SUBJECT z distinct from x which contains both x and either the governor of x (if x is governed) or the governor of the minimal maximal category dominating x (if x is not governed), where if z is accessible to x, z need not be an actual SUBJECT unless x is PRO or a lexical anaphor, which makes a lot of intuitive sense to me. I think it is reasonable to see in Brody's formulation a refinement and sharpening of insights implicit in traditional grammar.

NLLT 3.4 arrived, and I saw that Tom Wasow had dared to say in print in his TOPIC . . . COMMENT contribution that linguistics was not a science. I had crossed myself and said a brief prayer for his soul before I remembered that I was not a Catholic.

But the most extraordinary reading experience I had in my hours of browsing among the library's acquisitions was when I discovered the first issue of David Crystal's new journal *Linguistics Abstracts*. Right at the beginning there is a shock for those accustomed to the once solid scholarship of Peter Matthews, Professor of Linguistics at the University of Cambridge (the *real* Cambridge). Matthews offers a literature-survey article (LA Surveys 1: 'Whither linguistic theory?' *Linguistics Abstracts* 1.1, 1–7, 1985) that *doesn't have a list of references!*

How do you survey the literature without citing your references? Matthews simply says things like "in a book by David Allerton . . .", "in two books by Roy Harris . . .", and so on, and then leaves you on your own to figure it out from old book catalogs. Just like an undergraduate student who takes books out of the library but doesn't remember what they were called. Whither bibliographical courtesy, I wondered? Whither Peter Matthews?

But there was more to come, and it would (mercifully) wipe all thoughts of Peter Matthews from my mind. Flipping through the body of the issue, I glimpsed my own name, and found, to my utter astonishment, that *Linguistics Abstracts* publishes abstracts of TOPIC . . . COMMENT columns! There, carefully worded and painstakingly shrunk from 2,700 words to 150, like miniaturized ghosts from my former life of freedom, were abstracts of columns I had contributed to *NLLT* over the previous year. This oasis, this last respite from the seriousness of professionalized linguistics, this space reserved at the end of each *NLLT* for a piece of writing flippant and inconsequential enough to give an exhausted assistant professor the strength to get up and do what needs to be done, had been mistaken for mere research, and was being indexed and abstracted.

And what a shock to read those abstracts! Where was the soupçon of whimsy, the twinkle in the commentatorial eye, the stylish levity I imagined I had occasionally attained? The graceful, leaping gazelle of the prose I recalled had been transformed into a squat, humorless, pygmy hippo. 'Chomsky on the *Enterprise*', according to the abstract I read, was merely a critical paper alleging that Noam Chomsky had made "a number of suprising and dubious statements". Are we talking about the same piece? I recall a piece of science fantasy— remember Spock? And Scotty? Was the abstracter insane, or was I? How had my whimsical vision of a parallel universe been mistaken for a stodgy critique of the scholarly work of one of the twentieth century's leading theoretical biologists?

There were other abstracts of TOPIC . . . COMMENT pieces too, just as solemn, written in a tone for which the only known word is *plonking* (Stephen Potter, *Some Notes on Lifemanship,* Penguin Books, Harmondsworth, England, 1962, p. 41). Ironically, there was an abstract of 'Punctuation and human freedom', the piece that had led me into big-time campaign-fund management and my present situation. Almost as if to satirize a discipline which so often has difficulty maintaining the illusion of intellectual standards, the policy of *Linguistics Abstracts* seems to be to abstract everything it can get its hands on, regardless of scholarly content, or lack of it.

But there, of course, I suddenly saw, lay the seed of the policy's undoing. The threat of paradox. How can Crystal get someone to write an abstract of a column discussing *that very abstract itself?* What could the putative abstract of this issue's TOPIC . . . COMMENT say, for example, about this paragraph, the one you are now reading?

Twisting the logical knife, consider the following claim, which I hereby make: that *any abstract of this sentence is false.* The part of the abstract corresponding to this paragraph has no way out: if it summarizes truly, it attributes falsehood to itself; but if it is a false abstract of my claims, then it only shows how true my claims are; but if so, then by being false, it reports them falsely, yet even so must *ipso facto* confirm their truth, which means . . . But you get the point.

I told Leroy of my plan to scupper the abstracting of TOPIC . . . COMMENT columns. He chuckled at the subtlety of the logical trap. "ræɾõ", he enthused; "ɪɾcɪnoʊweɪdozkætsgõgɪɾa:ɾɔdæ?". "Do you think so, Leroy?" I asked, pleased that he took such a supportive view.

"ʃowdu", he confirmed; "degõlʊkdəmnomææwətdedu."

It was good to know that Leroy thought that. I had come to value his opinion greatly. It is wrong that the TOPIC . . . COMMENT column, last refuge for those who find linguistics in the eighties a little too lugubrious and self-important, should be slurped up and regurgitated by abstracting services, the mill into which so many dull recitations of the obvious disappear, only to reappear shorter but even duller. A TOPIC . . . COMMENT column that can be abstracted simply isn't doing its job.

Chapter Eleven

Seven deadly sins in journal publishing

This is a sequel to 'Stalking the perfect journal'. The usual uneasy mixture of fact and fiction is present: the offprint requests from M.D.s in Kansas *are* real; the friendly communications quoted *are* real; the FRIENDLY COMMUNICATIONS box is *not* real (too few letters to make it worthwhile starting a file); Eugene Garfield *is* real (some readers seemed to think he was just a figment of my imagination); *Current Contents* is likewise real; the Campaign for Typographical Freedom is *not* real.

Finally, the curse I purport to have placed on *Glossa* to force it out of business is also not real, but a strange thing has since happened. *Glossa* does seem to have ceased publishing. It never put out another issue after this column appeared, and may have disappeared for ever. This is a thoroughly Twilight-Zone thing to happen, and makes one completely reevaluate one's position on extrasensory perception, precognition, telekinesis, Pollock's analysis of the auxiliary system, etc. I do hope it is not anything to do with the chickens' blood and wax models that Leroy and I did fool around with at one point. I would feel awful to have sealed the fate of a living, breathing journal, however badly typeset.

The daily mailbag at the TOPIC . . . COMMENT office is an unedifying assortment of personal insults, solemn critical tirades with Massachusetts postmarks, vague blitherings about the scientific method, book catalogs, offprint requests from M.D.s in Kansas, and crudely crayoned death threats. But every now and then, something foreign appears. I don't mean foreign like an air mail letter from a stranger behind the Iron Curtain asking you for a free copy of your book, or a package from France containing a manuscript submitted to *Cognition* for you to referee when you never agreed to be a referee for them. I mean foreign in the sense that the word *exotic* had very briefly in between its original meaning 'introduced from abroad' and its present meaning, 'lewd and titillating'. I mean, in other words, out of the ordinary run of things.

What counts as out of the ordinary for the hard-working TOPIC . . . COMMENT staff is a letter of *support:* somebody out there agreeing with what has been said in one of the columns, and urging us on. I'm sure readers will be able to believe that this does not happen often.

In fact there is really only one column that has ever appeared that got a major flood of friendly communications as a response, causing my staff to start a new file labeled "FRIENDLY COMMUNICATIONS". I wonder if any reader would be able to guess which column it was that elicited this inflow of good feeling.

Well, the supporting remarks were inspired (and it really goes to show that you never can tell) by 'Stalking the perfect journal', three years ago now (*NLLT* 2.261–67, 1984), in which I presented a survey of a number of well-known linguistics journals, assessing their policies with regard to those matters of publishing style that affect the ability of scholars to use them effectively. I listed nine desiderata for a perfect journal (perfect in respect of not having annoying features of format and house style, that is; never mind the metaphysics).

The survey, you will recall, was a large and wide-ranging one. My research team surveyed no fewer than seven journals. If this does not seem very large and wide-ranging to you, think again.

- The median number of speakers on whom the entire corpus of examples in an English syntax paper is checked before publication, including its author, is zero.
- The median number of informants used for a study on a foreign language is one. (The person in question is known in the trade jargon as "my principal informant", which means that on the way to your informant's hut you were in the habit of saying good morning to one or two other villagers whom you met along the way, and sometimes you took note of a phrase or two that they said, if it seemed interesting.)
- The median number of children used in an acquisition study is one.
- The total number of experimental subjects used in Lieberman's study of the perception of intonation by linguists (*Word* 21.40–54, 1965) was two.
- The total number of Russian forms cited in Chomsky's classic presentation of the Hallean argument against phonemics (*Current Issues in Linguistic Theory,* section 4.3) is four.

• The number of languages adduced in support of Postal's claims about universals of reflexivization in his 1971 paper 'The method of universal grammar' (Paul Garvin, ed., *The Place of Method in Linguistics,* Mouton, The Hague, 1971) is two, and this is the same as the number of languages given detailed discussion in 'The category AUX in universal grammar' by Akmajian, Steele and Wasow (*LI* 10 [1979], 1–64).

Seven is a *big* number by the standards of linguistics. And in such a big survey as the one undertaken by my staff some four years ago, it is only natural that there should be some minor errors in the data gathered. Even the supportive letters went so far as to point out a few. One mistake was pointed out in a letter from the editor of *Journal of Linguistics,* Nigel Vincent. He wrote:

> I enjoyed your piece on the desiderata of a good journal in *NLLT* recently, and I was glad to see *JL* near the top. It would have been top if you (well, your research assistant) had noted that we do print our style sheet on the inside front cover of each number. I agree with you about the value of authors' full addresses—it's something I want to introduce in *JL.*

Well, the criticism must be accepted. But you have to admit that the general tone of this is friendly. Nigel's missive was duly added to the FRIENDLY COMMUNICATIONS file.

The same is true of the letter I received from Francis Jeffry Pelletier of the University of Alberta. Said Pelletier:

> I read with interest your column on the Perfect Journal. I was so taken with your completely reasonable suggestions (at least those on the "form" of the journal), that I was taken aback to discover that the *Canadian Journal of Philosophy* (of which I am an editor) did not already implement them all. Of your first nine recommendations (the stylistic ones), the *CJP* failed on
>   (a) inconsistency about printing dates of acceptance/revision, etc.
>   (b) author's *full* address
>   (c) page numbers on spine
>   (d) first/last page numbers on first page of each article
>   (e) announcements of forthcoming articles
> At an editorial meeting 3 Nov. 84, we rectified these shortcomings (and also changed Roman volume numbers to Arabic volume numbers), effective with the 1985 volume. Thanks for your sound advice.

Sound advice! All of us at the T . . . C office felt like the ugly duckling the day the swans came by and remarked approvingly on its swanhood. Actions on the part of whole editorial boards: what a change from the usual diet of whining and abuse. I was carried back to the days—it seems so long ago—when the Campaign for Typographical Freedom was in its heyday, before the IRS and the FBI became so interested in my admittedly rather California-style accounting practices, and arranged for my sabbatical in Soledad.

But the most impressive item in this minor avalanche of friendly and supportive mail had yet to come. I opened it with caution, as it was bulky, and from an address I did not recognize, but it was not booby-trapped; no frightening spring-loaded paper bat jumped out when I opened it (I wish those MIT students wouldn't do that). Instead, there was a letter, plus a couple of offprints, from none other than Eugene Garfield.

Now, don't tell me that you have not heard of Eugene Garfield, or I really am going to get irritable. President of the Institute for Scientific Information, based in Philadelphia, Eugene Garfield edits, and writes a regular column in, the vitally important archimetajournal *Current Contents.* I call it an archimetajournal quite seriously. *Current Contents* is an archijournal because it is a theoretical abstraction obtained by neutralizing the contrasts between the various specialized editions of it, such as *Current Contents: Social and Behavioral Sciences,* that have tangible manifestations on library shelves. And these specific instances are metajournals because, rather than containing information about their ultimate subjects, they contain information about sources that contain information about them.

The *Current Contents* suite of metajournals plays the role with respect to the scientific literature that the directory-listing program plays in your disk operating system; that the phone book plays in the telecommunications industry; that the photo of the reviewing stand at the annual May Day parade plays in Kremlinology (if someone less than six persons away from the Party Chairman writes to ask you for a free book, *send him one*). In (the specific instantiations of) *Current Contents* you will find the actual tables of contents of hundreds of recently published journals. It's not a handbook like the *Bibliographie Linguistique* or the MLA bibliography, listing everything that has appeared in a given year, but appearing long after that year is history, you understand; it is a weekly in which you can see the latest contents-lists of all the latest journal issues that had arrived by last week. It is a wonder of modern library science and photolithography.

What Eugene Garfield wanted to point out to me was that he has repeatedly used his editorial position to call upon publishers to shape up their journals and print authors' addresses and other helpful information in an accessible place. He has been writing about this for twenty years. He last wrote about it in the October 17 and 24 issues of *Current Contents* in 1983, which I had somehow missed. He is fighting mad about the issue. Yet with the whole weight of the Institute for Scientific Information behind him, he cannot achieve the changes he thinks are necessary. He cannot even get publishers to give their contributors' proper mailing addresses. He says he needs peer pressure support. His clarion call rings out (*Current Contents,* October 17, 1983, p. 13): "Scientists of the world, unite! You have nothing to lose but your delayed reprint postcards, returned letters, and much wasted time." How right he is.

Well, we have seen above that journals can be persuaded to make changes, and Garfield acknowledges that this is so ("In recognition of journals which prove that change *is* possible . . ." *Current Contents,* May 8, 1978, pp. 5–10). It *is* possible to change the world, to win a victory for common sense and the needs of the humble scholar.

I was moved to pay a visit to the university library and take another look at the situation, this time casting the net even wider. And I found out something: there are perfect journals in the linguistic sciences! If one looks far enough along the racks, one can find them. I will cite some data below.

But first, for the benefit of any bewildered reader who may have forgotten what 'Stalking the perfect journal' said, let me give a reminder of what we are talking about here. Let me remind you that "perfect" is a technical term. I will restate almost immediately the criteria for journal formats that I am advocating, but first, some negotiations, to make me appear flexible and conciliatory, and to lull the enemy into a false sense of security. It seems to me that the last two of the nine desiderata I talked about can be treated as less significant than the others. I suggested that journals should list in each issue the titles of papers known to be forthcoming, and that they should also publish their style sheets in each issue.

The advertising of forthcoming papers is a practice that is adopted by two Reidel linguistics journals (*NLLT* and *Linguistics and Philosophy*) and also by, e.g., *Romance Philology.* Although I like to see this, I think it could reasonably be argued that the scholar is not exactly inconvenienced by a journal that elects to keep the contents of future issues a surprise, and that it might not suit every publisher's modus operandi to keep an issue ahead with publishing plans in this way. For journals with long intervals between issues (like *JL*, published only twice a year) or short ones (like the *Journal of Philosophy*, published every two weeks), it might not even be possible to say at press time for issue *n* exactly what issue *n + 1* will contain. I can forgive this. I'm a reasonable man.

And in the matter of style sheets, we have to take into account that (i) some style sheets are very big (*NLLT*'s *Guidelines for Authors* is seventeen pages long, and wouldn't fit on the inside back cover, as Journals Manager Patrick Wharton points out to me in yet another friendly letter), and (ii) some journals don't really have a style sheet (*Glossa, Linguistics and Philosophy*, and *Studies in Language* seem to get along without telling authors where to put their commas and brackets). So again, this doesn't seem to be a relevant criterion.

So let me put those two issues aside, and turn to the seven remaining points. I will express them negatively: seven deadly sins of academic journal publishing.

1. **Omitting** the date of receipt and/or acceptance of a published article.
2. **Failing** to announce in an issue its month of publication.
3. **Concealing** the mailing address of an author by not printing it with the article.
4. **Lacking** a contents page for each issue on its cover.
5. **Neglecting** to print on the spine of each issue an indication of the page numbers covered in it.
6. **Forgetting** to include a statement of reference details (including first and last page numbers) for each article on its first page.
7. **Hiding** footnotes at the end of the article rather than printing them at the foot of the page.

In 'Stalking the perfect journal' I complained about the pain and frustration that the commission of any one of these sins could bring to the life of the poor library researcher. (Garfield disagrees with just one of them, the last, but his reason will not appeal to most linguists: he believes that footnotes "should be abolished". I say if people can't learn to write without footnotes, at least the publication should be organized so that we get their afterthoughts on the same page as their thoughts.)

I have personally re-examined recent issues of all the journals in
the language sciences that I can readily get my hands on, and compared again the records of sinfulness they instantiate. And I have
learned quite a lot. For one thing, I have learned that there can be
such a thing as a journal that commits all of the seven deadly sins
(*Glossa* is in this shameful state; I have accordingly had a curse
placed on it, and I expect it to be out of business within a year). And
for another, as I said above, I have found some Perfect Journals, with
plusses all the way down. Interestingly, two quality phonetics jour-

Table 2: Some journal policies as of early 1987

	Date rec'd	Month pub'd	Author address	Con-tents on cover	Pg. nos on spine	1st/ last pg. nos	Notes on page
Folia Linguistica	−	−	+	+	−	−	−
Glossa	−	−	−	−	−	−	−
IJAL	−	+	−	+	+	+	+
Journal of Linguistics	+	+	−	+	+	+	+
Journal of Phonetics	+	+	+	+	+	+	+
Language	+	+	−	+	+	−	+
Language and Speech	−	−	−	+	+	−	+
Language in Society	−	+	−	+	+	+	−
Linguistic Analysis	+	−	−	+	+	+	+
Linguistic Inquiry	−	−	+	+	−	+	+
Linguistic Review	−	+	+	−	−	+	−
Lingua	+	+	+	+	+	+	+
Linguistics	+	−	+	+	−	+	−
NLLT	+	+	+	+	+	+	+
Phonetica	+	+	+	+	+	+	+
Romance Philology	−	+	−	−	−	−	+
Studies in Language	−	−	−	+	−	+	−

nals (*Journal of Phonetics* and *Phonetica*) are in this class; perhaps phoneticians are a little more organized and competent than the kind of general linguist who has forgotten what a kymograph tracing is?

My current data base is shown in Table 2. Contrary to normal practice in phonological markedness, plus means good, minus means bad.

The scores, with the best-scoring (most helpful) journals at the top, can be summarized as follows:

7: *Journal of Phonetics*
   Lingua
   NLLT
   Phonetica
6: *Journal of Linguistics*
5: *IJAL*
   Language
   Linguistic Analysis
4: *Language in Society*
   Linguistic Inquiry
   Linguistics
3: *Language and Speech*
   Linguistic Review
2: *Romance Philology*
   Folia Linguistica
   Studies in Language
0: *Glossa*

There you have it. Tell the editor of your local journal to look upon this list and weep. There is not a single serious reason why the journals on the list should not all have a score of 7 out of 7, making life a little easier for all linguistic scholars. Why don't they clean up their acts? Several explanations come to mind as one looks down the original list of the seven deadly sins, namely (1) pride, (2) covetousness, (3) lust, (4) envy, (5) gluttony, (6) anger, and (7) sloth. Linguists are occasionally smitten with (1), and often with (6) when their hypotheses are criticized; they are as prone to (2) and its cousin (4) as anyone else, I suppose; they display a certain amount of (3) at LSA Linguistic Institutes in the summer, and suffer severe attacks of (5) during most conferences; but as to why linguistics editors do not get around to perfecting their journals in the respects listed earlier, I would suggest that (7), already a familiar failing of linguists when data have to be re-checked or consequences of constraint statements verified, is surely the most plausible candidate of all.

Chapter Twelve

The linguistics of defamation

For some reason I cannot recall, in the Christmas vacation of 1976 I went to the law library of University College London and took out a stack of books on the law of libel and slander to study over the holiday period (the University of London would completely close all its buildings and their heating plants for a long, dreary period of up to two weeks in order to save fuel, exactly the sort of climate-driven miserliness that made life miserable for a 365-day scholar like me and caused me to dream even then of living in California one day).

I became fascinated by the topic of defamation law, and have read avidly about it ever since. The English law of defamation, supposed to insure every citizen against having anything said about him that might cause him to be held in "hatred, ridicule, or contempt," has grown over the centuries into a forbidding tangle of precedents based on all sorts of crazy cases brought by offended millionaires and eccentrics. It has an appealing linguistic pedantry to it, but also an ugly underside suggestive of a major threat to the freedom of the press.

I began writing about the topic, and in 1979, at the spring meeting of the Linguists Association of Great Britain, I presented an invited lecture called 'Language, libel and the linguist'. It was never published; I tried to get the British humanities journal *Encounter* to take it, but, revealingly, the editor was a bit worried about republishing some of the libels that (of necessity) I quoted.

In the United States, the wackier excesses of the libel laws are held in check by the First Amendment to the Constitution, and by case law built on it—such as the judgment that gave rise to what is now known as the *New York Times* rule. When in 1984 I found it was actually being assumed that two comment-sullied generals, Ariel Sharon and William Westmoreland, had a chance of winning their libel suits against major organs of the mass media despite such safeguards to liberty, it got me thinking about libel again, and I wrote the following column, most of which is cannibalized out of the first half of my LAGB lecture.

Later I learned of another linguist who has taken a serious interest in the linguistic aspects of defamation law: Peter Meijes Tiersma (Ph.D. UC San Diego, 1980; J.D. UC Berkeley 1986). The reader who wishes to pursue the topic further might start with Tiersma's paper 'The language of defamation', *Texas Law Review* 66.2 (1987), 303–50.

As 1985 began, two major libel suits were in progress in New York. General Ariel Sharon was suing *Time* magazine over an article alleging that he had talked of revenge with the bereaved family of Bashir Gemayel just before the massacres in the refugee camps at Sabra and Shatila; and General William Westmoreland was suing CBS over a program claiming that he had lied to superiors about the strength of communist forces during the Vietnam war. The monetary claims were unprecedentedly enormous; in the case of Westmoreland, $120 million in damages was at issue—enough to damage even a TV network.

By mid-February 1985, both Sharon and Westmoreland had failed in their mammoth attempts to punish the news media. Sharon took his case through to the end, watched a jury find that he had not been libeled, and left telling reporters that he had nonetheless achieved a moral victory. Westmoreland did not wait for a conclusion; halfway through, he did what many thought the United States should have done in Vietnam in the sixties: he declared victory and pulled out to save further embarrassment.

I found it most surprising that there was talk in the press of *Time* and CBS having been lucky to get off so lightly—no judgment against them, just a few million dollars of legal costs to pay. The news media are generally, for obvious reasons, somewhat biased against libel suits; yet in this case it seemed widely accepted that these tarnished plaintiffs—Sharon with his long history of involvement in violent reprisal raids (see Noam Chomsky, *The Fateful Triangle: The United States, Israel and the Palestinians,* South End Press, Boston, 1983, especially pp. 382–85), and Westmoreland bearing the stigma of responsibility for waging a brutal war under an administration whose duplicity became legend—had some likelihood of winning libel suits against news sources that had discussed their official and public activities.

I cannot recall the law of defamation ever having been used to reach so aggressively for prizes so large in cases so clearly without merit. Under the British law, which is favorable beyond belief to those who wish to drag the freedom of speech of others into a courtroom for smothering, I could imagine such cases being taken seriously, but I was taken aback to see such a reaction in the United States. The American legal system has for many years offered scant encouragement to libel suits brought by the famous and the powerful, and from what I have been able to determine about the general content of the case law, this is just as well. I have spent a little time studying the laws of libel and slander from a linguistic standpoint. I find it a fascinating but rather scary topic. For anyone with an ounce of concern about guarantees for freedom of expression, it is highly thought-provoking. But most people, linguists included, know relatively little about it.

It would be reasonable for someone who had heard of libel informally, and had read a few newspaper reports of cases, to have formed something like the following view of what is involved in a libel:

1. The act of libeling involves writing down words in a natural language.
2. The words are apprehended and understood by some other person, the libeled person, who has grounds for objecting to their content.
3. The utterance contains some expression that refers to the libeled person.
4. The libeler intended the words to refer to the libeled person.
5. The utterance was issued in some nonconfidential form, published or addressed to people other than the libeled person.
6. Some claim the utterance makes about the libeled person is false.
7. The utterance has some intended interpretation in the context under which its claim reflects discredit on the libeled person.
8. The facts in the context that make the utterance defamatory of the libeled person are known to the libeler.
9. The facts in the context that make the utterance defamatory of the libeled person are known to the libeled person.
10. The libelous utterance has the form of a declarative sentence that makes some claim about the libeled person.
11. The libeler believes that the utterance asserts something unfavorable about the libeled person.

12. The libeled person believes that the utterance asserts something unfavorable about him/her.
13. The publication of the libelous utterance caused some kind of damage to the libeled person.

The legally sophisticated might spot that some of these conditions do not have to hold in a libel case. What relatively few people realize, however, is that under the English law (which at root provides the case-law basis used by the American courts too) *not a single one* of this baker's dozen of claims need hold.

Naively, it seems fantastic that a libel action might technically be brought without any words being written; or (if there are words) without the libeled person being referred to in the libelous words; or without the utterance saying anything false, or anything that either the libeler or the libeled regard as offensive; or without any attempt to let the libel be seen by a third party. Yet all these things are so in English law.

Whether the same is the case under American law is a very difficult question—at least fifty different difficult questions, in fact, because every state has different statutes and definitions. I will make some reference to the laws of the United States in what follows (mainly through references to Robert H. Phelps and E. Douglas Hamilton's useful survey, *Libel: A Guide to Rights, Risks, Responsibilities,* Collier Books, New York, 1969; henceforth P&H), but my remarks are based on British case law in the first instance. Note also that civil libel, criminal libel, slander, and malicious (nonlibelous) falsehood are all distinct topics. Unless otherwise specified I am talking about civil libel, the tort usually alleged in actions against newspapers and other publications.

One reason no written words need exist for a libel action to be brought is that spoken words are considered to be published in permanent form if they are broadcast (though normally spoken allegations can only lead to an action for slander, not libel). Notice that Westmoreland was complaining solely of spoken words, but his was a libel suit.

More startlingly, though, no utterance of any sort need exist in a libel case. Completely nonlinguistic signs have been held libelous in previous cases. Any picture or effigy can constitute a libel. So can other objects. In one 1809 case (Jeffries v. Duncombe (1809), 2 Camp. 3), a lamp hung outside a house was held libelous because in hanging it the defendant was "intending to mark out the dwelling-house of the plaintiff as a bawdy-house." The English courts have considered cases based on defamatory gramophone records, flags at sea, and parrots (yes, parrots). The definition of libel (for criminal libel) in the New York penal code (P&H, p. 6) covers any "publication, by writing, printing, picture, effigy, sign, or otherwise than by mere speech," which probably allows for most of these.

If a language is involved, it does not have to be one of which the plaintiff knows a single morpheme. If Bernard Comrie writes foul things about my personal habits in unglossed Chukchee, Wiyaw, or Maltese, I can sue, without being able to read a word of it. (Quine's thesis of the indeterminacy of translation, incidentally, is presupposed false by the English courts; I must provide exact English translations of the original Chuckchee, Wiyaw, or Maltese for the court, and they must be sworn to by the translator.)

It is much more surprising that there need be no definite description referring to the plaintiff. The key point here is that "it is not essential that there should be anything in the words complained of to connect them with the plaintiff if, by reasons of facts and matters known to persons to whom the words were published, such persons would understand the words to refer to the plaintiff" (P. F. Carter-Ruck, *Libel and Slander,* Faber and Faber, London, 1972, p. 67). Thus, as I have noted elsewhere (in chapter 15), the indefinite NP "a certain factory in the south of Ireland" cost a newspaper some money in 1848.

And this does extend to American law: a gossip columnist's reference to "the story that one of the resort's richest men caught his blonde wife in a compromising spot with a former FBI agent" was the grounds for a $58,500 settlement against the Hearst corporation in 1958 (Hope v. Hearst Consolidated Publications, Inc., 294 F. 2d 681). Notice that there is no uniqueness entailment to the offending sentence: Palm Beach could in principle have a slew of multimillionaires with blonde wives who fool around with FBI men. It makes no difference, if one of the millionaires complains that people have assumed the newspaper meant him.

Where an actual name is used, it makes no difference in principle whether the libeler intended the reference or knew that the plaintiff bore that name. The literature contains numerous cases in which an author accidentally picked a real person's name for a character in a story and got stuck with a libel suit, often a successful one. The Defamation Act of 1952 in England introduced a defense of "unintentional defamation" to deal with just this kind of case, but that defense failed the first time it was used [Ross v. Hopkinson and Others (1956), *The Times* (London), October 16–17, 1956] because "all reasonable care" had not been taken by the publishers to make sure there was no real person going by the name the author had chosen and bearing similarities to the fictional character.

The libelous statement must be published, but it is surprising how little it takes to achieve this. It does not matter that the words complained of were written down in a private letter addressed only to the complainer; in Theaker v. Richardson 1962 (All E.R. 229; cited in Carter-Ruck 1972, p. 30) it was successfully held that when a letter to the plaintiff was opened in error by the plaintiff's wife, that was enough to publish it. Moreover, "A communication is not privileged merely because it is confidential" (Lord Lyndhurst C.B., in Brooks v. Blanshard (1833) 1 Cr. & M., p. 783, cited by *Gatley on Libel and Slander,* 7th edition, Sweet and Maxwell, London, 1974, p. 211, n. 89), and in the case of *criminal* libel, "an action will lie if the libel has been published to the person defamed and to no one else" (Carter-Ruck 1972, p. 76)—so it would have done the Marquis of Queensberry no good to seal his visiting card in an envelope after inscribing it "To Oscar Wilde, posing as a sodomite": Wilde would still have been within his rights to have a criminal libel prosecution brought. (Note that Wilde did not lose his case; he withdrew after being publicly humiliated in a devastating cross-examination.)

Does a libel have to be in the declarative mood in order to make its libelous statement? Not at all. A libel can be in the interrogative. In a 1963 case in England [Jones v. Skelton (1963) 1 W.L.R. 1362 (P.C.)] the libelous words were in the form of a rhetorical question: "It is beyond understanding. Or is it?"

Another interrogative example is the sentence "Is this the woman who came and took the things away?", which was cited as a defamatory utterance in a 1902 case (though a technicality about being uttered on a privileged occasion prevented the action from succeeding; see Collins v. Cooper (1902) 19 T.L.R. 118 (C.A.), discussed in Gatley, pp. 55, 205). Notice that here the libel is not only in an interrogative, it is buried as a presupposition carried by a restrictive relative (*who came and took the things away*).

A libel can also be in the imperative. A 1936 case hinged on the following telegram:

EDITH HAS RESUMED HER SERVICE WITH US TODAY . PLEASE
SEND HER POSSESSIONS AND THE MONEY YOU BORROWED ,
ALSO HER WAGES .

Notice that again the libel, [*you borrowed* [$_{NP}$ *e*]], is only a presupposition of the sentence; and in fact, in this case the crucial phrase *borrowed the money* does not even appear in the surface string.

Suppose some defamatory material were embedded in a way that made sure it was *not* entailed by the sentence. Could it nonetheless make the sentence libelous? The answer is yes. Here is an example of a libel embedded under a non-factive inside an interrogative: "Have you ever heard that Fox was reported twice as a spy?" (Fox v. Goodfellow (1926) *N.Z.L.R.* 58; cited by Gatley, pp. 55, 205).

Could even the exact opposite of a libelous statement be held libelous on the grounds that it had an ironical interpretation? Yes again. Words of praise and approbation have been held defamatory in numerous cases because they appeared to have been published ironically (Gatley p. 58, n. 52).

Clearly, then, we have left behind questions of the literal meaning of sentences. What is suggested by the foregoing is that even the conversational implicatures of a sentence have to be taken into account in determining whether it is a libel; and this is exactly correct. An utterer is responsible not only for what the utterance says but also for everything that it implicates in the context of utterance, including those things that are implicated by virtue of background knowledge unknown to the utterer but known to the audience. The complete set cannot, of course, be computed by the average nontelepathic utterer; it is infinite under most accounts.

The morass of case law that has built up this almost unbelievable situation places very few limits on rich plaintiffs who wish to sue over something they have taken exception to. Almost anything anybody says is likely to be defamatory under some construal. The defamatory content does not have to be something inherently objectionable, because the law regards some predicates as inherently defamatory—"homosexual" is one of them, for example.

Finally, note that the utterance of the defamatory words need not have done any particular damage to the person defamed; hurt feelings or wounded esteem will be quite sufficient for the plaintiff to be entitled to his or her millions. (Recall the $1.6 million settlement in favor of actress Carol Burnett, who was falsely reported by a trash-stuffed weekly tabloid to have been a bit tipsy in a restaurant one night. $1.6 *million?* Even judges couldn't stomach that. In 1983 the California Appellate Court chopped it back to a mere $200,000.)

The only thing keeping the American legal system from getting like the British one, where an amazing battery of weapons is arrayed against the freedom of the press, and the abuse of the libel laws by the rich and influential is a national disgrace, is the well-known doctrine that says public figures should get out of the kitchen if they can't take the heat: the *New York Times* rule (The New York Times Co. v. Sullivan, 376 U.S. 254). Because of this rule, the news media in America since 1964 have remained free to do what has had to be done over the last few decades—uncovering the mendacity and criminal misdeeds of presidents, vice presidents, attorneys general, senators, congressmen, and generals—by publishing freely and fearlessly under no constraint more severe than a desire to be recognized as a reliable source of information.

If the news media in America were exposed without protection to the full lunacy of the 400-year-old jumble of defamation case law, much of the power of the American people to keep a watchful eye on their government would disappear like morning mist. And for a while back there, in early 1985, as two politically powerful generals tried to show the civilian media where the power really lay, I was worried. But the *New York Times* rule prevailed, and free linguistic expression lived to fight another day. I celebrated by getting a bit tipsy in a restaurant.

Chapter Thirteen

Trench-mouth comes to Trumpington Street

This piece is a sequel to 'The linguistics of defamation'. Its content derives largely from the second half of the lecture 'Language, libel, and the linguist' that I gave to the Linguistics Association of Great Britain in 1979. It concerns a real live example of a book about linguistic theory that was almost suppressed forever because of a fear about whether—and I swear this is what the unwilling publisher was worrying about—the example sentences might represent a risk that a libel action might be brought by a person or persons unknown who might claim that the examples were about them. After all, *John hit Mary with a stick* might be just a transitive clause with instrumental adjunct to you, but to someone called John married to someone called Mary . . .

Yes, it's completely cuckoo. But as I explain, the worry that Cambridge University Press's lawyers conveyed was soundly based in an understanding of the English libel law. You really could be libeled by an example sentence. It could happen at any time. It might be happening right now in the pages of *Natural Language and Linguistic Theory*. Tremble, and read on.

One evening in the summer of 1974, during the LSA Linguistic Institute at the University of Massachusetts, I sat watching TV with a roomful of American linguists in a house in Amherst as Richard M. Nixon resigned the most powerful post in the world. It was a kind of climax to an extraordinary period.

Over the preceding ten years, escalating violence in Southeast Asia had physically devastated three countries and killed hundreds of thousands of people. The stress of containing the domestic opposition to this had morally and politically torn the USA apart. Many linguists had quite recent memories of teaching on campuses disrupted by riots and tear-gas attacks. The beleaguered Nixon administration had been disgraced by the resignation of Vice President

Spiro Agnew on a tax evasion charge, and then had blundered during the 1972 election campaign into criminal activities and the ludicrous cover-up attempt that became known as Watergate.

In the same ten years, linguistics had been expanding dramatically as an academic subject in the United States, doubling or tripling in size.[1] In places such as the midwest, in relatively new departments without long-established traditions of pomp and gravity, linguists joined in with the rebellion and ridicule of government that was characteristic of the times, mingling their personal reactions with their professional lives.

What could linguists do about the things that were happening in the early seventies? The only weapons they had were words. But Chomsky had written hundreds of thousands of words in furious polemical writings about American politics and foreign policy, and still the same people were in power. Many linguists took to rather desperate ways of thumbing their noses at authority, studding their published research papers with defiant and satirical examples—the *Fuck Lyndon Johnson* school of example construction.[2]

For linguistic theory, the period in question was the heyday of "generative semantics". In fact, the first serious exploration of this hypothesis at book length, Georgia Green's *Semantics and Syntactic Regularity,* was still not published but had been announced by Cambridge University Press (C.U.P.). By April 1973, the first printing was complete, the first four specimen copies had been sent to the author, and a few other copies had found their way into booksellers' hands via publishers' representatives. The book had almost but not quite appeared. But then something very odd happened.

Georgia Green received a letter dated April 17 from Jack Schulman, manager of C.U.P.'s American branch in New York. Schulman said:

> After long and serious deliberation, it seems clear to us that we cannot publish your book as it stands. We must ask you to take out

1. See Frederick J. Newmeyer, *Linguistic theory in America,* Academic Press, New York, 1980, 52ff, for some figures.

2. See Quang Phuc Dong, 'English sentences without overt grammatical subject', in Arnold M. Zwicky, Peter H. Salus, Robert I. Binnick, and Anthony L. Vanek, eds., *Studies out in left field: Defamatory essays presented to James D. McCawley on the occasion of his 33rd or 34th birthday,* Linguistic Research Inc., Edmonton, Alberta, 1971, 3–10. P. Newman has some perceptive comments on the origins of such politicized linguistic behavior in his review of Claude Hagège, *La grammaire générative, Language* 54 (1978); see p. 928.

references to identifiable people, or we will run the risk of being
sued. It is one thing to use them in a classroom lecture, but it is an
entirely different matter to put such references in cold print. I am
sure you will agree that the same linguistic point can be made by
using examples which cannot be considered libelous or offensive.

Accompanying the letter was a list of example sentences that C.U.P.
had decided must be changed on the grounds that people identified in
them might sue for libel.

After consultation with her lawyer, a Mr. Dobbins, Green sent
C.U.P. a four-page memo outlining the reasons why she thought the
request was utterly unreasonable. It was closely followed by a letter
from Mr. Dobbins warning C.U.P. that it would be breaking a legal
agreement by not publishing.

Green developed twelve arguments for her position. (In those
days, no one in linguistics presented a claim without a dozen independent arguments to support it.) She argued that (1) the cost of re-
printing the book would be enormous; (2) a disclaimer on the flyleaf
would suffice; (3) no actually identifiable reference to a real person
was made by any example in the book; (4) the example sentences
were not even assertions but merely data; (5) there were no discourse
relations between adjacent examples despite fortuitous appearances;
(6) other publishers had got away with near-the-bone examples for
years; (7) the book had technically already been published when her
personal copies were sent to her; (8) she had already signed an agreement indemnifying C.U.P. against libel actions; (9) C.U.P. had already published books containing example sentences that could bear
a defamatory interpretation; (10) imagined referents could be found
for *any* linguistic example, which was a *reductio ad absurdum* of the
publisher's fears; (11) in many cases the example complained of had
to have the allegedly offensive properties in order for its point to be
made; (12) C.U.P. had signed a legally binding agreement to publish
after perusing the manuscript for seven months, during which time
she had changed some examples at their request, but they had not
complained of the material they now objected to.

On May 4 a letter from the University Publisher, R. W. David,
C.B.E, was sent from C.U.P.'s head office in Trumpington Street,
Cambridge, where Schulman was visiting and had been discussing
the matter with the C.U.P. directors, to Green's lawyers in Illinois.
Mr. David dealt with three main points: whether the Press had any

right to require modification of work it had agreed to publish, whether there were risks attendant on publishing the text as it stood, and whether it could be argued that the Press had already set a precedent by publishing earlier works containing risqué examples. The authority to require changes, he argued, was contained in the memorandum of agreement that Green had signed. On whether the material was defamatory he said:

> Opinion may differ as to whether a libel action by any of the persons so clearly indicated by Professor Green would or would not succeed in the U.S.A. But that is only one of several considerations. The Press is a world publisher, and the book will be published in many countries where the laws of libel are more stringent than in the U.S.A.; and if some of the "characters" are domestic to the U.S.A. and so unlikely to take action outside it, there are others who are not. Furthermore the sentences, even if in the event they were not taken to be libellous, are certainly offensive, and quite gratuitously so: a textbook of linguistics is not an appropriate stalking-horse from which to issue innuendoes against public figures. To use the book for this purpose would be likely to cheapen the reputations of author and publisher alike.

As to the sentences that Green had cited as precedents (e.g. George Lakoff's famous examples showing the purported grammatical relevance of his beliefs about whores, Republicans, virgins, and lexicalists: *John called Mary a Republican, and then she insulted him,* and so on),[3] Mr David said:

> It is true that the Press had already published material to which the same kind of objection can be made, though in our opinion the sentences in Steinberg and Jakobovits's book are more direct and less wounding. It is, however, to be noted, first [that] the Steinberg/Jakobovits book is a book of readings—that is, it consists of material that has already been published elsewhere and for which the Press takes no primary responsiblity; secondly, that we regard our publication of the sentences that you quote as an error in judgment and taste that we do not wish to repeat.

(Amusingly, Mr David slipped up here: the Lakoff paper had *not* been published before.)

---

3. From D. Steinberg and L. Jakobovits, eds., *Semantics: An interdisciplinary reader,* C.U.P., Cambridge, 1971.

Mr David was, then, "offering to reprint, wholly at the Press's expense and with the utmost possible expedition, such sections as would be necessary," which he felt would be "a very simple task," one that would be "worth while to secure a book which, with all its existing merits, cannot be criticised as containing gratuitous personal insults." He also said that if Green would not agree, C.U.P. would be prepared to simply sell the stock to another publisher if she could find one; but he would "resist any claim that the Press is bound itself to publish the book without modification."

Schulman telephoned Green to ask her if she would reconsider her decision and change some examples, but positions were firm on all sides. Green sent a letter on June 1 saying simply, "No, I will not change any example sentences, for reasons outlined to you in the letter from my lawyer, Mr. Dobbins." Schulman replied politely later in June and said that he was awaiting a libel report from C.U.P.'s lawyers in London.

There followed a period for the law's delays; then Schulman returned reluctantly to his role as the insolence of office. On October 3 he sent Green a copy of a libel report on the book prepared by C.U.P.'s legal advisers. According to the libel report, the problem with the example sentences is this:

> In some instances, the names chosen are such that, even to readers in the United Kingdom, they would tend to be associated with people well known to the general public in such a way that we consider that it would be difficult for the author to say that she had chosen all the names used in these illustrative sentences completely at random.

The names Tricky Dick, John and Martha, Liz and Richard, Reagan, Ruby, and Oswald are cited. The report admits that "by no means all the illustrative sentences containing the names just mentioned are defamatory." The problem is, however, that "the use of names of actual people in this way could be used by any person whose name is used in a defamatory context in the book to support their argument that the words of which they complain would be understood by reasonable readers to refer to them."

This was the point that really worried C.U.P. And it was followed by a list of all the sentences in the book that the lawyers thought were defamatory. A sampling of this is necessary here to convey the flavor of this extraordinary legal document. I give the page and example numbers, the lawyers' comment, and also the original example out of the book. The list begins:

Page	Example		Remarks
30	(44)	John knocked Harry down again.	Defamatory of John
31	(45)	Ruby killed Oswald again.	Defamatory of Ruby
47	(75)b.	Pornography began to bore John.	Defamatory of John

Sure, the first and third examples involve the syntactician's mythical *John,* and the people named in the second are dead. Nevertheless, the lawyers believed that the publishers should "change the names in any case where they identify living people unless the risk of such people complaining in each case can be positively discounted." They felt the same about these examples:

54	(98)a.	John tried a flight to Cuba.	Defamatory of John
	(98)b.	John attempted a flight to Cuba.	Defamatory of John
64	(110)	*John endeavored the seduction of Sabina.	Defamatory of John
78	(29)a.	Sears delivered them the wrong sofa.	Defamatory of Sears
	(29)b.	They had guaranteed them prompt delivery.	Ditto
	(29)c.	But they telephoned them an apology.	Ditto
82	(37)b.	Mary gave John an inferiority complex.	Defamatory of Mary
	(37)e.	Mary gave John a broken arm.	
	(37)f.	Mary gave John a hickey.	
	(37)g.	Mary gave John a black eye.	
	(37)h.	Mary gave John a pain in the neck.	

(Note here that (110) is not even a sentence, if the asterisk is to be taken at face value.) As the list goes on, it gets crazier:

116	(163)c.	I heard John say that Bill was a coward.	Defamatory of Bill

117	(166)a.	John sent Mary the time bomb.	Defamatory of John
128	(199)	After John got married he became lazy.	Defamatory of John
136	(7)a.	When John comes home, Mary says she won't hit him.	Defamatory of Mary
143	(243)e.	He permitted his cronies positions of power until the BGA caught on.	Defamatory of any person identifiable as he in these illustrations
144	(246)a.	John almost sold his ward to some white slavers, but the notary was out of town.	Defamatory of John
171	(10)a.	Barney gave Helen a kick, and then she gave him one.	Defamatory of Barney and Helen
177	(28)e.	The ride Mack gave to Ellen ended in disaster.	Defamatory of Mack
218	(3)e.	Sheldon kicked Shirley into the river.	Defamatory of Sheldon
	(5)e.	Sheldon kicked Shirley.	Ditto
218	(3)b.	Wayne shot Marvin dead.	Defamatory of Wayne
218	(5)f.	Sheldon shot Marvin.	Defamatory of Sheldon
227	(3)b.	John gave Harry a punch in the nose.	Defamatory of John
227	(1)	John gave Harry a well-deserved punch in the nose.	Defamatory of John and Harry

Now, it may seem completely loony to take the sentences just quoted as libel risks (think carefully about (7a) from page 136, for example). But there were, of course, obvious references to real American political figures in the book. C.U.P. and its lawyers did not like the look of this block of examples on page 47:

(77)a. Agnew believes that he is persecuted.
(77)b. Agnew believes himself to be persecuted.
(78)a. We know that he is the vice-president.
(78)b. We know him to be the vice-president.
(79)a. We expect that he will attack us again.
(79)b. We expect him to attack us again.

(80)a. We want [that he grow up].
(80)b. We want him to grow up.

The pronouns in the latter examples seemed to be anaphoric, referring back to Agnew, and the sentences seem to predicate persecution mania, belligerency, and immaturity of the disgraced ex-Vice President.

A sometime governor of California likewise made a cameo appearance amongst the examples:

95   (79)a. They're going to kill a hippie for Reagan.
       b. They're going to kill Reagan a hippie.

This pair was judged defamatory of Reagan (though not of the unspecified would-be killers). And legal eyebrows were also raised at:

170   (4)a. Martha gave John trench-mouth, and he gave it to Ted.

which was judged defamatory of Martha, John, and Ted. Could the *John* be the indicted Attorney General John Mitchell? Could *Martha* be his wife Martha Mitchell? Was *Ted* perhaps Senator Edward Kennedy? C.U.P. couldn't take risks with the names of people this well-known. It was 1973; Nixon was still in power, and for all C.U.P. knew he might bring suit with all the ferocity he had shown in his foreign policy.

And the lawyers were quite correct in recognizing that it was the English law of defamation they had to contend with. In England, public figures, even crooks, do not have to submit to the sort of public vilification that American ones endure for the sake of the First Amendment. Harold Evans, editor of the *Sunday Times,* once commented that "the crimes of Watergate could never have been exposed in Britain because our laws of contempt and confidence" (and defamation, one might well add) "would at several stages have prevented newspapers doing what the Washington Post did."[4]

Schulman was forced to tell Green: "It is still our wish to publish your scholarly work but we cannot do so unless you are willing to at least change the references which are easily identifiable, (Nixon, Agnew, the Mitchells, the Burtons, Rostow, and Kennedys, Reagan)

4. Harold Evans, 'Ever-increasing shackles on the freedom of the press', *The Guardian,* 17 February 1979, p. 11.

and to take out the sexual innuendos about "infections" in the context of identifiable people. We would rush these corrections through at our expense so that we could publish the book before the end of the year." Green, in her reply of October 9, made a last stand:

> Dear Mr. Schulman,
>
> I hereby affirm that no example sentence refers to any human being, living or dead. I hereby deny that I had any individual whatsoever in mind in composing any examples, and I deny that there are any references whatsoever to any Mitchells, Kennedys, Burtons, or Rostows. All names used are used merely to instantiate Noun Phrases—to make natural-sounding sentences to exemplify abstract formulae.
>
> Any name-changes will be utterly pointless, for, from what you say in your letters, anyone named John, Martha, Mary, Mack, Agnew, Ellen, etc. could sue, complaining that (s)he had been defamed, and produce a witness to testify (in bad faith) that the plaintiff had been referred to. There is no way to predict what 'names' are not the names of real people, especially since in many places, one can use any name one wishes, with no restrictions on the choice of name, and with no legal procedure required. Thus the problem of references to individuals in example sentences is from the point of view you have taken insoluble. It implies that you ought to get out of the linguistics-publishing business, since example sentences are our stock in trade, and restrictions on what they can include constitute control on the definition of the field imposed by non-practitioners.

With a flash of inspiration, she cited a C.U.P. book in which it had been argued that an isolated example sentence without illocutionary force could not possibly refer to anyone:

> I continue to maintain . . . a point of view, which, if adopted by Cambridge University Press, would allow them to put their minds at rest and release the book immediately, namely: that no *numbered* sentence (i.e. example sentence) makes an assertion, or has any other illocutionary force, as Searle has argued in print (John R. Searle, *Speech Acts,* p. 94. Cambridge University Press, 1981), that no noun phrase in any such sentence refers to any individual at all. Since none of the noun phrases in any of the example sentences refers, it follows that *none* of the example sentences could possibly be libelous.

A nice try. Especially nice to cite a C.U.P. book as the linguistic authority, a simultaneous *ad hominem* and *ad auctoritatem*. But in vain. This kind of argument, as I have shown elsewhere,[5] is quite without legal validity in England; it is whether someone *thinks* they have been referred to, and whether others think so too, that counts.

Green actually made one last offer, which she stressed was non-negotiable, to permit some changes: she would allow C.U.P. to change *Agnew* to *Wenga* throughout; alter the gender of several pronouns that looked anaphoric; and replace the names *Reagan* and *Nixon* in nine cases by the name *Fagin*. She added forcefully that she was "tired of this screwing around", and expressed the hope that they would now either publish the book or release the copyright back to her by November 1.

Schulman conducted "a very full dialogue" with Cambridge over the following four weeks, and wrote back four days after the deadline, on November 5, asking her to alter some further examples referring to John, Mary, Martha, Ted, Liz, Richard, Christine, Alex, and trench-mouth. Green replied, by return mail, that she had said non-negotiable and she meant non-negotiable. Eventually, on December 3, R. W. David wrote from Cambridge that they had "no alternative but to accede" to her request: the rights were released to her, leaving C.U.P. with all the stock of a book they could not distribute.

Green unsuccessfully approached the Univerity of Illinois Press and Academic Press in the USA but both were a little daunted by the C.U.P. tale. Indiana University Press finally bought the plates, and although even they wanted one or two minor changes (altering certain apparent allusions to Ronald Reagan so that they became allusions to Adolf Hitler or Jesse James), they published the book in 1974, under their imprint but in C.U.P.'s familiar and elegant typeface. The book was made available in Britain too. No libel case ever ensued.

Does the story have any significance? Not really, I suppose. It's an unsatisfying tale, worthy of telling here only because (to me) there is an appealingly surrealist quality to the idea of a legal battle about whether John can safely be alleged to have given Harry a punch in the nose in a Dative Movement example. C.U.P. was technically right about the law. Georgia Green stood her ground bravely on the freedom of speech issue, but did in fact have to compromise and change some example sentences before she got published.

Once the threat of libel has reared its ugly head, it becomes quite

---

5. 'The linguistics of defamation', *NLLT* 3.371–77 (1985).

difficult to illustrate some points of syntax. To demonstrate that the verb *give* as used with infectious diseases—*Martha gave John trench-mouth* and so on—requires the double-accusative construction (back then, it would have been called a positive absolute exception to Dative Movement), one certainly has to construct examples involving disease transmission, and it can be verified from the standard text[6] that the imputation of having *any* infectious disease (let alone transmitting it) is defamatory. (It is explicit in *Gatley* that the disease need not be sexually transmissible. Trench-mouth, in case you were wondering, has nothing to do with being naughty; the word is a First-World-War term for Vincent's gingivitis, a painful, bacteriogenic inflammation of the gums, with an aetiology relatable to lack of oral hygiene and possibly to nicotinic acid deficit. It isn't actually clear that it is transmissible at all.) If the name *John* or the pronoun *he* might be taken to refer to some complaining member of the public and if the assertion that someone passed on an infection is a defamatory assertion, it is indeed unclear that Green could ever have literally complied with C.U.P.'s legal advice. Readers of 'The linguistics of defamation' (chapter 12) will realize how difficult it would be to devise an example that had this property but could not be taken as defamatory of anyone.

The content of the disputed material in this case may matter very little. But the crazy agglutination of eccentric case law that nearly suppressed Georgia Green's linguistic monograph still stands, and threatens every publisher or distributor with an office in the United Kingdom, and every author, journalist, or scholar whose work appears there. Good luck with your example construction.

6. *Gatley on libel and slander,* 7th edition, section 37, p. 16, and references cited there.

Chapter Fourteen

Here come the linguistic fascists

During the 1980s, a nationwide movement began in the United States to amend state constitutions so that they explicitly lay down that English is the official language. In California, the most populous state in the union and one with a massive 20 percent Hispanic population, it was like shooting fish in a barrel: the measure enacting the constitutional amendment was approved by three-quarters of the voters. The people positively flocked to the polls to pull the lever for this useless yet still insulting affirmation of the pragmatically obvious. I felt the TOPIC . . . COMMENT column would not be doing its polemical duty if it did not lash out at the monolingual bigots responsible.

Since I wrote, the official-English snowball has kept on rolling. Where constitutional amendments have not been proposed, legislative resolutions have been passed or statutes have been enacted. State constitutions have been amended to establish English as the official language in Arizona, Arkansas, California, Colorado, Florida, Georgia, Hawaii, Illinois, Indiana, Kentucky, Mississippi, Nebraska, North Carolina, North Dakota, South Carolina, Tennessee, and Virginia. By the end of the 1980s, action was pending on making English official in Alabama, Connecticut, Kansas (a threat of multiculturalism in *Kansas?*), Missouri, New Jersey, New York, West Virginia, and Wisconsin, and additional unsuccessful attempts had been made in Maryland, New Hampshire, Oklahoma, Texas, and Utah. (These facts are reported in Geoffrey Nunberg, 'Linguists and the official language movement', *Language* 65 (1989), 579–87, citing an English Plus Information Clearinghouse report.) That's seventeen states with English language laws already, and thirteen present or recent attempts to pass similar laws, making thirty of the fifty states either in the official-English camp or seriously thinking about it. And the ultimate goal of the people who are pushing official-language initiatives in the different state legislatures is to have the United States Constitution itself amended to enshrine English (and insult Spanish, Vietnamese, Navajo, and four or five thousand other languages, most of them spoken somewhere in the USA).

The word 'fascists' in my title is used ironically, in the style of 1960ish political rant, of course. It is not used in its sense as a technical term. Fascism in the technical sense involves "the presence of a charismatic leader, a high degree of militarism, the endeavor to create a monolithic nation and to include all institutions within a single political party, and intensive propaganda in a collectivist ideology" (P. L. van den Berghe, *Race and Racism: A Comparative Perspective,* John Wiley, New York, 1967, p. 109).

No, it is not really fascists who are pushing the idea that the United States, traditionally a country of tolerance, should enact a discriminatory addition to its Constitution. It is ordinary people, many of them educated, some of them linguists, some of them from originally non-English-speaking minorities, who think they are taking a stand for the language of Shakespeare and Milton and Dickens, and encouraging immigrants to learn the language of power and influence in American society.

I think otherwise. I think they are playing into the hands of an ugly group of immigrant-haters (originally the Federation for American Immigration Reform, FAIR by acronym but not by intent), and embarking on a thoroughly un-American road toward legal impediments to diversity. The column that follows makes a start on explaining why.

Perhaps the tide has begun to turn in favor of the views I present here. In February 1990, in one of the first signs of a break in the English-only fanatics' run of luck, a judge in Arizona ruled that the Arizona English-only constitutional amendment was itself unconstitutional, and he struck it down.

But there is a lot of road still to travel, and the need for linguists to be better informed on this issue will continue to be very great. For a head start on some of the literature, see Nunberg's *Language* article and reference cited there, and also Susannah MacKaye, 'California Proposition 63: language attitudes reflected in the public debate', in Courtney B. Cazden and Catherine E. Snow, eds., *English Plus: Issues in Bilingual Education* (*The Annals of the American Academy of Social and Political Sciences* 508, March 1990).

In mailboxes all across the United States of America early in 1987 appeared a document headed "ENGLISH FIRST." For one such as I, caring about English and being a native speaker thereof, this looked like it could be good news, so I examined my copy with care. At the letterhead was a list of three officers and an advisory board composed of elected lawmakers from the legislatures of nearly twenty states. Big guns. I started to read the text. In short, strident paragraphs, it opens up with a number of frightening claims about what is happening in the United States, a great but now apparently imperilled country.

> Tragically, many immigrants these days refuse to learn English!
> They never become productive members of American society. They remain stuck in a linguistic and economic ghetto, many living off welfare and costing working Americans millions of tax dollars every year.
> Incredibly, there is a radical movement in this country that not only promotes such irresponsible behavior, but actually wants to give foreign languages the same status as English—the so-called "bilingual" movement.

Those damned radicals! Condoning expenditures from my taxes to institutionalize the unproductive torpor of linguistically stunted, welfare-scrounging aliens! It made my blood boil just to think about it.

The purpose of the document is to solicit signatures on "a Petition calling for a Constitutional Amendment to make English the official language of the United States." The issue is much more important than mere respect for the language of Shakespeare and Milton, however: "This Amendment will stop a direct attack on our American way of life." Indeed, English First is, the bottom of the notepaper reveals, a project of the Committee to Protect the Family. Ah, the family! How could any American not want to protect the family?

The document continued, in the underlined mode that daisywheel printers use to represent urgency:

> If you and I fail to pass this Amendment now, the fragmentation of American society along language lines will be complete. We'll create a permanent underclass of unemployable citizens.

My disposable income; the English language; welfare scrounging; the American way of life; the sanctity of the family; a horrible linguistic underclass of ne'er-do-wells lurking in our cellars; it was enough for me. I reached for my signature pen and my checkbook.

And then, for some reason, I paused for a moment to think. Not the intended reaction, surely: English First nearly had me where it wanted me, checkbook spreadeagled on the desk, veins standing out in my neck, pen poised. But the habits of the intellectual die hard, and unlike perhaps thousands of other readers who already had their checks in the envelope, I decided to read on through the two further pages of choppy, excited prose before endorsing the petition. And (curse of the educated) I found that knowledge I had gained during my linguistic education began to conspire with elementary logic and common sense to render disappointingly blunt the at first sharp edge of the English First attack. The adrenalin rush over, my customarily calm and analytical nature returned. I read on, and my reactions began to be less sympathetic.

> Look what's happened in Canada, where radical bilingualists have held power in Quebec. It is now a criminal offense for companies not to give French equal billing with English. It's doubled the paperwork load, driven up the cost of doing business and forced businesses out of the province.

Now, hold on a minute: the Parti Québécois (PQ) is not a party of radical bilingualists. It is a party of radical *anti*-bilingualists. Its language policy, first promulgated in April 1977, was described the following year by the *Encyclopaedia Britannica* as "a brutal challenge to Prime Minister Trudeau's cherished aim of establishing official bilingualism as a reality across Canada" (*Britannica Book of the Year,* 1978, 236). The language policy of the PQ was very much like the one being proposed under this Amendment. It was not the result of allowing state assistance for minority language groups in a nation dominated by English. Their policy was not bilingualism but francization. They made education in English illegal except under certain very narrow circumstances, and began *imposing* French as the language of business. Canada's language problems arise first and foremost from the underlying economic and demographic disparity, and secondly through intolerance. In Quebec, the francophone majority want a French First policy, and in the rest of Canada French (like its speakers) is treated with utter contempt. (I saw a brief notice in a post office in Vancouver that was in French as well as English, as the Federal government requires, but it was so atrociously spelled and so stuffed with insultingly elementary grammatical errors that the French side might just as well have said "Frogs not welcome.") English First proposes that English speakers in California should embark on a language policy exactly equivalent to the one adopted by the PQ when it attained power.

There are only 11 states that require English to take a driver's license test.

Isn't this for the Department of Motor Vehicles to decide? Are you sure, given that the number of visitors and short-stay temporary residents of the USA at any given time is in the millions, that you wouldn't rather have drivers examined on driving in a language they handle fluently, rather than excluded from the legal driving community and forced to drive as outlaws? Isn't it in the interests of the residents to have immigrants tested for driving fitness even during the period they are trying to learn English? How will they drive to their English classes? Isn't competence in English a rather different issue from safety on the roads?

The leaders of the bilingual movement . . . have already forced 30 states to use foreign language ballots in national and local elections. If this continues, the next American President could well be elected by people who can't read or speak English!

Couldn't these people still elect their choice of President, regardless of whether English is the official language? The names are on the ballot, and proper names do not change under translation in most cases. Generally, even in Chinese and Japanese, specific foreign personal names are inserted without transliteration, as one can see from a glance at any linguistics article that has been translated into a language with a different script. One only has to be able to tell *Gomez* from *Gephardt*, or *Jimenez* from *Jackson*, or *Quan* from *Quayle*, or whatever turns out to be the choice.

In California, one county was forced to spend $3600 per ballot to satisfy bilingual laws. Another shelled out $6619 and *no one used them at all.*

No one used them? Where's that unemployable underclass? Why weren't they out voting in the candidates of choice for their particular linguistic subcastes, trying to ensure that the next American President is elected by people who can't read or speak English?

Radical activists have been caught sneaking illegal aliens to the
polls on election day and using bilingual ballots to cast fraudulent
votes.

Not in the county where no one used the bilingual ballots, I assume.
Anyway, why was it necessary for these sneaks to use bilingual ballots? Why could they not just sneak people in and use any ballot that
was going? It's representing the selected warm body as correlated
with some name on the electoral roll that's crucial. What does this
voter fraud have to do with language in any way at all?

The National Education Association, the nation's largest teachers
union [*hey, shouldn't that be* teachers' union *if we really care about
English?—GKP*], sees bilingual education as a means to force schools
to hire more teachers and swell the union ranks. Even the textbook
publishers, who have visions of doubling their business, have gotten
into the act.

Why would business double, for either group, assuming student-
teacher ratios remain stable? Why would the English-speaking group
of students need the Spanish version of the textbook, or vice versa?
    The English First document I am quoting from is signed by Repre-
sentative Jim Horn of the Texas legislature. Rep. Horn has many
more strident paragraphs of undocumented assertion to offer, but
even a cursory glance shows that the logic of his alarmist conclusions
from those assertions is so faulty that one can have little faith in the
rational basis for the proposition argued—namely that a 27th Amendment to the Constitution of the United States is needed as "a simple
and direct solution to the dangerous spread of 'bilingualism' in our
society." So what is going on?
    Alas, it is all too clear. I well remember the last time I heard rheto-
ric like that with which Horn's letter is stuffed. It was in Britain in the
late 1960s; the subject matter was oddly devoid of reference to language problems (a real problem in some of Britain's urban schools at
that time), but harped solely on race. The voice was that of Enoch
Powell, a right-wing junior government minister who overstepped
the bounds of what even the Conservative Party would tolerate and
was expelled from the government for embarrassing it with his in-
flammatory anti-immigrant speeches. If Britain went on this way,
Powell intoned, there would be terrible trouble. Dark, alien people
were flooding the land. They could not be assimilated. They must be

sent back to where they came from, before they engulfed us. He had anecdotes with all the power to render the hearer indignant that Horn's tales of sneaky radicals have, and with a similar lack of documentation and explicitness. And it struck a chord in the hearts of some of the nastiest people ever to don an armband.

Yes, the fascists are back. The hallmark of the English First literature is not a desire to cherish the English language and the democratic traditions of the United States, but a hatred and suspicion of aliens and immigrants—the Puerto Ricans of New York, the Cubans of Miami, the Chicanos of East Los Angeles, the Chinese of San Francisco, the Vietnamese in San Jose, the Hmong refugees in Denver, whichever huddled masses have most recently been crowding through the golden door—"Hispanic and other", as the document puts it, guardedly. Sociolinguist John Baugh tells me that indeed the organization originates with an anti-immigrant group that was told by their market research consultants that people didn't get particularly steamed up about immigration, but they *did* get steamed up about the English language. The support for the English language issue started right there—a marketing decision by a P.R. man for a group of bigots.

Horn's document plays on the fears of the xenophobes, emphasizing the "irresponsible" and "sneaky" behavior of the "radicals", and the "dangerous spread" of ideas that favor "people who can't read or speak English". But the proposed amendment looks so reasonable when printed up as House Joint Resolution number 96. Section 1 reads simply:

> The English language shall be the official language of the United States.

How innocuous. And section 2 merely forbids either the United States or any state to require the use of another language for any purpose; section 3 provides that this shall not prohibit laws requiring instruction in some other language if it is "for the purpose of making students who use a language other than English proficient in English" (English but not math may be taught in Spanish, in other words); and section 4 allows the Congress and the states to enforce the above provisions by legislation. Most people in the USA would probably be surprised that these proposals are not part of the law already. How deceptive the proposed Amendment is.

In all of its history, the United States has had English as its language by custom, not by legal stipulation. Legal stipulations can be overturned by plebiscites; customs are immune to such measures. No one has ever previously suggested that the English-speaking character of the USA is a matter for legislators to debate or determine. While other countries have language policies set out in their constitutions, and regularly enjoy language riots, the USA has never considered such a thing, and the sovereignty of English has been the result.

Indeed, the rise of English across the entire world is utterly amazing. At international academic meetings in Bonn or Bologna, in Tokyo or Tbilisi, all papers are given in English. Japanese teenagers wear clothing with English words (chosen at random) emblazoned on them, because the look of written English is fashionable. Multinational corporations in Europe use English for all their business correspondence. India uses English as one of its major official languages. Bantu schoolchildren rioted in the streets in South Africa when it was proposed that they should be offered bilingualism (in the guise of obligatory Afrikaans classes); they wanted English. The world is just cuckoo bananas about English. People learn it even if they are discouraged—and surely it is easy to be discouraged from learning a language with a spelling system so insane it makes the underlying representations in *The Sound Pattern of English* look sensible.

The plain fact is that making English the official language of the United States of America is about as urgently called for as making hotdogs the official food at baseball games.

Are the supporters of English First deaf and blind to such facts? I have no idea. But the marketing strategy they have chosen for their ideas is likely to work like a charm with electors, as California found out in a recent election. A well-organized faction with aims related to those of English First put a proposition (i.e. a referendum measure) on the ballot that was to make English the official language of California, which it had never previously been. And despite a certain amount of opposition from groups who realized what this was really going to mean, it swept the board, with 76% of the electors voting yes.

Now, for the first time in its history, California has a statement in its constitution that says English is its official language. Hitherto, it had just been a blindingly obvious and socially immutable fact. Now, it is enshrined in the fickle fabric of a referendum outcome. Some time early in the next century, California will find, given present demographic trends, that it has more Spanish speakers than English speakers. Given what has been done so far, it will be the Spanish speakers' right to call another referendum, this time to declare that Spanish is the official language of California. (And why not? It certainly was that a mere 150 years ago.) I hope the English Firsters realize what they have done. The indisputably English-speaking character of California as a state has been reduced to a mere matter of law, and could be changed in a day. Yo soy learning to hablar Español (y trying to get the hang del code-switching).

Nor were the consequences of the vote in California merely symbolic. The first lawsuits to try and get state money pulled back from multilingual services to immigrants were filed within weeks of the election. The angry parent who once telephoned a college provost after a California graduation ceremony to complain bitterly about the minute or two that was in Spanish (many students being Chicanos) has a new option now: he can sue the college for being out of compliance with the state constitution.

The English First organization, with its highly un-American hostility to immigrants (immigrants other than Anglos like me, of course), is bent on doing for the entire United States what has already been achieved in California and several other states. And an incredibly large percentage of the population, including lots of legislators and a curiously large number of foreign immigrants, is with them to the hilt, apparently not understanding what is really going on.

As far as I can see, the only thing that can stop this wave of linguistic chauvinism, with its ugly political undertones, is a huge (and doubtless very costly) effort by those who know about the disadvantages of legally enforced language policies to get their side of the debate widely heard. And even then, the way things are going, they may lose, which will mean that the most powerful nation on earth will have, in a single decade, refused to affirm in its Constitution the equal rights of women, but agreed to affirm (pointlessly but symbolically) the lack of equal rights accorded to its large non-English-speaking population. I hope the sociolinguists and applied linguists who have more specialized knowledge in this domain than I do will get a chance to be heard in the coming debate, and will seize it.

Part Three

Unscientific Behavior

Chapter Fifteen

The revenge of the methodological moaners

In this piece I rail against the tendency of linguists to write about the philosophy of science as applied to their subject instead of writing about what languages are like, which is what linguists are supposed to be good at. Unsympathetic critics will no doubt charge that by doing so I instantiate the very kind of behavior that I am railing against. This is not so. I am complaining about unproductive metalevel discussion, which consists of linguists talking about doing linguistics instead of doing it. By offering a critique of such work, I am operating at a meta-metalevel, talking about linguists talking about doing linguistics instead of doing it. There is a difference.

Of course, in presenting a defense of my stance here in this prefatory note, I am operating at yet a different level, the metametameta-level, talking about talking about linguists talking about doing linguistics instead of doing it. The difference between these four levels can be clarified by a diagram. Mercifully, however, I have no interest whatsoever in showing you this diagram, so you will not find it here. This introduction has already gone on long enough; the philosophically sophisticated reader will sense an infinite regress of self-referential blather developing.

This column did not put a stop to methodological discourse by philosophically unqualified linguists; there has been plenty more of it since I wrote (including a letter of wounded concern about this very piece, by Michael Kac in *NLLT* 2.427–28, 1984). If one found one's Toyota repair mechanic writing analyses of Toyota repair argumentation instead of fixing the damn carburetor trouble, one would naturally and rightly get quite annoyed. And in the actual car repair world this does not happen. But trying to keep linguists from philosophizing inexpertly about their craft when they ought to be practicing it is like trying to keep a dog from barking at the mailman. I don't know why I bother.

In 1978, I published in *Language* a review of a rather dull book about linguistic argumentation, filled with uninspiring papers that fruitlessly raked over the ashes of arguments long gone cold. I thought it was regrettable to see linguists spending their time mulling over the logic of tired old arguments when there was so much linguistics to do, and I said so quite bluntly, using phrases like "self-indulgent methodological agonizing".

This brought down on me a certain amount of abuse. *Language* took the unusual step of publishing a letter to the editor about the review—a letter in which ugly phrases such as "ostrich-like" and "avoid facing up to foundational problems" are to be found (Kac 1980). And there were much angrier responses elsewhere. The angriest I know about was from Bruce Derwing of the University of Alberta, who in 1979 published an article in which my name appeared alarmingly close to a rash of phrases like "failure to recognize the nature of the problem", "pure sloth and accompanying ignorance", "arrogance", "narrow and inflexible mind", "thoroughly anti-scientific", and "disreputable and isolated". All I had said about Derwing in the review was that he represented an excellent example of the way the linguists who make the most noise about the coming methodological disaster seem also to be those who do the least linguistics. Derwing quotes this with the gratuitous insertion "formal" in front of my word "linguistics", but I wasn't singling out work that offers a mathematical definition of its claims (if there is any; cf. chapter 7, 'Formal linguistics meets the Boojum'). I mean any sort of linguistics at all. I was thinking of Derwing's book *Transformational Grammar as a Theory of Language Acquisition*, which contributes nothing to transformational grammar, and every bit as much to the study of language acquisition. It has essentially no linguistics in it. That seems a waste to me. Even if linguistics *is* in troubled waters, what we need is all hands to man the pumps. What we don't need is the likes of Derwing striding around the heaving deck shouting that we're all doomed.

Even people I did not mention at all have come forward obligingly to argue that they aren't guilty when I never said they were. This happens sometimes. In 1848 a factory in Portlaw, Ireland, brought a libel action against a newspaper for accusing "a certain factory in the south of Ireland" of cruel labor practices. The owners argued, most revealingly, that readers of the paper would be likely to assume it referred to them. (Incidentally, they won their case, and a lot of money, the judgment being upheld on appeal to the House of Lords; see Carter-Ruck 1972, 60.) One person who did something similar with my tirade against the methodological moaners is Geoffrey Sampson, who quotes the phrase about methodological agonizing in his book *Making Sense* (1980, p. 205) and attempts to defend himself against the potential charge that he is engaged in this activity. (Too disgusted to mention my name in the text, he refers to me by a contemptuous epithet, "One enthusiastic British proponent of Postal's theories" (!), revealing my identity only in a footnote on p. 206.) Well, I am not aware of having had Sampson in mind at the time, but if he thinks the cap fits, he is certainly welcome to insert his head. Certainly, he does seem to be another example of an erstwhile linguist who has deliberately decided not to do any more linguistics, but merely to stand around and kibitz.

In 1978, I had no idea of the direction that the next half-decade's developments would take. I merely hoped to discourage linguists from engaging in philosophy of science and encourage them to do something they are good at. I failed, as ever. Since I wrote the 1978 review, we have witnessed a new flowering of methodological moaning and self-serving cracker-barrel philosophy of science in the work of people who actually *do* produce publishable work in descriptive and theoretical linguistics. Many linguists now refuse to let their linguistic work stand on its merits. They garnish it with epistemological homilies, and serve it with a side salad of little sermons on the essence of scientific inquiry. While handing you their linguistic hypotheses they take the opportunity to stuff a few tracts on the philosophically correct view of falsifiability into your pocket, in case you should be so misguided as to suggest a counterargument, or to fail to see that what they are doing parallels precisely what Einstein and Newton did.

Jan Koster's 1978 article 'Conditions, empty modes, and markedness' is a fine example, and introduces to *Linguistic Inquiry* readers a useful term of abuse: "naive falsificationism" (p. 566). There is a substantial amount of serious and interesting linguistic argumentation in the article. But along with the grammar we get homilies on how to live as a Good Scientist, dressed up with references to Dijksterhuis, Feyerabend, Feynman, Holton, and Moscovici on the philosophy of science. And the drift of most of these didactic excursi into general studies of scientific method is purely defensive. Here are a few interpreted examples:

TEXT	INTERPRETATION
One can hardly imagine the development of an explanatory science without the discovery of entities that are unknown in prescientific experience. . . .	Don't be alarmed if I introduce some pretty weird little invisible doohickeys to get my explanatory payoff; it's O.K., real scientists do it.
It is necessary for the growth of a theory to work out several alternatives. . . .	I may seem to be disagreeing with Chomsky here, but don't worry, I really am a good guy.
Interesting theories do not avoid conflicts with data, but rather create clashes on purpose. . . . Idealization involves counterfactual representation, by definition. In general, improvements in the structure of theories may lead to a (temporary) loss of descriptive adequacy. . . .	I'm saying some things that look as if they're completely wrong, but what you've got to understand is that real scientists do this all the time, and it's completely kosher. My account is so much nicer, it's just mean to try and show that it's wrong about the mere facts.
it is entirely pointless to list arbitrary data from arbitrary languages in order to refute principles. . . .	Don't waste my time bringing me your weird data from languages no one ever heard of when I'm trying to do some theory, O.K.?
Mathematical order is not directly reflected in the common sense classification of any domain of reality. . . .	If you look for my beautiful constraints to leap out at you from your grubby field notes, you're in for a disappointment.
classical mechanics . . . *makes assertions which not only are never confirmed by everyday experience, but whose direct experimental verification is impossible.*	In physics they say things that no one can possibly check up on. I just don't see why you trust those nerds in their white coats more than you're prepared to trust me.

What is so hilarious here is not the anodyne views in the left column. It is seeing them defensively plugged in as interlinear glosses in an actual research paper. It's quite true that real working physicists ignore facts incompatible with their theory, operate with idealizations (like perfect vacua) that render their claims untestable, refuse to consider certain phenomena relevant because of deliberately imposed limits on scope of theories, and so on. But what they don't do is comment self-consciously on this in their actual technical publications, or drone on about how wrong it would be for anyone to come along and try to say their hypotheses were not correct.

There are far wilder examples than Koster's article. For a really splendid one, look at Carlos Quicoli's 'Some issues on [sic] the theory of clitics' (1982). This is a reply to Postal (1980), which itself was a critique of Quicoli (1980). The reader will have to be rather alert to keep straight about what is going on in the empirical dimension. Quicoli (1980) was supposed to be describing the standard French dialects discussed in such work as Kayne (1975), but cited some data from speakers who permit two dative clitics in one clause (e.g. Je te le lui laisserai donner 'I will let you (dat.) give it to him/her (dat.)') and thus do not instantiate the dialects Kayne was talking about. Quicoli did not initially appreciate that his informant was not giving him standard French, and thus was operating under a misconception in devising his analysis (see p. 231 of his article). Postal's allegation is that Kayne wrongly predicts *no* French speakers accept double-dative sentences, and Quicoli wrongly predicts that *all* French speakers should accept them. Quicoli's (somewhat baffling) response is to accuse Postal of holding the view that grammars should be able to describe mutually inconsistent dialects simultaneously. But before this, the reader has to suffer a whole section, nearly eight pages, about "conceptual issues". All Postal is saying is that Quicoli's paper is a wretched piece of descriptive linguistics, wrong at many points in its account of the syntax of French, and thus a very poor exemplar of the alleged merits of the theory in whose terms it is couched. He wants to get down to facts. But Quicoli leaps straight to the philosophy of science shelf, not the French grammar shelf, as if he had got out of the library elevator on the wrong floor. The quotation at the head of his section 3 reads

> There is no falsification before the emergence of a better theory
> (Imre Lakatos).

and the following section, about the data, has another quote, from Gerald Holton:

> Not only do brute facts alone not lead to science, a program of enthusiastic compilation of facts *per se* has more than once delayed the progress of science. . . . As the scientist-educator J. B.

Conant has pointed out, "Science advances not by the accumula-
tion of new facts . . . but by the continuous development of new
and fruitful concepts".

Again one wonders who would doubt the truth of these platitudes.
Why are they dragged out, and heavily embroidered on, by Quicoli,
who is only supposed to be responding to the charge that his analysis
of French grammar is a crock? Does Quicoli really think Postal wants
just to amass facts and not develop concepts? Surely not. Postal
spends his life devising theories. (Sampson reports me as an enthusiastic proponent of them, remember?) Who can Quicoli be preaching
to? Why is he rummaging through philosophy of science paperbacks
to flesh out his protest? Linguists might listen if he presented a suc-
cinct account of the French facts that not only described them accurately but also revealed principles of some generality underlying that
account. But I for one do not want to wade through eight pages of
Quicoli raving about verification, theoretical constructs, quantum
physics, raw data, falsifying experiments, conceptual voids, and so
on (which has led, I noted with alarm more recently, to a further ten
pages of philosophical discussion in a 56-page counterattack by
Postal (1983)). I want to see linguistic research in the journals I subscribe to, not philosophy term papers.

It wouldn't be so bad if it were good, creative philosophical analysis. But in fact the term papers one finds embedded in the work of the
methodological moaners would in many cases get a B-minus at best.
Many linguists have a rather uncertain grasp of philosophy.

I discern three main factions in philosophy of science. The first
contains the logicians. They study topics like the logic of confirma-
tion, the empirical status of counterfactual conditional claims, and so
on. They cite Hempel and Popper, and their examples are about
swans being white. The second faction contains the sociohistorians.
They study issues like the emergence of scientific revolutions and the
sociological preconditions for acceptance of new theories. They cite
Kuhn and Lakatos, and their examples are about brave physicists and
chemists struggling on despite recalcitrant data and the disapproval
of friends and relatives.

The third faction consists of Paul Feyerabend. What Feyerabend
offers is not so much philosophy as guerilla theater for philosophers.
His work is marvellous reading: bubbling wit, boiling invective,

deep erudition, a constant twinkle in the eye—to read Feyerabend is to experience an intellectual analog of what dogs seem to enjoy when they get a chance to roll on their backs in a patch of fresh, crisp grass. But make no mistake: reading Feyerabend without appreciating that he is sending the whole business up is like mistaking Monty Python's Flying Circus for the Ten O'Clock News. In his celebrated book *Against Method,* for example, Feyerabend offers, tongue in cheek, a recipe for the destruction of science. Deadpan, he presents a purported methodology for modern scientists that will allegedly take them in the footsteps of their great heroes such as Galileo: develop theories that are in conflict with known facts; lie about the observational support for them; maintain them stubbornly in the face of objections; defend them by means of dishonesty and bluster. Feyerabend seems to be alternately amused and disgusted to see that there are people who read his satirical proposals as if seriously put forward (see e.g. his 'Marxist fairytales from Australia', 1978). He would really get a kick out of seeing how linguists are solemnly citing him (see Hornstein and Lightfoot 1981, p. 29, note 5, for a wholly serious reference to *Against Method*), and how some seem to be actually trying to live by his ironically proposed principles.

If linguists understood a little more philosophy, we might be spared such things. And we might be spared the sight of Quicoli solemnly quoting Feyerabend's old friend Lakatos on the impossibility of "falsifying" (Lakatos really means "overthrowing") a theory without devising another theory to put in its place, confusing utterly his own job (defending hypotheses about the structure of French) and the job of future historiographers of linguistics.

Tomorrow's historians of linguistics might conceivably be interested in unraveling the psychological and sociological mystery of why Quicoli and Postal held on to their theoretical preconceptions so tenaciously, finding not one atom of agreement in the course of the 54 pages of Quicoli's original article and the 168 printed pages (so far) of debate about it. But they will not fall for the nonsense more and more fierce transformational grammarians are prepared to dish out, about it being a "conceptual error" to suppose that the observation $\sim P$ falsifies a theory that predicts P. Of course it isn't a mistake to think that if you discover that $\sim P$ you have falsified a theory that entails P. It is, however, a mistake to suppose that anyone other than your enthusiastic proponents will listen to you.

REFERENCES

Carter-Ruck, Peter F. 1972. *Libel and slander.* Faber and Faber, London.

Derwing, Bruce L. 1973. *Transformational grammar as a theory of language acquisition.* Cambridge University Press, Cambridge.

——. 1979. Psycholinguistic evidence and linguistic theory. In Gary D. Prideaux, ed. *Perspectives in experimental linguistics.* J. Benjamins, Amsterdam, pp. 113–38.

Feyerabend, Paul. 1975. *Against method.* New Left Books, London.

——. 1978. Marxist fairytales from Australia. In *Science in a free society.* New Left Books, London, pp. 154–82.

Hornstein, Norbert, and David W. Lightfoot. 1981. Introduction to *Explanation in linguistics: The logical problem of language acquisition.* Longmans, London, pp. 9–31.

Kac, Michael. 1980. Note in *Language* 56.919.

Kayne, Richard S. 1975. *French syntax: The transformational cycle.* MIT Press, Cambridge, Massachusetts.

Koster, Jan. 1978. Conditions, empty nodes, and markedness. *Linguistic Inquiry* 9.551–93.

Postal, Paul M. 1980. A failed analysis of the French cohesive infinitive construction. *Linguistic Analysis* 8.281–323.

——. 1983. On characterizing French grammatical structure. *Linguistic Analysis* 11.361–417.

Pullum, Geoffrey K. 1978. Review in *Language* 54.399–402.

Quicoli, A. Carlos. 1980. Clitic movement in French causatives. *Linguistic Analysis* 6.131–85.

——. 1982. Some issues on the theory of clitics. *Linguistic Analysis* 10.203–73.

Sampson, Geoffrey R. 1980. *Making sense.* Oxford University Press, Oxford.

Chapter Sixteen

Footloose and context-free

This column actually has an underlying thread of content, an unusual thing in the context of TOPIC . . . COMMENT. It is about a mathematical discovery concerning human languages: construed as stringsets, human languages are not necessarily context-free.

A set of strings of symbols is context-free in the mathematical linguistics sense if and only if there is a correct grammar for it that contains only rules of the simple form $\alpha \to W$, where α is a category (a part-of-speech label) and W is a string of categories and/or words. A rule like 'a verb phrase may consist of the verb *show* followed by two noun phrases' is legitimate in such a grammar; so is a rule like 'a noun phrase may consist of a single noun'; but a rule like 'a verb phrase must contain a singular verb if the nearest noun phrase to its left is singular' is not allowed.

There are some curious, counterintuitive truths about context-freeness. For example, if there were a language in which the two noun phrases occurring with *show* had to be different, a context-free grammar that could guarantee the difference could in principle (and ceteris paribus) be provided; but if there were a language in which the two noun phrases occurring with *show* had to be identical, no context-free grammar could possibly handle the job. Call me eccentric, but I find that intriguing and strange.

But never mind these technicalities. This piece is not about the issue itself, which many linguists care nothing about. It is about the location of the discovery in time, and the publication of the discovery. It turns out that linguists are so extraordinarily sloppy in their work and their publication and citation practices that if there were a prize for the discovery of the non-context-freeness of human languages it would be completely unclear who to give it to.

When I wrote this chapter I was unaware of a crucial reference, and thus missed a vital point in the story. No excuses: I'm sloppy too, and I missed a relevant item in my reading. In the next chapter (chapter 17) I apologize for this and tell the rest of the story.

It was not an isolated believe-it-or-not coincidence when a Cambridge mathematician (Adams) and a Paris mathematician (Le Verrier) both predicted the discovery of Neptune at the same time through similar but entirely independent calculations of Uranean orbit wobble. Similar things happen all the time. Ideas often seem to be hanging from the tree of science like ripe fruits ready to fall, and several hands may grasp at the bough simultaneously.

A number of things are necessary to make it nonetheless possible to identify the discoverer(s) of a given truth: careful record-keeping about research activity, fair and efficient management of the peer-review and research publication enterprise, and above all, generally accepted standards about what constitutes a result. If things that have not by any stretch of a disordered imagination been demonstrated are claimed to have been demonstrated, clearly it will be hard to establish later that a given person discovered a given thing. If standards of evidence are set ad hoc to ensure rhetorical victories over critics, and alliances determined more by sociological groupings than by problems shared, there is little hope of being able to look back and see progress.

Let me give a case history. It is not pretty; in fact, it is a mess, but we must face our world as it really is.

By 1985 it had become clear that not all natural languages are context-free. In 1955 the question could not have been formulated, because context-free languages (CFL) and the context-free phrase structure grammars (CF-PSG) that by definition generate them, had not yet been defined. So the discovery that certain natural languages are not CF occurred some time between 1955 and 1985. Yet although the result in question was widely believed true by the middle sixties, it does not seem to have been validly and publicly shown to be true until quite recently, and the question of who deserves the credit is a morass of unclarity.

The question was first formulated by Noam Chomsky. In his 1956 paper 'Three models for the description of language' (*I.R.E. Transactions on Information Theory* IT-2.113–23), he reported that he didn't know the answer. During the wave of activity which was the start of the whole field of formal language theory (now an important part of theoretical computer science) a number of people started looking for the answer. Several early efforts are reviewed in R. T. Daly, *Applications of the Mathematical Theory of Linguistics* (Mouton, The Hague, 1974) and G. K. Pullum and G. Gazdar, 'Natural languages and context-free languages' (*Linguistics and Philosophy* 4.471–504, 1982).

Paul Postal gave a non-CF-ness argument for Mohawk in his 1962 Yale University doctoral dissertation (*Some Syntactic Rules in Mohawk*, Garland, New York, 1979), and later in a 1964 paper ('Limitations of phrase structure grammars', in Jerry A. Fodor and Jerrold J. Katz, eds., *The Structure of Language*, Prentice-Hall, Englewood Cliffs; pp. 137–51), and Chomsky proposed one himself ('Formal properties of grammars', in R. D. Luce et al., eds., *Handbook of Mathematical Psychology, Vol. II*, Wiley, New York; see pp. 378–79). Like most of the early arguments, these had both formal and empirical failings. Although suggestions were made for patching some of them up (see especially D. Terence Langendoen's paper in *Studies in Descriptive and Historical Linguistics: Festschrift for Winfred P. Lehmann*, ed. by Paul J. Hopper, Benjamin, Amsterdam, 1977, pp. 159–71), the case still seemed to Gazdar and me not to have been made.

In one argument we discussed, neither the mathematics nor the facts are in dispute, yet the issue still seems hard to resolve. Arnold Zwicky claimed in 1963 ('Some languages that are not context-free', *Quarterly Progress Report of the Research Laboratory of Electronics, MIT,* 70.290–93) that number systems in human languages are not CF. What he showed entails that if (say) *zillion* is the highest monomorphemic number-name in English, the set of all number names will be non-CF, because in a well-formed number name the zillions follow the zillion zillions, which follow the zillion zillion zillions, and so on, and a CF-PSG cannot handle this pattern if length of strings is unbounded (as it surely must be with number names). Gazdar and I took the view that this is merely a fact about the number system. We have to be taught it in math classes at school, and we do not acquire it with our language per se. On odd dates I still think this is right, but on even dates I think the argument has been unjustly overlooked. Zwicky thinks we were correct to dismiss it, but maybe he is wrong and it was the first valid argument that English is non-

CF. The problem here is that we are not entirely sure what is a fact about a language and what is a fact about the culture associated with it (more on this below).

The most fascinating new material uncovered during the recent debate about CF-ness was the Dutch construction first discussed in this context by M. A. C. (Riny) Huybregts in 1976 ('Overlapping dependencies in Dutch', *Utrecht Working Papers in Linguistics* 1.24–65). Dutch subordinate clauses with meanings like 'Al saw Bo make Cy let Di help Ed shave' come out (or can come out) with the word order *Al Bo Cy Di Ed saw make let help shave*. This rather surprising fact leads to the conclusion that this construction in Dutch exhibits what has become known as a cross-serial dependency: the nth verb takes the nth NP as its direct object. (If you believe in small clauses, this is incorrectly put, and I have no idea what superficial structure you might assign; but then, if you believe in small clauses you probably eat steak with a spoon. Even Edwin Williams doesn't believe in small clauses.)

What Gazdar and I maintained about the Dutch case was that the purely syntactic facts seemed unproblematic. All the grammar had to do was provide the right number of NPs to go round—one per verb, in the simplest case. A context-free grammar could easily do that. However, to show this, we used grammar fragments whose chances of being associated with valid semantic rules were similar to Mr. T's chances of being offered an honorary doctorate at Harvard. There was clearly something disturbing and potentially very relevant to the issue afoot, for we could not exhibit a context-free grammar which both generated Dutch and seemed likely to be able to support a semantics. (This is in essence the point that Bresnan, Kaplan, Peters, and Zaenen pursued in 'Cross-serial dependencies in Dutch', *Linguistic Inquiry* 13.613–35, 1982, though they put things in terms of syntactic motivation for tree structures.) Huybregts had put his finger on the reason why Dutch was a problem, but Dutch didn't quite allow for his argument to be completed.

Now the plot quickens its pace a bit. (It should, I hear you cry; nothing has happened yet.) At a conference in Brussels in June 1983, Tom Wasow was told by Richie Kayne that Swiss German had a similar word-order pattern to that of Dutch in clauses of the relevant sort, but also had, like standard German, certain verbs which took a visible dative case on their objects. That would mean there could be a morphologically indicated syntactic link between the nth verb and the *n*th NP, which would be very likely to allow a non-CF-ness proof to be constructed. As luck would have it, a native or near-native speaker was available right there at the conference: Henk van Riemsdijk has mother-tongue knowledge of Swiss German. Wasow had a lot of trouble pinning van Riemsdijk down for even a cursory interview; van Riemsdijk was very busy, and apparently uninterested in the issue at hand. Wasow did not get very far with the investigation, but by the end of the conference he had extracted one example which at least suggested there was a case to answer.

In August 1983, after having been told of this by Wasow, Stuart Shieber, then a computer scientist at SRI International in Menlo Park, California (now at Harvard), set off on a trip to Europe to attend a conference in Switzerland. Finding himself in Zurich, he started working with informants in that area to see what he could find out about the crucial syntactic property-cluster Swiss German was reputed to have.

Meanwhile, in western Mali, a hundred drought-stricken miles southwest of Timbuktu, Christopher Culy, a recent linguistics graduate who had decided to do two years in the Peace Corps before embarking upon graduate school, was commencing lessons in the language of the area, Bambara. While working on the language, he came upon something that took him back to his classes in linguistics and mathematics at Stanford. The device Bambara uses for forming an expression meaning 'whatever dog' is reduplication of the noun-stem meaning 'dog' with an *o* separating the two halves. But, Culy noticed, the construction appears to work the same for noun stems of any length, including compound nouns with internal syntactic complexity. It looked, therefore, as if the Bambara lexicon had an infinite subset with the form *xx*, where *x* could be of any length. This could be used to argue that Bambara as a whole was not CF.

On August 24, 1983, Culy wrote a letter to Tom Wasow and Ivan Sag, his former teachers at Stanford, describing the Bambara situation and sketching an argument that it made Bambara non-CF. Wasow wrote back encouraging Culy to construct the argument explicitly and write it up for publication. Culy proceeded to do this, though there were great difficulties, one being the mail delays involved in communicating with Stanford, and another being that as a government agency employee, Culy had to get permission from the Peace Corps to publish.

Whether Shieber had his results on Swiss German by the time

Culy's letter was mailed from Mali is not clear to me. But a further strand complicating the story must now be mentioned. Considerably earlier, in 1981, it had occurred to Alexis Manaster-Ramer that one could develop a non-CF-ness argument using the contemptuous reduplication of Yiddish-influenced English (transformation, schmansformation). In the spring of 1983 he presented his argument at the Chicago Linguistic Society's regional meeting, and in the summer, with Culy in Mali and Shieber in Switzerland, it was published in the CLS proceedings volume for the year ('The soft formal underbelly of theoretical syntax', *CLS 19*.256–62, 1983).

Now, to me, the construction Manaster-Ramer refers to looks like a game one plays *with* the language rather than a construction *within* the language (the difficulty of knowing what's language and what's culture again), and thus I was not immediately impressed with the argument. Moreover, the paper is distinctly equivocal about whether a valid non-CF-ness argument exists (see pp. 259–61). Manaster-Ramer does note that similar reduplication constructions are found in several other languages, but he does not give any examples. Manaster-Ramer's CLS paper could be seen as a prior publication of essentially Culy's point, though it isn't entirely clear.

Culy and Shieber both wrote papers and submitted them to *Linguistics and Philosophy* some time in the first half of 1984. Culy's was submitted first, but owing to various delays, Shieber's paper was accepted first. Eventually both papers appeared in the same issue of *Linguistics and Philosophy.*

But before they did, in the spring of 1984, a wild card was played. Out of the blue, a paper by James Higginbotham appeared in *Linguistic Inquiry* 15, 225–34; its title was, 'English is not a context-free language'. It cited none of the previous literature on the subject; one would have thought that Higginbotham had invented the issue on his own. The argument it offered involved applying a mathematical result known as Ogden's Lemma to a set of strings involving the relative clause-like construction with *such that*. The crucial empirical premise was that in an NP of the form 'Det N *such that S*', S must contain a pronoun of the right number, person, and gender to refer back to N. It had already been pointed out to Higginbotham before he published that this didn't really appear to be true (phrases like *any triangle such that two sides are equal* had been cited by Barbara Partee), but he was not deterred, and dismissed such examples in a footnote as ungrammatical but interpretable as ellipses (p. 229, n.1).

I published a response arguing that Higginbotham was entirely wrong about the facts (*Linguistic Inquiry* 16.291–98, 1985), and he replied indignantly in the same issue of *LI* that I was completely wrong about him being wrong (*LI* 16.298–304), and naturally I believe that he is completely wrong about me being wrong about him being wrong. (These things tend to drag on; in future work, Higginbotham will argue that my eyes are too close together, and I will argue that on the contrary, his head is too round.) But if he were right about what is and is not grammatical, then he would be the first person to have published a valid demonstration that natural languages are not context-free in a refereed journal, because it was 1985 before Shieber and Culy saw their papers in print.

Before I try to draw a moral from this historiographical chaos, let me point out what happened when a situation with some similar characteristics arose in another discipline, mathematics. In 1985, no less than five distinct groups of mathematicians hit on essentially the same result: a beautiful new way of characterizing knots in terms of polynomials. As Ivars Peterson reports in *Science News* (128.17, October 26, 1985, 266), the *Bulletin of the American Mathematical Society* saw to it that the results were amalgamated, and a single paper with six authors was published, with summaries of the proofs achieved by four of the five groups (the fifth group, two Polish mathematicians, missed out because of mail delivery delays). All mathematicians agreed that the five groups had achieved essentially the same result, and no attempt was made by any of the mathematicians involved to claim priority over the others in the discovery.

Linguists seem not to behave so well. The chaotic thirty-year history of our efforts to decide whether there are non-CF natural languages has no air of clean professionalism about it. And although Ivars Peterson wrote a report on the Culy and Shieber results in *Science News* (128.20.314–15, November 16, 1985), his report was promptly attacked twice in the letters column: Robin Ault of Newtonville, Massachusetts (128.24.371, December 14, 1985) burbled incoherently that languages were really finite, and was in turn incoherently attacked by Gary R. Lavine (129.4.57, January 25, 1986), and Michael Kac (129.2.19, January 11, 1986) protested that Manaster-Ramer had priority over Culy and Shieber.

The non-CF-ness result itself, Chomsky has repeatedly told us (see chapters 6 and 7), is of little importance. But then hardly anything in linguistics is important, in a way: if invalid arguments or incorrectly substantiated results are reported in linguistics, society suffers no particular ill, whereas if the same thing happens in marine toxicology, we eat poisoned fish. Probably the most interesting thing about the whole debate is the view it affords of how linguists do business.

I find myself feeling chastened by the words of Columbia University mathematician Joan Birman (quoted by Peterson) about the polynomial knot results:

> I felt very proud of mathematicians for the nice way that those competing announcements were handled. It had the potential for a big argument, but there was none.

For those who share my feeling that we linguists, in our disunity, may not have left quite such a good impression, a different epigraph: the closing lines of D. H. Lawrence's poem, *Snake*.

And I have something to expiate:
A pettiness.

Chapter Seventeen

Nobody goes around at LSA meetings offering odds

This is the sequel to "Footloose and context-free' (chapter 16). It was embarrassing to find that I had overlooked a crucial publication in a column devoted to flaming at people who don't respect scientific publication conventions, but there we are: I'm sure I'm a better person for having humiliated myself like this.

In telling the rest of the tale, I also recanted in part my portrayal of mathematicians as a higher race of beings whose behavior is vastly superior to that of linguists. When I wrote 'Footloose and context-free', I had just read about the joint discovery and publication of the polynomial knot characterization result. When I wrote this sequel, I had just read about the brouhaha over the purported Rourke Rêgo proof of Poincaré's conjecture. There is a world of difference. I actually began to think a little better of linguists' conduct, in fact. Read on, and you will see why.

I believe that if you try hard enough, and steel yourself against the initial pain, you can almost bring yourself to almost enjoy finding that you have been refuted; there can be something salutary or even cathartic about the experience of having your pronouncements and predictions wrecked by the chariot of history as it thunders past, trampling over what you have done. There is an element of masochism in this, no doubt, but at least anyone who gets refuted isn't being *entirely* ignored, and that's worth something.

Nonetheless, I must confess I was taken aback at how fast my claims were covered with wheel ruts and hoofprints after the appearance of 'Footloose and context-free' (chapter 16; originally *NLLT* 4.409–14, 1986). Almost as soon as it was published, I learned that my best efforts at chronologizing and attributing the discovery that there were non-context-free human languages had not been good enough. Ger de Haan wrote to inform me that a crucial publication had been overlooked.

Readers of the saga will recall that Riny Huybregts was mentioned in passing as the originator of an argument from Dutch that introduced the most interesting new class of data to emerge in the whole affair, but I noted that the facts he cited were not sufficient to establish a valid argument about the character of the Dutch stringset. Shieber was cited as having later developed a valid argument by extending the Dutch argument into the realm of Swiss German. Well, quite unknown to me, a book published in Holland in 1984 contains something highly relevant.

The book is *Van Periferie naar Kern,* edited by Ger de Haan, Mieke Trommelen, and Wim Zonneveld [Foris, Dordrecht, 1984]. The title is in Dutch; the title page is in Dutch; the preface is in Dutch; the heading of the preface where it should say "Preface" is in Dutch (it says "Voorwoord"); twelve of the seventeen papers included are in Dutch; even the Foris catalog description is in Dutch. I mention all this in a pathetic effort to mitigate the blame that will attach to me for being unscholarly and ill-read in this matter.

Dutch happens to be a language in which my unfettered human capacity for free expression and comprehension of thoughts is rather fettered. In fact, all I can convincingly say in Dutch is that I would like to have een broodje met warme worst en een koffie met melk alstublieft. (This ability once saved me from starving to death during a GLOW conference in Amsterdam when no one would have lunch with me because of my position on the bounding of movement rules.) So left to my own devices, I would not have tried to read any of *Van Periferie naar Kern,* thinking that it was all in Dutch and thus beyond my competence. I would guess that the title had something to do with the fabled but unexplicated core and periphery distinction. It doesn't seem to imply that there might be any mathematical linguistics inside.

But in fact, among the five papers in English is one by Riny Huybregts entitled 'The weak inadequacy of context-free phrase structure grammars'. In this paper, Huybregts answers the arguments that Gazdar and I made in 1982 concerning the failure of the case made in his 1976 paper (for references, see chapter 16). He not only fleshes out the Dutch argument with some new data involving subcategorization of adverbs that appear to defeat one strategy we employed, but he also brings up the Swiss German data (specifically,

Zürich German or *Züritüütsch*), and makes an argument based on those facts.[1]

This gives Huybregts clear publication priority over Shieber. Below the voorwoord, indicating when it went to press, the volume has the date 'januari 1984'. (Sometimes, as here, Dutch looks remarkably like English as typed by the guys at the Computer Center.) Shieber's independent publication on Züritüütsch appeared in the August 1985 issue of *Linguistics and Philosophy*, though it is not possible to tell when the paper was received, because *Linguistics and Philosophy* is a journal which, to its lasting shame, still does not print the date of receipt with each article published (see chapter 8, 'Stalking the perfect journal', originally *NLLT* 2.261–67, 1984).

Huybregts' first publication of the Züritüütsch argument can be tied down to an even earlier date, in fact. His paper is marked with a postposed ° on the contents page, and at the bottom of that page, it says, "(De met ° aangeduide bijdragen werden op 20–22 december 1983 als lezingen gerepresenteerd op Biltstraat 200)". Now, this is Dutch again, but I'm not so inept at my craft that I can't puzzle it out with a little help from the dictionary. It means, plainly, that the with ° indicated contributions were upon December 20–22 1983 as readings represented upon Biltstraat 200.

Biltstraat 200? The book is coy about this. "De Biltstraat, het woord zegt het al," begins the voorwoord disingenuously. Of course the word doesn't say it all; who are they trying to fool? But I have figured out that it's an address in Utrecht, the address of the Instituut A. W. de Groot voor Algemene Taalwetenschap, where Huybregts gave his paper as a lecture just before Christmas 1983.

This leaves little doubt that Riny Huybregts has an unassailable claim to being the discoverer of the Swiss-German argument that languages with the peculiar word-order properties that Dutch and Züritüütsch seem to have will never submit to context-free phrase structure description. Indeed, he is perhaps the first person to publish a valid non-context-freeness argument about a natural language—though I have not yet gone over his work with a fine-tooth comb looking for errors and loopholes, and this really needs to be done.

---

1. Huybregts even wrote to Gerald Gazdar on September 16, 1983, asking for xerox copies of some relevant articles, and was duly sent them. Huybregts' letter added, "Perhaps I could return the favor some day". But he never returned the favor in the obvious way, by sending his paper, and Gazdar never learned of Huybregts' work until I showed him *Van Periferie naar Kern*.

It is a pity, in fact, that Huybregts' result did not undergo the scrutiny of referees and appear in a recognized international journal; perhaps the social pressure on him to regard the result as "unimportant" because it was about weak generative capacity was sufficiently strong that he did not want to risk making the work too visible (see chapters 6 and 7 for some evidence of the kind of negative energy that Noam Chomsky has been directing against work in mathematical linguistics, for example). I, for my part, consider Huybregts' result significant and interesting, and I regret the fact that although I regularly read seven or eight journals and attend numerous conferences, neither I nor anyone I knew in the field was aware of Huybregts' result until Ger de Haan sent me his book and told me where to look. Our techniques for communicating results should be working better than this.

There is a second respect in which the views I confidently enunciated in 'Footloose and context-free' turned out very rapidly to elicit a refuting knuckle-rap from the cosmos. I suggested in that column that mathematicians constituted a group of academics who behaved in a much more orderly and responsible way than their bumbling, amateurish, and ungracious linguistic counterparts. I was thinking of the chaotic publication policies of linguists ("see Snodgrass, unpublished manuscript"), their erratic grasp of what was or was not a result ("Snodgrass's example is dubious at best"), and their habit of squabbling wildly over not only whether something had been shown but even what we were supposed to be talking about in the first place ("Snodgrass's arguments do not even bear on the issue"). And I was moved by one recent sterling example of comradeship in mathematics to suggest that mathematicians behave much better.

Dream on. Mathematicians, as I guess I knew all along, are people too. And sometimes . . .

Well, let me begin at the beginning.

In 1986, in the March 20 issue of *Nature,* it was reported that two mathematicians had announced a proof of Poincaré's conjecture. Such a proof, let me make it clear, would be Big News. The conjecture, about as old as this century, says that what is true of the 2-dimensional surface of the (3-dimensional) sphere is also true of the 3-dimensional surface of the 4-dimensional analog of a sphere: each is the only simply connected surface with that number of dimensions. (A surface is simply connected if and only if any loop on it can be shrunk down to a point without cutting through the surface.)

The problem is celebrated, and quite fascinating to the sort of person who thinks so abstractly that they see no difference at all between the shapes of a ring doughnut and a coffee mug, or between either one and a needle or a door key.

The two mathematicians who claim to have proved the conjecture are Colin Rourke of the University of Warwick, England, and his graduate student Eduardo Rêgo, now of the University of Oporto (Portugal). And all unseemly hell has broken loose about the alleged proof. According to the *New York Times* of September 30, 1986, Rourke and Rêgo "have circulated, withdrawn, revised and reissued several versions since January", and there is still no refereed publication in sight. Their latest version was a 123-page manuscript issued in late September 1986.

And has sweet reason and respectful acknowledgment been their reward for their willingness to get their latest results out to their colleagues via semipublication? Not a bit of it. Rourke told *Nature* and *New Scientist* about the result before there was consensus in the topological community that it was really a result, and other mathematicians are clearly incensed. Joan Birman of Columbia University remarks that "There's some skepticism in the community because there have been many false proofs [of Poincaré's conjecture]" (*Science News* 129.14.215, April 5, 1986). Indeed there have. In fact, Wolfgang Haken spent some time struggling with the problem fifteen years ago, using exactly the techniques Rourke and Rêgo were now using, but was able to show that at a certain point the approach failed and the result could not be achieved. So mathematicians were indeed skeptical. "Too sketchy to confirm", was the sort of comment they made to the *New York Times*.

Michael Freedman, of the University of California, San Diego, told the *New York Times* that people are betting "as high as 200 to 1" that the proof is not correct. This is even more cruel than I can remember linguists having been; nobody goes around at LSA meetings offering *odds* that the *Barriers* framework can't account for English parasitic gaps. And keep in mind that Michael Freedman was presented with the Fields Medal in August 1986 for proving that the 4-dimensional case of the Poincaré conjecture is true; if even he cannot understand the proof of the 3-dimensional case, we are in deep trouble.

Meanwhile, Rourke defends himself against the charge of having laid claim to an important result on the basis of an unverified proof.

He apparently feels that the mathematics community ought to buckle down and figure out that his proof is correct. "They're sort of sitting back and waiting for someone else to do the work", he is reported as saying; "Mathematicians are sort of lazy". (Rourke sort of uses the *sort of* construction sort of excessively.)

Rourke's position, in other words, is that the duty of mathematicians, when faced with a couple of hundred pages of a proof so difficult that Michael Freedman cannot understand it, is not to toss it back and demand a better exposition, but to sit down and do the hard work of verifying that it really does all make sense, and then hand the credit to the author of the obscure material from which they painstakingly hewed out the crucial nuggets of truth. If they fail, he retains the right to accuse them of having been too "lazy" to discern the merit of his leading ideas. But if they succeed, he can claim full credit for the proof that thereby emerges, and point to the clarified version as simply a restatement of his own original thinking. Does this sound at all familiar to you?

The whole episode sounds to me a lot like the behavior we regularly see in linguistics. The unrefereed manuscripts circulated to a circle of initiates; the fixes and alterations as initial objections are raised; the vague and sketchy arguments; the early announcements of victory; the rapid onset of doubt in the community at large; the indignant rebuttals; the bitter accusations of a biased or lazy profession; it's all so familiar. "His [Rourke's] approach is not technically complete. He hasn't been careful about the technical details", says William P. Thurston of Princeton. "There just wasn't a proof there", says Robion Kirby of Berkeley. This is the way linguists talk about each other (with good reason, of course, in many cases).

Thus it might look from this example as if mathematics is not quite the perfect exemplar of scholarship that I might have appeared to seem to tend to imply that it was. They bicker, just like us, and can't even manage to settle what is or what is not a proof or a result.

Well, not quite. Mathematicians are not gods, to be sure, and they get mired down in vicious disputes sometimes like scholars in any other field. In fact, there was a dispute in algebraic topology that led to a year-long period in which conflicting proofs had been published, each entailing that the other was erroneous, and one Rutgers University mathematician (on the side that proved to be right) became so disgusted with the state of things that he resigned his tenured post and left the field. But I still think there is a contrast to be pointed up; mathematicians still don't run quite as shabby an operation as theoretical linguistics.

In November 1986, Rourke visited Berkeley to spend a week presenting his supposed proof. Heavies from Southern California came up to listen and participate, among them David Gabai of Cal Tech, who tells me that about three months of his research time during 1986 was spent in trying to understand Rourke's work. On the fourth day of Rourke's presentation, which was confusing and even sloppy at many points, Gabai asked a question about a particular diagram on the board, in an attempt to clarify exactly how it was to be understood in the light of the reply to an earlier clarificatory point. Rourke attempted to address the matter, but as he worked, it suddenly became clear that the example, when analyzed closely, was a counterexample. A series of entities each greater than some of the others had to exist, but clearly could not exist. The lemma could not be established, and the proof had collapsed. What's more, the problematic part of the proof was exactly the bit that Wolfgang Haken had warned about years earlier. Rourke mumbled something about being sure the difficulty could be overcome and the hole patched, but no one took this seriously; the whole episode is over, the proof is dead.

For in mathematics, the force of counterexamples is different. They are not to be rebutted with rhetorical defenses. Linguists dismiss facts as "mere facts"; they distinguish between counterexamples and mere exceptions; they point out loftily that apparent counterexamples and unexplained phenomena should be carefully noted, but that it is often rational to put them aside pending further study when principles of a certain degree of explanatory power are at stake; they assign selected phenomena to the marked periphery; they will digress into philosophy of science and point out that there have been cases in history of apparent counterevidence that turned out not to be such (cf. chapter 15); they will do anything, up to and including telling flaming lies, to avoid being in the situation that up to time t they thought that p was a principle of linguistic theory but at time t' a counterexample was adduced which showed that $\sim p$.

I was certainly wrong if I implied that mathematicians always behave in a civilized and organized way while linguists are slugging it out with abuse, vagueness, and obscure methodological defense mechanisms. But I think it's still true that we would be better off if linguists behaved a bit more like mathematicians at their best, and I think it still looks as if mathematicians at their worst don't sink quite so low as linguists.

In the world of linguistics, Rourke and Rêgo would have been published without question in any of the student linguistic society conference volumes, and quite possibly in a refereed journal. What's more, they would probably have replied to the subsequent critical rejoinders, accusing the putative refuters of myopic empiricism. I'll lay odds on it.

Chapter Eighteen

Citation etiquette beyond Thunderdome

This essay focusses on the origins of the Unaccusative Hypothesis. Despite the pseudo-objective mathematics of citation analysis with which the column begins, that is secondary. The primary topic is the way in which (as with the claim that natural languages are non-context free, discussed in chapters 16 and 17) it seems impossible to figure out from the linguistic literature, even with some knowledge of the background and chronology, who thought of the idea.

The Unaccusative Hypothesis says that in some simplex clauses but not others, e.g. in the sentence *Two seconds elapsed* but not in the sentence *Two secretaries eloped*, the NP that appears to be an ordinary subject of an intransitive verb is really the direct object of that verb at a more abstract level of syntactic analysis. (A familiar way to say that would be to say that it's a grammatical subject but a logical direct object; but that's not very precise, since most modern theories of grammar embrace the logical part as well.) Once connected to other facts by some general theoretical principles, this becomes a truly deep and fruitful idea. In my opinion, it is one of the most interesting new ideas in syntax this century.

Now try and find out from the literature who thought of it. I still haven't decided. What follows is an attempt to explain why.

Despite my concern with bibliography in what follows, I wasn't able to get it right myself, and I made a fairly serious bibliographical booboo in the original publication: I said that Dave Perlmutter's paper in *NLLT* 1 (1983) was the first journal article on the Unaccusative Hypothesis. But it was not; Perlmutter waited long enough to deny himself even that distinction (rushing into print is not one of Dave's vices). The first paper in a refereed journal that used the words 'Unaccusative Hypothesis' was (as far as I currently know) Alice Harris's paper 'Georgian and the Unaccusative Hypothesis', which appeared in *Language* 58.290–306 in 1982, a year earlier than Perlmutter's paper. Hence her name would appear in any more fully developed version of the tangled tale that the following piece relates. Apologies to you, Alice, for having forgotten about your work the first time round.

Take any mutually relevant set of works on a specific problem. Construct a matrix with the works listed, down and across, in chronological order of appearance. For each cell in the lower left quadrant, enter a plus if the work at that row cites the work at the column on the problem or topic in question. Enter a minus for each case of no citation. Discard the upper right quadrant of the square (since a work cannot be cited before its appearance). Also discard all self-citation cells. (i.e. remove the diagonal, because no work cites itself), and also eliminate any other case of authors citing work of their own (because self-publicizing activities are not quite the same as respect for the previous literature).

Now compute the ratio of pluses to minuses. What you have determined is the Citation Integrity Matrix Analysis (CIMA) score for the selected set of works (see Pullum 1988). In a world of sound and reliable scientific publication, where later works on a problem duly cite earlier results, CIMA scores approach 1.0 for typical clusters of contributions to the literature. Keep this in mind; we will return to it. First, I have to summarize the background[1] to a perplexing case of citation etiquette, one concerned with the following familiar hypothesis: *In some intransitive clauses (typically with nonvolitional predicates) but not others (typically volitional), the superficial subject corresponds to a direct object of the clause in a more abstract subjectless structure.*

During 1974 and 1975 a torrent of research notes and telephone conversations was flowing in both directions between Paul Postal and David Perlmutter. The foundations of relational grammar were being developed in the aftermath of the celebrated Linguistic Institute course at the University of Massachusetts, Amherst, in 1974. My box of linguistic memorabilia from this period, filled with correspondence, papers, squibs, postcards, restaurant menus, napkin doodles, annotated coasters, and other items, contains a note that Paul Postal sent to David Perlmutter on October 20, 1975. Here, lest Garland Publishing should try to reproduce its blotchy imperfection in fac-

---

1. I had help from a number of people in doing the research for this column. I am not at liberty to divulge who they were.

simile, is the text of the note, quoted in full by permission of its author. (As usual in relational grammar, '1' means subject and '2' means direct object. Typographical errors in the original have been silently corrected.)

Relational Remorse I   October 20, 1975

Two Types of Underlyingly Intransitive V

We have, without any argument or even discussion, assumed that 'intransitive' V like <u>sleep</u> and <u>exist</u> will <u>all</u> have initial structures with:

(1) a. A single term.
    b. This term marked a 1.

(1a) is not in question. But I think (1b) should be called into question, and that we should seriously consider the consequences of representing some 'intransitive' V initially with a term which is a 2. Some indications that this may be required are as follows.

In Mohawk, it is regular for transitive 2 to incorporate, and <u>some</u> 1 of intransitives do too, <u>but not all</u>. Recalling that incorporation in Mohawk involves <u>initial</u> terms, we could reduce this to a simple regularity:

(2) In Mohawk, only initial 2 incorporate.

Interestingly, those terms of 'intransitive' V which do not incorporate in Mohawk are roughly the 'agentive' ones. I.e. <u>sleep</u>, etc. don't but <u>fall</u>, <u>be black</u>, etc. do.

In French, we have noticed that some intransitive V permit Extraposition of Indefinite, while others permit Impersonal Passive. Which which? Guess: Extraposition of Indefinite goes with initial 2, that is why it works with <u>arriver</u> and with 2 of passive and reflexive passive V. Impersonal Passive will go with initial 1. Thus, <u>dormir</u> will take Impersonal Passive, <u>arriver</u> Extraposition of Indefinite. Note the hint of a correlation between French and Mohawk here, which is crucial since we want the assignment of 1 or 2 status to the single term to be universally predictable on semantic grounds; a V meaning 'sleep' should take a 1 everywhere therefore.

I am now suggesting, of course, that an English sentence like:

(3) Three people arrived.

is derived from an initial V-2 structure, in which case the 2 must become a 1 by some rule. This seems an unnecessary burden internal to English, but when we look at French it begins to pay off. One thing I have always worried about is why so many English V have reflexive correspondents in French, in a nonrandom fashion— e.g. English <u>happen</u> going with <u>se placer</u>, <u>se produire</u>, <u>se passer</u>, and others. If the underlying term of such V is a 2, then there is finally an answer: the rule which makes it a 1 is a reflexive passive rule in both languages, but, as usual (compare That book is selling well, Ce livre se vend bien), reflexive passive reflexives are deleted in English.

Moreover, we now finally also have a way of expressing similarity between V like turn out, happen, in English and seem, appear, etc., that is, those V which don't permit their complements to be cyclic 1. These are all V which take underlying 2 complements. Now, my hope is that this arrangement will aid us in dealing with Ruwet's arguments in his paper about seem, etc. It will turn out we partly agree with him in that it will now be the case that the complement of, e.g., paraître, etc. never are 1, and Extraposition does not come into play in these derivations. This has to be worked on.

It may also now be possible to have a grammatical account of the V which Ruwet calls "neutre," like les branches se brisent. These, according to him, are derived lexically. But I am sure that it will be cross-linguistically found that among the uses for reflexives is this one, i.e. as a marker that a V which is lexically apparently a causative is used noncausatively. If we take les branches to be the underlying 2 in such cases then we can say that lexically the meaning of briser is (CAUSE) BECOME BROKEN, and when there is no 1, reflexive passive must operate. Obviously, what is being assumed here is that, at least in English and French, there must be a cyclic 1 (though we no longer insist on an initial 1). Whether this is a universal or not is open as it has always been (recall our early discussion of a law to this effect whose name now eludes me).

This is all fairly thin but I am internally convinced that there are two different types of initially single term V and that a pursuit of this is going to help with a lot of things. One question that is raised involves the Ergative-Absolutive dimension. It is not clear how this will work with respect to the then three possible types of configuration (at early stages anyway):

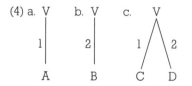

My feeling is that the first type will be more ergative than the second, and that in some languages they will be marked the same (I recall this as being the so-called agentive case in some American Indian languages, discussed in Fillmore's 'The case for case').

Another question is why, in these terms, if any rule makes the 2 in b into a 1, it is always Reflexive Passive and never Plain Passive. This suggests that the two rules, though sometimes apparently overlapping in function are actually rather different; Plain Passive aims to make an initial 1 a non-1, while Reflexive Passive aims to make an initial 2 a 1.

Notice that in what I am now suggesting, cases like There are apples over there, etc. are such that nothing but there is ever the 1. There is introduced as a 2 (to meet the successor condition), and then goes to 1; apples is a 2 chomeur.

We now, moreover, are in better shape to deal with those languages where the chomeur in such cases turns genitive or partitive or whatnot in the negative, etc. I.e. it may be possible to say this happens only to sometime 2 (probably not initial 2, but I don't know).

But I have saved the best for last. Can't it now be said in Portuguese that Tough Movement works only on sometime 2, since cases like 'These things are difficult to happen', which were the only counterexamples if I remember right, now fall under the 2 story?

Cryptic though this note is at several points, especially to those not familiar with relational grammar of this period, it clearly contains the seeds of many more recent developments.

A year later, as the idea was slowly being developed in a certain amount of terminological fog, I wrote to Postal (on October 30, 1976) suggesting that new terms with *un-* should be struck: if a 1 in a stratum with a 2 is an ergative, a 1 in a stratum with no 2 should be called an *unergative* 1, and likewise, if a 2 in a stratum with a 1 is an accusative, a 2 in a stratum with no 1 should be called an *unaccusative* 2. Thus emerged one of my more superficial contributions to linguistics: I developed the brand name of what has become known as the Unaccusative Hypothesis (henceforth the UH).

But what of the content? Did it come down to Postal in a flaming pie as he munched his breakfast cereal on October 20, 1975? I do not know. I was eating lunch on another continent at the time. But earlier sources are known to me that at least hint at the UH.

A possible example is the unpublished doctoral dissertation of Robert Fiengo, submitted to MIT on August 12, 1974; on p. 80, Fiengo, citing no previous work in this connection, considers deriving *The ice melted* by object movement from [$_S$ [$_{NP}$ *e*] [$_{VP}$ melted [$_{NP}$ the ice]]]. But although prepared to run this idea up the flagpole, he isn't really prepared to salute it. The theory "cannot yet be formulated" in his terms (because of semantic difficulties), and so he drops the matter. And his 1980 book pours cold water on the idea (1980, 57), adding: "In a previous work (Fiengo, 1974) I discussed the alternative analyses of the intransitives, but no conclusion was drawn. I continue to consider this question to be open." Not exactly a clarion call. Moreover, his structure is not truly subjectless. It is transitive, with both a subject and an object node, though not every NP is phonetically realized.

But wait. Apparently unknown to Fiengo, just up Massachusetts Avenue at Harvard University, Donna Jo Napoli had presented a year earlier a dissertation on Italian which derives some intransitive subjects from objects by movement, in order to get an explanation for the occurrence of *si* in certain clauses that do not have a reflexive meaning (1973, 103–5). Could Napoli be the source?

But wait. The unpublished doctoral dissertation of John Bowers, submitted to MIT in January 1972, analyzes a nonvolitional clause like *The soap slipped into the closet* (discussed by Emonds 1970) in terms of a deep structure $[_S [_{NP} \Delta] [_{VP} slipped [_{NP} the soap] [_{PP} into the closet]]]$. Moreover, Bowers explicitly refers to a class of verbs including *burn, disperse, drain, drop, grow, improve, melt, move, open, roll, slip, split, turn*—a whole gang of indubitably unaccusative verbs (1972, 53ff); he makes the point that "it does not seem to be the case that we can predict [their] syntactic properties solely on the basis of their semantic properties" (1972, 55), anticipating an issue that is still a topic of debate (see Grimshaw 1987, 248–52); and he specifically refers to "intransitive Verbs which take Direct Objects"—a veritable contradiction in terms until one adopts the viewpoint of the UH. Could Bowers be the source?

But wait. An earlier influence cited by Bowers (in addition to Emonds 1970) is Fillmore (1968), which clearly shows *The door opened* represented with an Objective case NP but no subject in the deepest layer of structure (p. 33). Could Fillmore be the source?

But wait. Bowers also cites an even earlier work: the MIT dissertation of Barbara Hall (now Partee), from 1965. She discusses the possibility "that 'break' and the other verbs of that class are basically transitive, i.e. always require a following NP in the underlying structure" (p. 29), and gives a full tree diagram for a deep structure of *The window broke* that looks like $[_S [_{AUX} Tns\text{-}have\text{-}en] [_{VP} [_V break] [_{NP} the window]]]$, plus a transformation that will convert such a structure into the obvious surface form by fronting the NP. Notice that her structure is truly subjectless: no subject node at all. Could Hall be the source?

But wait. There is a yet earlier dissertation that introduces the idea of surface intransitive subjects that are deep objects in subjectless clauses:

> . . . thus far the rules of the phrase structure have been stated in such a way that the one nominal of intransitive verbs comes from the Subject node. But no formal justification for this has been presented and, indeed, I do not think there is any. And now it can be seen that there are, in fact, strong formal reasons to derive the one nominal of intransitive sentences from the same node as the Object nominals of transitive verbs.

And who is this, advancing the UH in 1962? Surprise! None other than Paul Postal again, in his dissertation *Some Syntactic Rules in Mohawk* (p. 289). And although Hall does not cite this work, she does mention "fruitful discussions with Professors N. Chomsky, E. Klima, and P. Postal" at the beginning of the relevant section (1965, 25). Could Postal's earlier ideas be the source?

But wait. Postal's dissertation does not in fact make any reference to the existence of intransitive verbs that *do* take subjects (i.e. unergative predicates). He asserts that incorporation of transitive clause objects "is found as well with intransitives" (1962, 288), but without a hint that some intransitive subjects *fail* to incorporate (which is true). Postal simply derives *all* intransitive subjects in Mohawk from the direct object position, and states incorporation in a way that implies that all direct objects incorporate (the simplification of incorporation constituting the "strong formal reasons" he mentions). The notion of two different *types* of intransitive clause is crucially missing.

But wait. An even earlier work does seem, to some, to hint at the two classes. Sapir (1917) implies what Perlmutter (1978, 186n) regards as "a form of the Unaccusative Hypothesis." (Fillmore (1968, 53) also cites Sapir.) The relevant remarks are these (p. 85):

> instead of interpreting the object of the transitive verb as a sort of subjective (in other words, deriving it from the intransitive or inactive case), one may, on the contrary, look upon the latter as an objective, the inactive or intransitive verb being interpreted as a static verb without expressed subject, but with direct or indirect object. Thus, forms like I SLEEP or I THINK could be understood as meaning properly IT SLEEPS ME or IT SEEMS TO ME (cf. such German forms as *mich hungert*).

Sapir adds that this seems very plausible "for those languages that, like Tlingit, Haida, Muskogean, and Siouan, distinguish between active and inactive verbs." He gives a further hint on page 86, with a table showing that Dakota subject pronouns in intransitive clauses look like object pronouns when the verb is inactive or nonvolitional, but like subject pronouns when the verb is active or volitional. Could Sapir be the source?

But wait. Deep though my respect is for the giants of yesteryear, this seems a bit vague to me. To say that a form "could be understood as meaning" something is not the same as saying that there are two different syntactic structures for intransitive clauses. And Sapir jumbles together impersonal dummy constructions and the inversion alternation (*I think* versus *seems to me*), without even mentioning verbs on the transitive-intransitive cusp like *melt* or *break*, on which the transformational analyses place such stress.

This stuff about classes of verbs is absolutely central to the UH. One way in which none of the works of the 1965–75 period truly represent espousals of the UH is that *all* the verbs they cite have corresponding transitive forms. The crucial thing about Postal's 1975 note is that it mentions predicates like *exist, be black, arrive,* and *happen,* which *never* have surface direct objects. This is what differentiates the UH from the proposals of so many earlier works. As correctly noted by Grimshaw (1987, 251), merely requiring that identity of thematic relationships implies identity of deep structural relationships (as in Baker 1985, 57) may entail the Hall-Bowers-Fiengo analysis of *break,* but it does not yield the UH. What really started things moving in 1975 was Postal and Perlmutter's recognition that some *strictly* intransitive predicates (like *exist*) had initial 2s.

As the two linguists probed around for evidence for the UH, they found that it did indeed promise solutions to many problems. Perlmutter began presenting evidence for the UH in class lectures at MIT and at various departmental talks across the country during 1976 and 1977. Several papers were planned by both Perlmutter and Postal, who regarded the topic as part of their ongoing relational grammar collaboration, but no publication strategy of any sort emerged. Nothing was even presented at a professional meeting until February 1978, when Perlmutter presented at the Berkeley Linguistics Society a paper called 'Impersonal Passives and the Unaccusative Hypothesis', centered around Dutch evidence, the paper most commonly cited today as the source of the UH.

On May 9, 1978, Perlmutter gave a talk called 'The Unaccusative Hypothesis and Multiattachment: the Italian Evidence' to the Harvard Linguistics Circle (the handout is in my memorabilia box). It showed how the UH shed light on reflexive unaccusatives, participial absolutes, past participles as adjectives, partitive *ne,* and auxiliary selection. But linguists all over the world who did not see the small-circulation litho-printed *BLS* volume for 1978 spent 1979 and 1980 still not knowing anything about the UH, because the journals still contained nothing.

In October 1980, Carol Rosen defended her Harvard dissertation, which adopted the UH and presented evidence for it from Italian. She was awarded the doctorate in 1981. Meanwhile, down the street at MIT, Luigi Burzio also drafted a doctoral dissertation on the UH in 1980 and received the Ph.D. for it in 1981. Burzio laid out the entire assemblage of Italian evidence for the UH that Perlmutter had presented at Harvard and elsewhere, with the arguments all translated from relational terminology into constituent structure, coindexing, and movement terms, and unaccusative verbs renamed—in a truly crackbrained piece of terminological revisionism—"ergative verbs" (sic; blessings upon those like Grimshaw (1987) who are returning the field to nomenclatural sanity). It is clear what had happened: Perlmutter had delayed writing up his results on Italian so long that others had done it for him.

Lines between the members of the small group of Italian unaccusativity specialists were less than fully open. Neither Burzio nor Rosen cited the other. When Perlmutter finally produced a paper on the Italian material for *NLLT*'s first issue in 1983, he cited Rosen (1981) throughout, but said of Burzio (1981) only: "I have not consulted this work, and make no attempt at cross-framework comparison." Burzio proceeded to return the compliment by not citing Perlmutter (1983) at all in his 1986 book.

Of course, Burzio was something of a prisoner of the multicultural linguistics scene. While some linguists talk of 1-arc successors of 2-arcs, and others describe noun phrases moving from deep structure nodes to places where little triangles are waiting, students and other innocent bystanders have to find a way of operating without unintentionally marking themselves as members of the wrong subculture.

Burzio's translation from relational to transformational terms provided a license for other linguists of nonrelational persuasions to take up the UH without giving any credit to its relational developers. For example, although Burzio does at least clearly acknowledge that his central theme was provided by Perlmutter in personal discussions,

Chomsky (1981) cites no one but Burzio and Fiengo on the UH (see e.g. p. 147, n.104), avoiding all mention of relational work on this topic. This set the tone for later practices. Even Grimshaw (1987), which does not overlook relational work, attributes Perlmutter's 1978 discoveries of the Italian auxiliary selection and partitive *ne* arguments solely to Burzio (1986). (It also attributes the past-participles-as-adjectives argument, the Italian version of which was on the handout for Perlmutter's 1978 Harvard talk, to Rappaport and Levin (1986).)

But what of the citation etiquette *before* GB took over the UH in 1981? The answer is that in the crucial period 1962–80, hardly anyone bothered to cite anyone on UH-style analyses. The CIMA score for Postal 1962, Hall 1965, Fillmore 1968, Bowers 1972, Napoli 1973, Fiengo 1974, Perlmutter 1978, and Fiengo 1980 is a staggeringly low 0.08. CIMA scores as low as this are seldom seen, even in linguistics. What it means is that, in this sample, relevant and accessible earlier works are cited at a rate of less than one case in twelve. Normal scientific standards have broken down.[2]

Citation etiquette cannot be seriously invoked at all in a context like this. The courtesies of scholarship are replaced by the me-first ethics of the post-apocalyptic society seen in movies like *Mad Max: Beyond Thunderdome*. "Two men enter, one man leaves." Raw strength, posturing, and self-promotion are what counts in wresting approval from the baying crowd. Crediting others is for wimps.

Given the trend of the times, and the difficulty of determining answers to vexed questions of priority from the literature I have surveyed, I recommend that anyone wishing to assume or discuss the UH should simply reintroduce it as their own, citing no one. For my

2. I stress that this is the pre-1981 literature. The CIMA score for a later sample would be significantly higher, so perhaps things are improving (despite what I have said about the relative disdain GB and RG have shown for each other's contributions). In particular, Burzio (1986) had an apparent attack of citation panic, and listed in a footnote (p. 74, n. 12), every single post-1965 work that could conceivably be thought relevant to deriving surface intransitive subjects from deep objects. The burst of marginally relevant references almost seems designed to imply that with so many previous potential claimants to the inheritance, any squabbling among the heirs would be pointless and unseemly. There are indeed many potential litigants; but their number should not be allowed to obscure the central fact that the work of Postal and Perlmutter should loom very large in any serious study of unaccusativity (somewhat larger than it does in the GB literature, I suggest).

part, I will certainly be attributing the UH to myself. Hell, I may even rename it.

REFERENCES

Baker, Mark. 1985. *Incorporation: A theory of grammatical function changing,* MIT dissertation.[3]

Bowers, John S. 1972. *Grammatical relations,* MIT dissertation. Published by Garland Publishing, New York, 1986.

Burzio, Luigi. 1981. *Intransitive verbs and Italian auxiliaries,* MIT dissertation.

Burzio, Luigi. 1986. *Italian syntax: A government-binding approach.* D. Reidel, Dordrecht.

Chomsky, Noam. 1981. *Lectures on government and binding.* Foris, Dordrecht.

Emonds, Joseph E. 1970. *Root and structure-preserving transformations,* MIT dissertation. Published by Indiana University Linguistics Club, Bloomington, Indiana, 1970.

Fiengo, Robert W. 1974. *Semantic conditions on surface structure,* MIT dissertation.

Fiengo, Robert W. 1980. *Surface structure: The interface of autonomous components.* Harvard University Press, Cambridge, Massachusetts.

Fillmore, Charles J. 1968. The Case for Case, in Emmon Bach and Robert T. Harms, eds. *Universals in linguistic theory,* 1–88, Holt Rinehart and Winston, New York.

Grimshaw, Jane. 1987. Unaccusatives—an overview. *Proceedings of NELS 17, 1986, Volume I,* ed. by Joyce McDonough and Bernadette Plunkett, 244–58. GLSA, University of Massachusetts, Amherst, Massachusetts.

Hall, Barbara. 1965. *Subject and Object in Modern English,* MIT dissertation. Published by Garland Publishing, New York, 1979, as by Barbara Hall Partee.

Napoli, Donna Jo. 1973. *The two Si's of Italian,* Harvard dissertation.

Perlmutter, David M. 1978. Impersonal Passives and the Unaccusative Hypothesis, *Proceedings of the Fourth Annual Meeting of the Berkeley Linguistics Society,* 157–89, Berkeley, California.

Perlmutter, David M. 1983. Personal vs. impersonal constructions. *NLLT* 1.141–200.

Postal, Paul M. 1962. *Some syntactic rules in Mohawk,* Yale dissertation. Published by Garland Publishing, New York, 1979.

3. "MIT dissertation" in this bibliography is short for "unpublished doctoral dissertation, Massachusetts Institute of Technology, Cambridge, Massachusetts." I abbreviate analogously with dissertations from Harvard (Cambridge, Massachusetts) and Yale (New Haven, Connecticut).

Pullum, Geoffrey K. 1988. Citation etiquette beyond Thunderdome, *NLLT*
      6.579–88.
Rappaport, Malka and Beth Levin. 1986. What to do with Theta-Roles, *Lexi-
      con Project Working Papers* 11. Center for Cognitive Science, MIT.
Rosen, Carol. 1981. *The relational structure of reflexive clauses: Evidence
      from Italian,* Harvard dissertation.
Sapir, Edward. 1917. Review of C. C. Uhlenbeck, Het Passieve Karakter
      van het Verbum Transitivum of van het Verbum Actionis in Talen van
      Noord-Amerika, *IJAL* 1.82–86.

Chapter Nineteen

The great Eskimo vocabulary hoax

Once the public has decided to accept something as an interesting fact, it becomes almost impossible to get the acceptance rescinded. The persistent interestingness and symbolic usefulness overrides any lack of factuality.

For instance, the notion that dinosaurs were stupid, slow-moving reptiles that soon died out because they were unsuccessful and couldn't keep up with the industrious mammals is stuck in the public consciousness. It is far too useful to give up. What insult are you going to hurl at some old but powerful idiot or huge but slow-adapting corporation if not 'dinosaur'? The new research discoveries of the last two decades concerning the intelligence, agility, endothermicity, longevity, and evolutionary robustness of the dinosauria have no effect on the use of the term 'dinosaur' and its supposed associations; no one wants to hear that the dinosauria dominated the planet with intelligence and adaptive genius for hundreds of millions of years and were far more successful than mammals have yet shown themselves to be.

It is in the scholarly community that we ought to find a certain immunity, or at least resistance, to uncritical acceptance of myths, fables, and misinformation. But sadly, the academic profession shows a strong tendency to create stable and self-sustaining but completely false legends of its own, and hang on to them grimly, transmitting them from article to article and from textbook to textbook like software viruses spreading between students' Macintoshes. Stephen O. Murray has pointed out to me a rather beautifully titled paper by John Shelton Reed, Gail E. Doss, and Jeanne S. Hurlbert of the University of North Carolina at Chapel Hill: 'Too good to be false: an essay in the folklore of social science' (*Sociological Inquiry* 57 (1987), 1–11). It is about the assertion that the frequency of lynchings in the American South in the early part of this century was positively correlated with the price of cotton, a 'fact' that has frequently been used as a key piece of evidence for frustration-aggression theory. Reed et al. show that nearly all

159

the numerous mentions of this 'fact' state the finding incorrectly, and
neglect to cite the works in which real doubt has been cast on whether
there is a fact there at all.

There are thousands of further examples, both within and without
academia; whole books have been published on commonly believed
fallacious (non-)knowledge (e.g. Tom Burnam, *Dictionary of Misinformation*, Crowell, New York, 1975). In the study of language, one case
surpasses all others in its degree of ubiquity, and the present chapter is
devoted to it: it is the notion that Eskimos have bucketloads of different
words for snow.

What I do here is very little more than an extended review and elaboration on Laura Martin's wonderful *American Anthropologist* report of
1986. Laura Martin is professor and chair of the Department of Anthropology at the Cleveland State University. She endures calmly the fact
that virtually no one listened to her when she first published. It may be
that few will listen to me as I explain in different words to another
audience what she pointed out. But the truth is that the Eskimos do *not*
have lots of different words for snow, and no one who knows anything
about Eskimo (or more accurately, about the Inuit and Yupik families
of related languages spoken by Eskimos from Siberia to Greenland)
has ever said they do. Anyone who insists on simply checking their
primary sources will find that they are quite unable to document the
alleged facts about snow vocabulary (but nobody ever checks, because
the truth might not be what the reading public wants to hear).

In this chapter, I take a rather more critical stance regarding the role
of Benjamin Lee Whorf than Laura Martin did; in fact, I'm rather cruel
to the memory of that fine amateur linguist. Since several readers of
this piece when it first appeared (and after it appeared in abridged form
in the inaugural issue of the academic magazine *Lingua Franca*), let
me be clear about this. Whorf has a lasting place in the history of
linguistics, a place few of us can aspire to. He is basically responsible
for opening up our access to an entire language that had previously
been inaccessible (the classical form of Mayan that lay behind the
Mayan hieroglyphs until Whorf deciphered them); he coined lastingly
useful terms (*allophone* is an example) and introduced intriguing new
concepts (the concept of a cryptotype, for instance); and he did important academic work almost entirely without having paid positions in
the academic world—an uncommon achievement then, and one almost unheard of now.

But he wasn't a god, and his contribution to Eskimo lexicography
looks shoddy to me, so I poke some fun at him in this chapter, just as I
am liable to poke fun at anyone who stumbles across my path. Lasting
though his place in the history of linguistics may be, Whorf was guilty

of his own small part of the amplification of a piece of misinformation, and deserves his own small share of opprobrium. Professor Martin has seen in writing numbers as high as *four hundred* (repeat, 400) given as the number of Eskimo words for snow. The four hundred figure came from a piece by a would-be author who admitted (under questioning by a magazine fact-checker) to having no source for the number whatsoever. The nonsense that Whorf unwittingly helped to foster is completely out of control.

"A silly, infuriatingly unscholarly piece, designed to mislead" is what one irate but anonymous senior scholar called this chapter when it was first published in *NLLT*. But this is not correct; rather, what I have written here is a silly, misleadingly unscholarly piece, designed to infuriate. There is a huge difference. If scholars of Boas, Whorf, and other giants of twentieth-century language study get angry enough at my flippancy, perhaps they will do some further research on relevant issues (finding out whether Whorf ever did do any informant work with speakers of the Inuit or Yupik languages, for example), and that is fine. I will read with interest whatever is published or sent to me on this topic. So will Professor Laura Martin, who continues to collect any and all citations concerning Eskimo snow terms, however misinformed or well-informed they may be; her address is: Department of Anthropology, Cleveland State University, Cleveland, Ohio 44115, USA.

Most linguistics departments have an introduction-to-language course in which students other than linguistics majors can be exposed to at least something of the mysteries of language and communication: signing apes and dancing bees; wild children and lateralization; logographic writing and the Rosetta Stone; *pit* and *spit;* Sir William Jones and Professor Henry Higgins; isoglosses and Grimm's Law; *Jabberwocky* and colorless green ideas; and of course, without fail, the Eskimos and their multiple words for snow.

Few among us, I'm sure, can say with certainty that we never told an awestruck sea of upturned sophomore faces about the multitude of snow descriptors used by these lexically profligate hyperborean nomads, about whom so little information is repeated so often to so many. Linguists have been just as active as schoolteachers or general-knowledge columnists in spreading the entrancing story. What a pity the story is unredeemed piffle.

Anthropologist Laura Martin of Cleveland State University spent some of her research time during the 1980s attempting to slay the

constantly changing, self-regenerating myth of Eskimo snow terminology, like a Sigourney Weaver fighting alone against the hideous
space creature in the movie *Alien* (a xenomorph, they called it in the
sequel *Aliens;* nice word). You may recall that the creature seemed to
spring up everywhere once it got loose on the spaceship, and was
very difficult to kill.

Martin presented her paper at the annual meeting of the American
Anthropological Association in Washington D.C. in December 1982,
and eventually (after a four-year struggle during which bonehead reviewers cut a third of the paper, including several interesting quotes)
she published an abbreviated version of it in the 'Research Reports'
section of AAA's journal (Martin 1986). This ought to have been
enough for the news to get out.

But no, as far as widespread recognition is concerned, Martin labored in vain. Never does a month (or in all probability a week) go
by without yet another publication of the familiar claim about the
wondrous richness of the Eskimo conceptual scheme: hundreds of
words for different grades and types of snow, a lexicographical winter wonderland, the quintessential demonstration of how primitive
minds categorize the world so differently from us.

And the alleged lexical extravagance of the Eskimos comports so
well with the many other facets of their polysynthetic perversity: rub-
bing noses; lending their wives to strangers; eating raw seal blubber;
throwing grandma out to be eaten by polar bears; "We are prepared to
believe almost anything about such an unfamiliar and peculiar group",
says Martin, in a gentle reminder of our buried racist tendencies.

The tale she tells is an embarrassing saga of scholarly sloppiness
and popular eagerness to embrace exotic facts about other people's
languages without seeing the evidence. The fact is that the myth of
the multiple words for snow is based on almost nothing at all. It is a
kind of accidentally developed hoax perpetrated by the anthropological linguistics community on itself.

The original source is Franz Boas' introduction to *The Handbook
of North American Indians* (1911). And all Boas says there, in the
context of a low-key and slightly ill-explained discussion of independent versus derived terms for things in different languages, is that
just as English uses separate roots for a variety of forms of water
(liquid, lake, river, brook, rain, dew, wave, foam) that might be
formed by derivational morphology from a single root meaning
'water' in some other language, so Eskimo uses the apparently dis-

tinct roots *aput* 'snow on the ground', *gana* 'falling snow', *piqsir-poq* 'drifting snow', and *qimuqsuq* 'a snow drift'. Boas' point is simply that English expresses these notions by phrases involving the root *snow,* but things could have been otherwise, just as the words for lake, river, etc. could have been formed derivationally or peri-phrastically on the root *water.*

But with the next twist in the story, the unleashing of the xenomor-phic fable of Eskimo lexicography seems to have become inevitable. What happened was that Benjamin Lee Whorf, Connecticut fire pre-vention inspector and weekend language-fancier, picked up Boas' example and used it, vaguely, in his 1940 amateur linguistics article 'Science and linguistics', which was published in MIT's promotional magazine *Technology Review* (Whorf was an alumnus; he had done his B.S. in chemical engineering at MIT).

Our word *snow* would seem too inclusive to an Eskimo, our man from the Hartford Fire Insurance Company confidently asserts. With an uncanny perception into the hearts and minds of the hardy Arctic denizens (the more uncanny since Eskimos were not a prominent fea-ture of Hartford's social scene at the time), he avers:

> We have the same word for falling snow, snow on the ground, snow packed hard like ice, slushy snow, wind-driven flying snow— whatever the situation may be. To an Eskimo, this all-inclusive word would be almost unthinkable; he would say that falling snow, slushy snow, and so on, are sensuously and operationally different, different things to contend with; he uses different words for them and for other kinds of snow. (Whorf 1940; in Carroll 1956, 216)

Whorf's article was quoted and reprinted in more subsequent books than you could shake a flamethrower at; the creature was already loose and regenerating itself all over the ship.

Notice that Whorf's statement has illicitly inflated Boas' four terms to at least seven (1: "falling", 2: "on the ground", 3: "packed hard", 4: "slushy, 5: "flying", 6, 7, . . . : "and other kinds of snow"). Notice also that his claims about English speakers are false; I recall the stuff in question being called *snow* when fluffy and white, *slush* when partly melted, *sleet* when falling in a half-melted state, and a *blizzard* when pelting down hard enough to make driving dan-gerous. Whorf's remark about his own speech community is no more reliable than his glib generalizations about what things are "sensu-ously and operationally different" to the generic Eskimo.

But the lack of little things like verisimilitude and substantiation are not enough to stop a myth. Martin tracks the great Eskimo vocabulary hoax through successively more careless repetitions and embroiderings in a number of popular books on language. Roger Brown's *Words and Things* (1958, 234–36), attributing the example to Whorf, provides an early example of careless popularization and perversion of the issue. His numbers disagree with both Boas and Whorf (he says there are "three Eskimo words for snow", apparently getting this from figure 10 in Whorf's paper; perhaps he only looked at the pictures).[1]

After works like Brown's have picked up Whorf's second-hand misrecollection of Boas to generate third-hand accounts, we begin to get fourth-hand accounts carelessly based on Brown. For example, Martin notes that in Carol Eastman's *Aspects of Language and Culture* (1975; 3rd printing, 1980), the familiar assertion that "Eskimo languages have many words for snow" is found only six lines away from a direct quote of Brown's reference to "three" words for snow.

But never mind: three, four, seven, who cares? It's a bunch, right? When more popular sources start to get hold of the example, all constraints are removed: arbitrary numbers are just made up as the writer thinks appropriate for the readership. In Lanford Wilson's 1978 play *The Fifth of July* it is "fifty". From 1984 alone (two years *after* her 1982 presentation to the American Anthropological Association meetings on the subject—not that mere announcement at a scholarly meeting could have been expected to change anything), Martin cites the number of Eskimo snow terms given as "nine" (in a trivia encyclopedia, Adams 1984), "one hundred" (in a *New York Times* editorial on February 9), and "two hundred" (in a Cleveland TV weather forecast).

By coincidence, I happened to notice, the *New York Times* returned to the topic four years to the day after committing itself to the

1. Murray (1987) has argued that Martin is too harsh on some people, particularly Brown, who does correctly see that some English speakers also differentiate their snow terms (skiers talk of *powder, crust,* and *slush*). But Martin is surely correct in criticizing Brown for citing no data at all, and for making points about lexical structure, perception, and Zipf's Law that are rendered nonsense by the actual nature of Eskimo word structure (his reference to "length of a verbal expression" providing "an index of its frequency in speech" fails to take account of the fact that even with a single root for snow, the number of actual *word forms* for snow in Eskimo will be effectively infinite, and the frequency of each one approximately zero, because of the polysynthetic morphology).

figure of one hundred: on February 9, 1988, on page 21, in the 'Science Times' section, a piece by Jane E. Brody on laboratory research into snowflake formation began: "The Eskimos have about four dozen words to describe snow and ice, and Sam Colbeck knows why." The *New York Times,* America's closest approach to a serious newspaper of record, had changed its position on the snow-term count by over 50% within four years. And in the *science* section. But hey: nine, forty-eight, a hundred, two hundred, who cares? It's a bunch, right? On this topic, no source can be trusted.

People cannot be persuaded to shut up about it, either. Attempting to slay the creature at least in my locality, I mentioned Martin's work in a public lecture in Santa Cruz in 1985, in the presence of a number of faculty, students, and members of the general public. I drove home the point about scholarly irresponsibility to an attentive crowd, and imagined I had put at least a temporary halt to careless talk about the Eskimo morpheme stock within Santa Cruz County. But it was not to be.

Within the following three months, two undergraduate students came to me to say that they had been told in class lectures about the Eskimo's highly ramified snow vocabulary, one in politics, one in psychology; my son told me he had been fed the same factoid in class at his junior high school; and the assertion turned up once again in a "fascinating facts" column in a Santa Cruz weekly paper.

Among the many depressing things about this credulous transmission and elaboration of a false claim is that even if there *were* a large number of roots for different snow types in some Arctic language, this would *not,* objectively, be intellectually interesting; it would be a most mundane and unremarkable fact.

Horsebreeders have various names for breeds, sizes, and ages of horses; botanists have names for leaf shapes; interior decorators have names for shades of mauve; printers have many different names for different fonts (Caslon, Garamond, Helvetica, Times Roman, and so on), naturally enough. If these obvious truths of specialization are supposed to be interesting facts about language, thought, and culture, then I'm sorry, but include me out.

Would anyone think of writing about printers the same kind of slop we find written about Eskimos in bad linguistics textbooks? Take a random textbook like Paul Gaeng's *Introduction to the Principles of Language* (1971), with its earnest assertion: "It is quite obvious that in the culture of the Eskimos . . . snow is of great enough importance to split up the conceptual sphere that corresponds to one word and one thought in English into several distinct classes . . ." (p. 137). Imagine reading: "It is quite obvious that in the culture of printers . . . fonts are of great enough importance to split up the conceptual sphere that corresponds to one word and one thought among non-printers into several distinct classes. . . ." Utterly boring, even if true. Only the link to those legendary, promiscuous, blubber-gnawing hunters of the ice-packs could permit something this trite to be presented to us for contemplation.

And actually, when you come to think of it, Eskimos aren't really that likely to be interested in snow. Snow in the traditional Eskimo hunter's life must be a kind of constantly assumed background, like sand on the beach. And even beach bums have only one word for sand. But there you are: the more you think about the Eskimo vocabulary hoax, the more stupid it gets.

The final words of Laura Martin's paper are about her hope that we can come to see the Eskimo snow story as a cautionary tale reminding us of "the intellectual protection to be found in the careful use of sources, the clear presentation of evidence, and above all, the constant evaluation of our assumptions." Amen to that. The prevalence of the great Eskimo snow hoax is testimony to falling standards in academia, but also to a wider tendency (particularly in the United States, I'm afraid) toward fundamentally anti-intellectual "gee-whiz" modes of discourse and increasing ignorance of scientific thought.

This is one more battle that linguists must take up—like convincing people that there is no need for a law to make English the official language of Kansas (cf. chapter 14), or that elementary schools shouldn't spend time trying to abolish negated auxiliary verbs ("There is no such word as *can't*"). Some time in the future, and it may be soon, you will be told by someone that the Eskimos have many or dozens or scores or hundreds of words for snow. You, gentle reader, must decide here and now whether you are going to let them get away with it, or whether you are going to be true to your position as an Expert On Language by calling them on it.

The last time it happened to me (other than through the medium of print) was in July 1988 at the University of California's Irvine campus, where I was attending the university's annual Management Institute. Not just one lecturer at the Institute but two of them somehow (don't ask me how) worked the Eskimological falsehood into their tedious presentations on management psychology and administrative problem-solving. The first time I attempted to demur and was glared at by lecturer and classmates alike; the second time, discretion for once getting the upper hand over valor, I just held my face in my hands for a minute, then quietly closed my binder and crept out of the room.

Don't be a coward like me. Stand up and tell the speaker this: C. W. Schultz-Lorentzen's *Dictionary of the West Greenlandic Eskimo Language* (1927) gives just two possibly relevant roots: *qanik,* meaning 'snow in the air' or 'snowflake', and *aput,* meaning 'snow on the ground'. Then add that you would be interested to know if the speaker can cite any more.

This will not make you the most popular person in the room. It will have an effect roughly comparable to pouring fifty gallons of thick oatmeal into a harpsichord during a baroque recital. But it will strike a blow for truth, responsibility, and standards of evidence in linguistics.

REFERENCES

Adams, Cecil. 1984. *The straight dope: A compendium of human knowledge,* edited and with an introduction by Ed Zotti, Chicago Review Press, Chicago, Illinois.
Boas, Franz. 1911. Introduction to *The handbook of North American Indians, Vol. I, Bureau of American Ethnology Bulletin* 40, Part 1, Smithsonian Institution, Washington, D.C. Reprinted by Georgetown University Press, Washington D.C. (c. 1963) and by University of Nebraska Press, Lincoln, Nebraska (1966).
Brown, Roger. 1958. *Words and things,* The Free Press, New York.
Carroll, John B., ed. 1956. *Language, thought, and reality: Selected writings of Benjamin Lee Whorf,* MIT Press, Cambridge, Massachusetts.
Eastman, Carol. 1975. *Aspects of language and culture,* Chandler, San Francisco, California. 3rd printing, Chandler & Sharp, Novato, California, 1980.
Gaeng, Paul A. 1971. *Introduction to the principles of language,* Harper & Row, New York.
Martin, Laura. 1986. "Eskimo words for snow": A case study in the genesis and decay of an anthropological example, *American Anthropologist* 88, 2 (June), 418–23.
Murray, Stephen O. 1987. Snowing canonical texts, *American Anthropologist* 89, 2 (June), 443–44.

Schultz-Lorentzen, C. W. 1927. *Dictionary of the West Greenlandic Eskimo language, Meddelser om Grønland* 69, Reitzels, Copenhagen.
Whorf, Benjamin Lee. 1940. Science and linguistics, *Technology Review* (MIT) 42, 6 (April), 229–31, 247–48. Reprinted in Carroll, ed., 207–19.

Appendix: Yes, But How Many Really?

Yes, but how many are there really? I can just hear you asking. I've told you a lot about how sloppy everyone has been on this subject, and about how they ought to be challenged to cite some data, and about how much ridiculous and unsupported exaggeration has gone on. But I haven't told you anything about the actual vocabulary of Eskimos and the range of snow terms they really use.

Well, to tackle this question we must, however reluctantly, move from our armchair, at least as far as the phone or the computer mail terminal. I contacted the best Eskimologist I was personally acquainted with, namely Anthony Woodbury of the University of Texas at Austin, and asked him. I will paraphrase what he said. Keep in mind that with true scholarly caution and modesty, he is quite diffident about giving conclusive answers; the crucial issues about many relevant forms, he feels, need to be resolved by research that has not yet been done. I take responsibility for this somewhat embellished sketch of the position he takes.

When you pose a question as ill-defined as "How many Eskimo words for snow are there?" Woodbury observes, you run into major problems not just with determining the answer to the apparently empirical "How many" part but with the other parts: how to interpret the terms "Eskimo", "words", and "for snow". All of them are problematic.

The languages that the Eskimo people speak around the top of the world, in places as far apart as Siberia, Alaska, Canada, and Greenland, differ quite a lot in details of vocabulary. The differences between urbanized and nomadic Eskimos and between young and old speakers are also considerable. So one problem lies in getting down to the level of specific lists of words that can be verified as genuine by a particular speaker of a particular dialect, and getting away from the notion of a single truth about a monolithic "Eskimo" language.

Then one needs to get clear about what one proposes to count when one counts "words". Even in English, the distinction between internally unanalyzable roots (like *snow* and *slush*) on the one hand

and inflected word forms of nouns on the other is worth noting. *Snow* is one word, but it is easy to generate another dozen directly from it, simply by applying inflectional and derivational morphological rules to the root: *snowball, snowbank, snowblower, snowcapped, snowdrift, snowfall, snowflake, snowlike, snows, snowshoe, snowstorm, snowy.* . . . You get the picture.

Now, this may not seem like too wild a profusion of derived words. But in the Eskimo languages there is a great deal more inflection (grammatical endings) and vastly more fully productive derivational morphology (word formation). For each noun stem there are about 280 different inflectional forms. And then if you start adding in all the forms derivable by word formation processes that yield other parts of speech (illustrated in a rudimentary way by English *to snow, snowed, snowing, snowier, snowiest,* etc.), you get an even bigger collection—indeed, an infinite collection, because there really is no such thing as the longest word in a language of the Eskimo type where words of arbitrary complexity can be derived.

So if you identify four snow-related noun stems in some Eskimo dialect, what do you report? Four? Or the number of actual inflected noun forms derivable therefrom, certainly over a thousand? Or the entire set, perhaps infinite, of relatable words of all parts of speech?

Finally, Woodbury points out that there is a real issue about what is a word for snow as opposed to a word for something else. Some concrete examples will be useful here. Take the form *igluksaq,* which turned up (misspelled) on a list of twenty alleged words for snow in a Canadian Inuit dialect that was sent to me by Edith Moravcsik of the University of Wisconsin, who got it from a correspondent of hers, who got it from a minister of religion, who got it from some Inuit people in the Kewatin region among whom he had worked as a missionary. *Igluksaq* was glossed 'snow for igloo making' on the list. But Woodbury points out that the word is a productive formation from *iglu* 'house' and *-ksaq* 'material for'; in other words, it means simply 'house-building material'. In Woodbury's view, this would probably include plywood, nails, perhaps bricks or roofing tiles. *Igluksaq* isn't a word for a special kind of snow at all.

Another word on the list (misspelled again) was apparently meant to be *saumavuq,* and was glossed 'covered in snow'. But this, Woodbury reports, is clearly just a verb form meaning 'it has been covered'. It doesn't appear to have anything specifically to do with snow.

Many similar observations could be made about the words on the list Moravcsik obtained. The unfortunate fact is that even lists of Eskimo words with meanings attached, written out by people with extensive acquaintance with the people and the language, have to be interpreted in a sophisticated way against the background of a full understanding of Eskimo morphology and etymology if we are to draw conclusions about whether they can be counted as words for snow.

So how many really? I know you still crave an answer. I will say only this. In 1987, in response to a request from some students at Texas who had read Laura Martin's article, Woodbury put together a list of bases in the Central Alaskan Yupik language that could be regarded as synchronically unanalyzable and had snow-related meanings. All of them are in Steven A. Jacobson's *Yup'ik Eskimo Dictionary* (University of Alaska, Fairbanks, 1984). Some of them are general weather-related words relating to rain, frost, and other conditions; some are count nouns denoting phenomena like blizzards, avalanches, snow cornices, snow crusts, and the like; some are etymologizable in a way that involves only roots unrelated to snow (example: *nutaryug-* is glossed as 'new snow' but originates from *nutar-* 'new' and *-yug-* 'what tends to be', so it means literally 'that which tends to be new' or 'new stuff'), but they have apparently been lexicalized as ways of referring to snow. The list includes both non-snow-referring roots (e.g. *muru-* 'to sink into something') and etymologically complex but apparently lexicalized stems based on them that are usually glossed as referring to snow (e.g. *muruaneq* 'soft deep snow', etymologically something like 'stuff for habitually sinking into'). The list has about a dozen different stems with 'snow' in the gloss, and a variety of other words (slightly more than a dozen) that are transparently derived from these (for example, *natquig-* is a noun stem meaning 'drifting snow' and *natquigte-* is a verb stem meaning 'for snow etc. to drift along ground').

So the list is still short, not remarkably different in size from the list in English (which, remember, boasts not just *snow, slush,* and *sleet* and their derivatives, but also count nouns like *avalanche* and *blizzard,* technical terms like *hardpack* and *powder,* expressive meteorological descriptive phrases like *flurry* and *dusting,* compounds with idiosyncratic meanings like *snow cornice,* and so on; many of the terms on Woodbury's list are much more like these terms than like simple mass nouns for new and unusual varieties of snow).

If it will allow you to rest easier at night, or to be more of an authority at cocktail parties, let it be known that Professor Anthony Woodbury (Department of Linguistics, University of Texas, Austin, Texas 78712) is prepared to endorse the claim that the Central Alaskan Yupik Eskimo language has about a dozen words (even a couple of dozen if you are fairly liberal about what you count) for referring to snow and to related natural phenomena, events, or behavior. Reliable reports based on systematic dictionary searches for other Eskimo languages are not available as far as I know.

For my part, I want to make one last effort to clarify that the chapter above isn't about Eskimo lexicography at all, though I'm sure it will be taken to be. What it's actually about is intellectual sloth. Among all the hundreds of people making published contributions to the great Eskimo vocabulary hoax, no one had acquired any evidence about how long the purported list of snow terms really was, or what words were on it, or what criteria were used in deciding what to put on the list. The tragedy is not that so many people got the facts wildly wrong; it is that in the mentally lazy and anti-intellectual world we live in today, hardly anyone cares enough to think about trying to determine what the facts are.

Part Four

Linguistic Fantasies

Chapter Twenty

No trips to Stockholm

What would linguistics of Nobel prize-winning caliber be like? I have absolutely no idea. We seem to have no prizes in our field—not even a best-paper-of-the-conference award given each December by the Linguistic Society of America, or something like that. (MacArthurs have gone to linguists in a few cases, but they are not really prizes but fellowships for support of research or creative activity.)

The lack of prizes in our field is probably because the discipline in its modern form is too young for any rich linguists (or admirers of linguistics) to have died and left enough money to make a regular sum of prize money available. But whatever the reason, I found myself ruminating one day on the effects, and on what things might be like if we did have a major prize—or even an academy awards ceremony for linguists . . . The following musings resulted.

Physics, chemistry, literature, peace, and physiology (including medicine). In those five subjects, the will of Alfred Nobel provides that your work can earn you a substantial monetary prize. Linguistics, one immediately notes, is missing from the list.

There are relatively few prizes that linguists can win for their work. One rather unwelcome one, accessible to you provided your linguistic research is done in the United States on public money, is the sarcastic "Golden Fleece" award, assigned by the odious Senator Proxmire to selected research projects that strike him as having been a waste of money to the extent of fleecing the tax-paying public. Proxmire's political sense tells him that there are cheap votes to be picked up from anti-intellectual Americans by accusing academic research of being a scam. And linguistics has won the Golden Fleece at least twice. Once it went to William Labov for his ongoing empirical studies on the speech of Philadelphians. Another time it went to

Robert M. McLaughlin for the research that went into his marvellous *Great Tzotzil Dictionary* (see *IJAl* 44 (1978), 156–59, for a review). Proxmire regarded it as a waste of his constituents' tax money for McLaughlin to devote over ten years of his life to compiling the best dictionary any Amerindian language ever had, for it was being done, as he saw it, for the benefit of just a few thousand Mexican Indians.

It might have been possible for us to tolerate this invidious position of being eligible for the Golden Fleece from an ignorant populist but not for a Nobel Prize from the hallowed podium in Stockholm if we could convince ourselves that our discipline was just not of the right sort to be regarded as endowed with the intellectual profundity that would merit a Nobel Prize. It might, had it not been for the institution in 1969 of a "prize to the memory of Alfred Nobel" in one more subject: economics. Economics has given mankind a meagre bundle of conceptual tools for essaying (generally unsuccessful) routine maintenance on capitalism. The first Nobel in economics went to Jan Tinbergen and Ragnar Frisch "for having developed and applied dynamic models for the analysis of economic processes." Tinbergen, for example, applied dynamic analysis to U.S. and U.K. business cycles. Prizes for this, and not for linguistics? I don't see it. It is no doubt as worthy and good to apply dynamic analysis to business cycles as it is to apply generative phonology to Russian stress cycles; but neither activity has the kind of impact on the history of the human race that, for example, the first Nobel in physics had. (It went to Wilhelm Röntgen in 1901 for the discovery of X rays.)

The most recent (1984) Nobel for economics went to a British economist whom economist friends of mine had never even heard of. His work had involved a sort of national-level accountancy, developing useful statistical measures of the extent to which rich countries were getting richer and poor countries were getting poorer. Well, I'm sorry; I really hate to cast aspersions on the work of my elders and betters, as those who know me will confirm; but it seems to me that such work hardly compares with the discovery of the background radiation from the birth of the universe that clinched it for the Big Bang theory of cosmology (another physics Nobel).

Maybe no activity in the social, cognitive, or linguistic sciences quite measures up as regards having "conferred the greatest benefit on mankind", as Nobel's will put it. Conceivably the labor of producing the *New English Dictionary on Historical Principles* (the *Oxford English Dictionary,* as it is now known) might be adjudged

Nobelworthy; maybe also Jespersen's *Modern English Grammar,* and a very few other monumental tomes that have taken people's lives to produce, and are genuine landmarks of achievement. But if one looks to the generative period with an objective eye, the truth is that major and permanent achievements that have permanently changed the state of our knowledge about human language stubbornly refuse to come to mind. Generative linguistics has so far produced a vast literature containing much that is ephemeral, and very few pieces of work that represent breakthroughs of permanent value or scholarly achievements of significant proportions, even within linguistics. And the transdisciplinary pretensions of the subject are so far mainly self-delusion. (Try to find a working geneticist who can be persuaded to agree that the outlines of the X-bar system are probably determined by the gene plasm.)

Perhaps, therefore, we would be flattering ourselves too much if we participated in an annual program of dishing out prizes for benefiting mankind. Linguistics is currently a tiny node in a congeries of related disciplines (mathematics, logic, philosophy, computation, psychology, anthropology, sociology) that may in due course bring forth fundamental insights into the nature of our species and its capacity for processing symbolic information, but we have not yet made any appreciable strides toward such a goal.

If that seems a little depressing, I suggest that perhaps what we need is a simple morale-lifting ceremony each year—something more akin to Hollywood's Academy Awards ceremony than the solemn rites of the Nobel Foundation in Stockholm. It would do us good.

UCLA, only a stone's throw from Hollywood, would be a good place to hold it. Each year we could enjoy months of tense speculation about the outcome of the voting. On the night of the ceremony, flocks of famous linguists would arrive at the auditorium dressed in their best Linguistic Institute T-shirts. Crowds of ordinary people (the "psychologists, philosophers, and anthropologists" mentioned on the publisher's announcements of nearly all linguistics books) would line the street outside, hoping to catch a glimpse of some famous Professor emerging from his limousine, or some Associate Professor getting out of his Honda, or some Assistant Professor dismounting from her bicycle. And inside: the glitter, the excitement, the anticipation, before the long-awaited dimming of the house lights, the soft whisk of the curtains, the buzz of anxious conversation dying away as master of ceremonies Bob Stockwell walks onto the stage, commanding rapt attention from the audience, and begins to pluck from large manila envelopes the cards bearing the names of the linguists who have won the coveted trophies.

There could be numerous categories of award. Hardly anyone would have to go their entire career without eventually winning in some category or other. I would like to see a James McCawley Prize for Profound Erudition, awarded for citing profoundly abstruse references or allusions. (Two of my favorites: W. S. Allen referring at the end of 'Structure and system in the Abaza verbal complex' (*Trans. Phil. Soc.*, 1956) to a 1944 lithograph by K. Lomatidze and citing the title *in the Georgian script;* and Gaberell Drachman's "Take for example the control of the postural muscles in the abdomen of the crayfish", in 'On the notion "phonological rule",' *Working Papers in Linguistics* 15, Ohio State University, 1973, 135–36.)

It would be nice to see an award for Withering Invective. Linguistics does so much better on this front than most subjects (apart from literary criticism, of course) that it would seem most appropriate to reward really top-flight practitioners. Private sneering, naturally, would not count. The invective in question would have to actually be published in a book, or in a refereed, or at least edited, journal (not a conference volume; as the printer's deadline approaches for some litho-printed conference volumes, the teams of graduate students who stay up all night to put the page numbers on the pages often don't actually get a chance to read the papers; they simply measure the margins). Chomsky's blistering use of the word "pathological" in *Lectures on Government and Binding,* p. 149, is a nice example of withering invective. F. J. Newmeyer might be a candidate for nomination; see his nice deployment of the word "bloated" (applied to grammatical theories) in *Linguistics* 18 (1980), 934. But most of the real award-winners would tend to be found in the book review columns of *Language.* Look at works like James Sledd's merciless vivisection of Morton Bloomfield and Leonard Newmark's *A Linguistic Introduction to the History of English (Language* 40 (1964), 465–83) or R. M. W. Dixon's assassination of Stephan Wurm's *Languages of Australia and Tasmania (Language* 52 (1976), 260–66) to see how it's really done. The acid is all the more pungent for being bottled up in such a respectable vessel as the journal of the Linguistic Society of America.

It might be reasonable to have a Captain Ahab Trophy for obsessive work on a one-person grammatical theory, though the large numbers of little-known theories currently receiving monomaniacal attention solely from their creators might make it very hard for the judges to decide between them.

Perhaps there could be a Linguistic Inquiry Cup for Generative Arrogance, awarded for contributions to the combination of lofty disdain with wild-eyed commitment to dogma that makes much generative work so interesting to read. It is not at all easy to achieve the combination I am referring to; it is extremely difficult not to let the wild-eyedness interfere with the loftiness. Nonetheless, there are steady streams of entrants. For example, I think Norbert Hornstein and Amy Weinberg might qualify for nomination, for boldly stating that "*Referred to in 1964* and *talked to Harry about* are not natural predicates" (*Linguistic Inquiry* 12, 66) without defining the notion *natural predicate*. And I fear someone might think of nominating Henk van Riemsdijk for the final footnote in his *A Case Study in Syntactic Markedness* (Peter de Ridder, 1978), which deals with preposition stranding in the Scandinavian languages with the words, "a quick glance suggests that they are rather similar to Modern English."

A Karl V. Teeter award for study of a language nobody else has ever heard of would be nice. This surely would have been captured around 1977 by Charles Li and Sandy Thompson for their work on "Wappo". But consider also "Spaka" (Randy Dichl and Katherine Kolodzey), "Kobon" (John Davies), "Jinghpaw" (La Raw Maran and J. M. Clifton), "Ozark English" (Suzette Haden Elgin), "Thompson" (L. Thompson and M. T. Thompson), "the secret argot of the Sontay boatmen" (Moira Yip), "Dutch" (Annie Zaenen) and so on. I swear I have not made up a single one of these fantastical purported languages. (Those who can identify the published sources on all of them without looking anything up are obviously promising future candidates for the McCawley Prize.)

There is apparently a minor competition in progress for inserting fictitious references in linguistic works, and this could be made official. These references generally occur in books, not in journals, because journals tend to have competent editorial assistants who catch them, but book publishers often do not. For example, there is a joke reference to an alleged forthcoming work by a young child in J. Emonds' *A Transformational Approach to English Syntax* (1976; p. 253), and it is echoed by F. J. Newmeyer in *Linguistic Theory in America* (1980; p. 258), which means that the Academic Press copy editors missed it twice; nyaah nyaah to them! But journal editors are

human too—yes, even the editor of *Language*. There is a reference
to a nonexistent 1982 book on page 637 of *Language* 58, which survived all through copy-editing and proofreading by the three dimwits
who published the article; and on page 653 of *Language* 53 one may
find an audacious citation of a fictitious trace-theory manuscript by
Canadian singer Gordon Lightfoot. To give some solace to the then
editor Bill Bright and his then assistant Lucy Stockwell in their grief
as they read these revelations, let me point out that the index page for
Linguistic Inquiry volume 8 refers to another totally nonexistent
work, "Features and Control" by Chomsky and Lasnik.[1]

A Janus Linguarum Prize for the most startling *volte face* in the
linguistics literature might well give rise to the hottest competition of
all. Among the award winners over the years we might have seen
Charles Hockett (whose introduction to the algebraic study of languages, *Language, Mathematics and Linguistics* (1967), has a preface retracting the whole algebraic approach); Jerrold Katz, who
wrote in 1964 ("Mentalism in linguistics") that "the linguist's theory is subject to the requirement that it . . . be consistent with the
neurophysiologist's theories concerning the type of existing brain
mechanisms", and then announced in 1981 that this was a category
mistake (*Language and Other Abstract Objects*); Paul Postal, for is-
suing in 1968 a vituperative attack on stratificational grammar for its
lack of a lexicon (*Aspects of Phonological Theory*, pp. 198–207),
and then announcing in 1980 a theory that also has no lexicon (cf.
Johnson and Postal, *Arc Pair Grammar*); and Edwin Williams, for
inventing in 1975 (*Syntax and Semantics* 4, ed. by J. Kimball, Academic Press) and attacking in 1983 (*Linguistics Inquiry* 14, 287–308)
the notion of "small clause". There would be candidates galore every
year, I am sure. Now that I come to think of it, I'm not sure I
wouldn't be among them . . .

The key thing about the Linguistic Awards ceremony, anyway,
would be that it could serve the function of gathering the whole linguistics profession together for a purpose less sombre than the depressing jobs mart of the annual meeting of the LSA each January. It
would be a pure celebration of the profession of linguist; a chance for

1. The last two items are noted in the wonderful collections of linguistics publishing errors amassed by the editors of *Utrecht Working Papers in Linguistics* and published in issues 10 and 11.

us to gather together without having to listen to anyone's revision of the definition of government; a conference without handouts.

It is sad that as yet there is no sign of any of this coming to pass. No glittering Linguistic Academy Awards night for us to look forward to. And no trips to Stockholm.

Chapter Twenty-one

A memo from the Vice Chancellor

This piece of whimsy, originally bearing the rather clumsy title 'Memo from AVC re divisional placement of Linguistics Department', arose from reflections on two things. One was the regular interdisciplinary bickering one encounters in most universities about whether the sciences are getting away with a light workload, whether humanities faculty are lazy about applying for grants, whether the fine and performing arts are being cheated of resources, whether the social sciences have enough intellectual content to make them deserve their slice of the pie, and so on. The other was the astonishing story of the rise of CSLI, the Center for the Study of Language and Information at Stanford University.

To launch CSLI, Stanford obtained a gift of about $20,000,000 from the System Development Foundation (formed to dispose of the unexpectedly enormous amount of money generated through the selling off of the System Development Corporation think-tank in Santa Monica). This was an unprecedentedly huge amount of money for research on language. It led me to imagine a new university without a linguistics department suddenly being the scene of a major turf battle between different divisions or colleges vying with each other to gain administrative authority over linguistics in case similarly huge grants of research money should come its way.

The premise was self-evidently silly (CSLI's millions were negotiated not by linguists but primarily by a philosopher, John Perry, and a mathematician cum logician, Jon Barwise; they and the computer science researchers who affiliated with CSLI were of considerably more interest to the System Development Foundation than the linguists); but it led to what I present here, an imaginary report by an imaginary Academic Vice Chancellor (or Provost, or Vice President for Academic Affairs, or whatever they call the equivalent person at your university) on the arguments of the humanities, social science, and natural science divisions that they should house the imaginary new linguistics department.

The ending is the best I could do to exit on a punch line from my little fantasy; the contrast between the Vice Chancellor's disdain for pecuniary motives and the last dozen words of the secretary's annotation on the end are supposed to be the stinger. But one Stanford colleague who had formerly exhibited many signs of being an intelligent life form, reading carelessly and irritably through a page on which he saw the words 'Stanford', 'lust', 'funding', 'Genghis Khan', and 'corrupted', became highly incensed; convinced that I was trying to insult his fine university (with which I have had a friendly association since 1981), he attempted to convince several senior administrators that I should be declared *persona non grata* there or something. I am delighted to report that this effort to ostracize me failed, and I am still welcomed every time I am able to drop by for CSLI's very civilized tradition of afternoon tea at three-thirty each working day.

I made a mistake in saying that the University of California Irvine campus counted linguistics among the social sciences. In actual fact (and this is a very strange fact), Irvine had two linguistics programs at the time, one in the School of Social Sciences and a quite separate one across Aldrich Park in the School of Humanities. Bernard Tranel wrote to *NLLT* to point this out and set the record straight ('L'embarras du choix', *NLLT* 3 (1985), 493).

To: CHANCELLOR

From: ACADEMIC VICE-CHANCELLOR

Subject: Divisional placement of proposed Linguistics Department

As requested in your memo of the 5th, I have attempted to arrive at a reasonable decision regarding the question of which of our three academic Divisions should contain the proposed new Linguistics Department at this University. I have to confess, however, that I have been unable to resolve the matter satisfactorily. The Divisional Deans have been quite forthright in the opinions I elicited from them, and they have each argued with the utmost cogency—with a forcefulness that even the plan for three new posts in the subject does not explain—that Linguistics should fall within their own Division. Since ultimately the matter is going to lie with you for a decision, I will simply present you with a digest, mostly composed of direct quotation or close paraphrase from the Deans' letters, of the three points of view whose relative merits you will have to determine. I regret not being able to offer you a clear advisory opinion in this complex and obviously controversial matter, but I must admit to a certain amount of bewilderment as a result of my study of the following powerfully argued opinions.

1. DIVISION OF HUMANITIES OPINION

Linguistics finds its natural place within the Humanities on numerous mutually reinforcing grounds. At many universities, linguistics teaching has originated within one or another department of foreign languages or literatures, and has thereafter attained autonomy without relinquishing its intellectual ties with those areas. At the University of Cambridge in England, Linguistics has always been a department within the Faculty (read Division) of Mediaeval and Modern Languages and Literatures. At the University of Washington in Seattle, linguistics developed into a separate department through the efforts of two scholars of Spanish in the Department of Romance Languages and Literatures, and there are also linguists there in the departments of Asian and Germanic Languages and Literatures. These two random examples may fairly be said to typify the normal pattern in universities in this country and overseas.

It might be noted in this connection that MIT's famous Department of Linguistics, now amalgamated with another Humanities discipline as the Department of Linguistics and Philosophy, sprang in the first place from the Department of Modern Languages; Noam Chomsky's post (before he became an Institute Professor) was for many years the Ferrari P. Ward Professorship of Modern Languages and Linguistics.

At other universities, linguistics was originally taught, or is still taught, within the Department of English; Brandeis in Massachusetts and Wayne State in Michigan are but two exemplars. Many linguistics programs that have Program or Committee rather than Department status are administered chiefly by departments of English, many of them tying linguistics activity to the teaching of English as a second language—surely a very natural connection to make.

On intellectual grounds, it is easy to support the assignment of the Linguistics Department to the Humanities here as has so often been done elsewhere. The study of language is inherently a Humanities discipline, of a piece with the analysis of literature, or with philosophical analysis, or with historiography, in that its concern is with the appreciation of the qualities and experiences that define our human existence. To think of the study of language being separated by major disciplinary and administrative boundaries from poetic analysis, or philosophical logic, or classics, or the study of modern languages, is a manifest absurdity, and one to which the Humanities division would take the strongest possible exception.

2. DIVISION OF SOCIAL SCIENCES OPINION

It can hardly be seriously questioned that linguistics is one of the social and behavioral sciences. There is almost universal recognition of this. In the United Kingdom, the former Social Science Research Council (now the Social and Economic Research Council) has been essentially the sole funding agency for linguistics research. In the United States, the massive Sloan Foundation effort in cognitive science has securely established the kinship of linguistics with the other disciplines of what has come to be known as the "Sloan area", and other funding agencies in the social sciences (the Ford Foundation, the Wenner-Gren Foundation, etc.) have clearly recognized that linguistics lies within their purview. The Center for Advanced Study in the Behavioral Sciences at Stanford has traditionally counted linguistics within the field it caters to, and continues almost every year to fund fellowships in linguistics.

Within the United States in particular, linguistics has grown almost entirely out of the social science discipline of anthropology. The great American anthropologist A. L. Kroeber speaks of his "first remembered purely intellectual pleasure" as having been "the demonstration of pattern in the classes of English strong verbs" (Foreword to Hymes' *Language in Culture and Society*)—and not for nothing; the rigorous analysis of the systematicities in human behavior and culture is what links the study of grammar to the study of human society, and anthropologists have rightly regarded the two as inseparable. Franz Boas was a central figure in the emergence not only of American anthropology but also American linguistics; something rather similar could be said of Edward Sapir; and so on.

Language is widely regarded as inherently a product of human societies. Wittgenstein has even suggested that on philosophical grounds the notion of a language inaccessible to a society—a "private language" accessible only to one individual—is incoherent. If this is so, clearly William Labov and others have the right to protest the marginalization (as "socio-linguistics") of that part of the language sciences most closely concerned with the study of language in its social context. But even those who do not protest it have recognized that the broader intellectual affiliations of linguistics are within the cluster of disciplines standardly brought together as the social, behavioral, and cognitive sciences. At the University of California, Irvine, linguistics is entirely (and very successfully) accommodated within the School of Social Sciences. At Berkeley, too, the Department of Linguistics is under the Dean of Social Sciences. At Brandeis University, linguistics is a program within the Department of Psychology. At the University of Manitoba in Canada, linguistics is entirely within the Department of Anthropology.

It is quite plain that close association between the scientific study of language and the human sciences is and should be the norm in a modern university. The Social Sciences Division would resist very strongly any move to institute at the very start of the linguistics program here a senseless administrative barrier between such closely related branches of learning.

3. Division of Natural Sciences opinion

If one looks at the actual practice of linguistics today, and at the actual intellectual affinities of the work that modern linguistics research involves, one rapidly sees that most universities in the world have their administrative structure wrongly designed, in a way that is at odds with the prevailing intellectual trends in the field. Here we have a chance to do things right, from the word go, by adopting the structure implicit in, for example, IBM's Thomas J. Watson Research Center at Yorktown Heights, where linguistics research has from the start been located in the Mathematical Sciences department.

Linguistics today employs the methods of mathematics, mathematical logic, and theoretical computer science. While it may apply them to a domain that can be linked to the social sciences and even the humanities indirectly, this does not determine or even affect the nature of the methodology or the intellectual affiliations of the work involved. Linguists do not in fact employ any of the methods of psychologists, sociologists, or economists; laboratory observation of small-group behavior and questionnaire-based sampling of societal trends may be used in some research on language by social scientists, but those kinds of research are grossly different from the theoretical reasoning and mathematical modelling of abstract systems that must characterize serious work in linguistic science, and which also characterize the most highly theoretical work in areas such as particle physics and molecular biology.

It is noteworthy that despite the early use made by Morris Halle of posts in foreign-language teaching to get faculty (in the most celebrated case, Noam Chomsky) into MIT, the real rise of the MIT Department of Linguistics has been intimately tied to the Research Laboratory of Electronics. The reasons are clear. From the very start, linguistics has had more in common with computer science and related fields than it could possibly have with instruction in foreign languages or with the study of literature. Chomsky's own work on the form of grammars for natural languages instantly generated spin-off in computer science (the notion of context-free grammars, the "Chomsky hierarchy," and the whole area of formal language theory). And today the drift of his position on the place of linguistics in the academy is that it actually forms a part of the growing area of theoretical biology, in that its true goal is the specification of certain (perhaps genetically determined) aspects of the structure of the human brain and its information-processing capacities.

The growing closeness of linguistic and mathematical investigations generates new areas of investigation all the time. Very recently we have seen extremely important results in denotational semantics arising out of parallel and crucially interrelated work on natural languages and computer programming languages (cf. the work on "Scott-Strachey semantics" for both).

More than ever, the activities of linguists involve interaction and collaborative work with mathematicians and computer scientists; and this should not be surprising: in the work of Zellig Harris, the key figure in the prehistory of generative grammar, it has always been quite explicit (see for example his book *Mathematical Structures of Language,* which derived from lectures given at the Courant Institute of Mathematical Sciences).

Linguistics is even generating engineering applications, as the focus of the computer industry moves toward the creation of software that will be able to match the sophistication of tomorrow's hardware. Indeed, in one subarea of the linguistic sciences, namely phonetics, the natural science nature of the work becomes so evident as to be undeniable. Modern phonetic research demands highly advanced laboratory equipment for wave-form display and manipulation, acoustic analysis, and computer simulation, and relates to physics more closely than to any other domain. (It also supports a multi-million dollar industry based on the machine analysis and synthesis of speech.)

It is important not to be misled by the human connections and importance of language and language use into thinking that the associations people have regarding the subject matter of linguistics must determine the content, methods, or administrative affiliations of the discipline. Nothing can be more sacred to human beings than the mystery of life itself, yet biology is a natural science; we are not tempted to move it into the Humanities. No question has more mystical profundity than that of the origin and fate of our universe, yet we locate physics and astronomy within the natural sciences, not in the School of Divinity.

A forward-looking university in this modern age will attempt to align itself with the demands of the future, responding to the real trends in intellectual affairs rather than to the meaningless traditions that may have arisen from earlier conceptions of the academic disciplines and their structure. At too many universities the dead weight of past traditions—the associations between the linguistics of the past with philology or with cultural anthropology—tie the hands of the institution in the present. Precisely because of the accidental circumstance of our never previously having had a linguistics program, we have the power to liberate ourselves from outmoded conceptions. An opportunity exists to recognize what is already an established alliance in modern science: the new complex of disciplines concerned with the theory of information-manipulating systems and their physical and biological instantiations. Recognition of this exciting and potentially revolutionary new line of evolution in the sciences demands that the Linguistics program here be located within the Natural Sciences Division.

4. CONCLUSION AND CAVEAT

As I warned you, Chancellor, I am not able to reconcile the viewpoints I have represented to the best of my ability above, and I feel I must leave the actual decision-making in the matter to you.

However, there is one thing that I feel I ought to point out. It has not escaped my notice, and doubtless will not have escaped yours, that a certain amount of publicity has recently been generated by the establishment at Stanford of a "Center for the Study of Language and Information" (CSLI) funded by the System Development Foundation to the tune of approximately twenty million dollars. (Estimates, and even insider reports, have varied; inaccurate first projections spoke of $45 million over about a decade; my best information at present is that about $19.5 million has so far been granted to CSLI, and new funding proposals are in the pipeline.) Much of the work of CSLI falls within the domain of linguistics, though a substantial amount of interdisciplinary work spread between philosophy, artificial intelligence, computer science, mathematics, and perhaps also psychology is involved.

I have to confess to a certain suspicion about whether some of the tone of advocacy in the Deans' opinions summarized above could not be attributed to a simple lust for a share of some of the large-scale funding that now appears to be becoming available for work in the linguistic sciences, broadly construed. I would prefer to think that our faculty and administration are guided by purer motives than mere desire for conference funds and laser printers when they consider important matters bearing on the administrative structure of our institution, but realistically we must face the fact that everyone is heir to human weaknesses. It is fairly clear that the status of Stanford University within the linguistic sciences at present is roughly comparable to the status of Genghis Khan in Asia during the mid-thirteenth century, except that Stanford has vastly better computational resources than were available to the Mongol Empire, while Genghis Khan certainly had superior numbers of horses (but not postdocs).

All power corrupts, and Stanford is clearly destined to become corrupted absolutely. Whether this should lead you to attempt to find a more objective source of advice and recommendations about the linguistics issue than our own faculty and their decanal representatives, I cannot say.

Academic Vice Chancellor

[Dictated by the AVC but signed in his absence; he is away this week at a conference at Stanford—JK]

Chapter Twenty-two

Some lists of things about books

This was really just a doodle; a compilation of some bits and pieces I had collected over a few years like cardboard boxes or old pieces of wire because I thought they might come in handy some day. Not wanting them simply to be found among my effects after my demise—a box of scraps of paper like the one that was posthumously published as Ludwig Wittgenstein's *Zettel*, a course of action that no doubt would have greatly embarrassed him—I pulled them together here with the feeble excuse of representing them as the beginnings of a linguist's version of the best-selling *Book of Lists* series.

For those who have found it difficult to distinguish my playful fantasies from my actual activities, let me note here that I am *not* planning a book-length project with color pop-up illustrations under the title *Noam Chomsky on the Enterprise: A Conversation with Spock* (chapter 6 of the present book is all you get), I am *not* attempting to publish a biography of Jay Keyser called *Look, I Have to Trust My Referees,* and I am *not* really going to produce a full-length linguist's book of lists, so don't ask.

It is necessary for me to mention this, because I still get quite a bit of mail from people who want to add to my lists. Linda Lombardi, for example, sent another entry for the very short list of books whose titles are not grammatical constituents: a mystery by Colin Dexter called *Last Seen Wearing.*

Several people have pointed out that my list of six science-fiction novels for linguists is nowhere near a complete enumeration or even a good sampling of this genre. Many have pointed out, quite correctly, that I made no mention of the novels of Suzette Haden Elgin, which are written by a linguist for linguists, with linguists as central characters. I felt that citing novels *by* a linguist was cheating. Naturally Suzette would put linguists in her stories; if she had been a lumberjack, I assume she would have written lumberjack stories.

What is much more surprising is that, for example, Samuel R. Delany, the black literary genius who had won no less than four Nebula awards by 1984, wrote a novel with a linguist heroine. Georgia Green thinks the novel in question, *Babel-17*, is awful; read it, and you will see that I am right and she is wrong.

Although I am right about Delany, I am (contrary to what so many people assume) not always right about everything. I make, albeit very rarely, occasional mistakes. Professor Charles-James N. Bailey (who may be known as 'Charles-James' to his mother and perhaps a few cousins and aunts, but is normally addressed as 'C-J' by nonrelatives) took the trouble to point out one in this piece. I nearly left it as an exercise for the reader, but in the end decided on revealing it here.

At one point in the piece that follows, I arrived at a point where I needed to use the plural of the noun *excursus*. Seduced by the pattern seen in such pairs as:

alumnus	*alumni*
bacillus	*bacilli*
cactus	*cacti*
calculus	*calculi*
emeritus	*emeriti*
focus	*foci*
fungus	*fungi*
gladiolus	*gladioli*
hippopotamus	*hippopotami*
incubus	*incubi*
locus	*loci*
nucleus	*nuclei*
octopus	*octopi*
radius	*radii*
stimulus	*stimuli*
streptococcus	*streptococci*
terminus	*termini*

and so on, I wrote *excursi*. I never thought for a moment about the awful warning implied by pairs like:

chorus	**chori*
circus	**circi*
genus	**geni*
minus	**mini*
omnibus	**omnibi*
opus	**opi*
ruckus	**rucki*
status	**stati*
surplus	**surpli*
walrus	**walri*

C-J wrote to me from Berlin on May 18, 1988, to say, "I could not escape a twinge of grief when I read *excursi,* which transmogrifies a ū-stem, which the word was and is, into an ŏ-stem . . ."

On realizing what I had done, I went into a paroxysm of agony and guilt that began a two-day episode of weeping, drinking, picking fights, smashing things, and reciting Latin noun paradigms while banging my head against hard surfaces. I remember very little about the two days in question, but Leroy tells me that at one point I had to be hauled out of the hot tub and physically restrained lest my anguished thrashing about should injure either me or the two young women who for some reason were with me at the time. At length, through hot and cold showers and a strict regimen of sedative-induced sleep and meals of tofu and alfalfa sprouts, I was brought back to some semblance of normal functioning, and after two months of counseling and massage therapy I was as right as rain.

But once recovered and able to face calmly and analytically the enormity of my morphological crime, I began to think about what the correct plural of *excursus* is supposed to be if you don't transmogrify it. Is one really supposed to say "one excursus, two excursuses"? Or slavishly follow the Latin and make it "one excursus, two excursus"? Nothing seems right. I wish now I had never fallen into the trap of using the word in a plural context at all. Not a trap, rather, a gap, a paradigm gap. Some words are better left unpluralized. I'm only sorry that this one cost me nine weeks of my life, many windows and ornaments, and five quart bottles of José Cuervo tequila.

Since 1977, somewhat before the craze for trivia quiz games began to sweep the United States in the early 1980s, a book called *The Book of Lists* appeared (David Wallechinsky, Irving Wallace, and Amy Wallace; New York: William Morrow, 1977). It contains lists of things: the ten longest-reigning dictators, the ten best forgers, the thirty best places in the USA to live, that sort of thing. Americans loved it; it sold millions, and it still does, and so does its sequel, *The Book of Lists #2* (Irving Wallace, David Wallechinsky, Amy Wallace, and Sylvia Wallace; New York: William Morrow, 1980).

Lists of 'mere facts' are supposed to be anathema to linguists. Linguists want principles, theories, rich deductive structure. There are few things (other than weak generative capacity and the United States government) on which Chomsky has poured such scorn as the mindless listing of mere facts. Simply listing facts will do us no good, it is argued. It is easy. It is boring. Anyone can do it. But ultimately it is useless to serious linguistic research.

The truth, of course, is very different. Linguistic facts are quite difficult to obtain in some cases (cineradiography; fieldwork in the Caucasus; clear judgments on quadruple extractions; monolingual elicitation; acoustic phonetics of basilectal creole), and often rather low grade when easily gathered (the assembled intuitions of everyone at the dinner table about one parasitic gap example). Some people are brilliant at finding new linguistic facts, and others are relatively weak at it. Facts are often very interesting, all by themselves: Haj Ross used to cry "Neat fact!" when someone found one. Chomsky is just being a killjoy.

Moreover, linguists need far more in the way of mere facts than is available to them, not less. So vast is the range of hypotheses about almost anything in connection with language that it would be enormously useful to be able to marshal more facts at earlier stages in the struggle to weed out hypotheses whose future is roughly comparable to that of disco. And in general they are extremely weak on general knowledge about languages (we shall see some evidence of that below).

The constant protestations by Chomsky and his sales force to the effect that this is not so can only be taken as a deep desire to escape from the slow agony of empirical endeavor into a fantasy world where great science can be done from an armchair without even putting down one's glass, let alone sifting great quantities of facts.

There are virtually no intelligent people who do not recall making lists of things during the fundamental years of their intellectual growth: ages 7 through 15. And although after the latter age (or when sex is discovered, whichever is the sooner) there is a decrease in most people's list-making activities, the urge does not go away. It is a fundamental human need. Wallechinsky et al. have tapped into an important part of the human psyche by publishing a list of lists. I once saw a cartoon in *Punch* in which a man was leaning out of a window high above New York, shouting out his own list through a megaphone: "*Attention, fellow citizens: the following is the Fenton T. Armbrewster list of the ten best movies of all time.*" All but the dullest of us have felt that impulse.

And linguists are no exception. Nothing would be more useful to linguists than a book of lists of things relevant to linguistics. Yet although Wallechinsky et al. have a chapter in *The Book of Lists* called "In a Word—Communications", it is full of the sort of drivel that gives lists of facts a bad name among haughty theoreticians: Wilfred J. Funk's 10 most beautiful words in the English language (all right, I know that you cannot restrain yourself from wanting to know what they are: *chimes, dawn, golden, hush, lullaby, luminous, melody, mist, murmuring, tranquil;* don't ask me, I do not answer for Wilfred J. Funk); 10 words that only one person in 100,000 can pronounce correctly (yes, of course I scored 10 out of 10; the words are *data, gratis, culinary, cocaine, gondola, version, impious, chic, Caribbean,* and *viking*); the 13 longest words in English (yawn . . .); the 12 most commonly used words in English (zzz . . .); 39 non-Indo-European languages with loanwords in English (. . .); the 10 languages of the world with the most speakers . . . Just garbage. You can't expect linguists to be interested in stuff on that level.

I have accordingly begun work on a new project, *The Linguist's Book of Lists.* Of course, it must take its place in line behind other projects. The color pop-up book version of *Noam Chomsky on the* Enterprise: *A Conversation with Spock* still has no publisher willing to risk it; one small press in south Boston did give me a contract and went so far as to print up some copies, but then they mysteriously decided to suppress the work and refused to release the stock for sale. I also have to see through the press my unauthorized biography of Jay Keyser, *Look, I Have to Trust my Referees.* Nonetheless, *The Linguist's Book of Lists* is scheduled for completion some time in the next two years.

Now, in the tradition of those bars in American cities that serve free hors d'œurves at happy hour in the hope that customers will drink more, I propose to offer the reader some tempting morsels: a sampler of what the book itself will contain. I have resisted my inclination to supply morsels from the chapter on well-known linguists' private and sexual lives. Nor will I reveal here any of the contents of the many chapters that will be stuffed with lists of things about languages. The selection here is from a relatively dull chapter called 'Things about books'. Even the dull material from this book has its scintillating little moments, as I hope you will see. *Bon appetit.*

10 Books Called *Semantics*

This list excludes books with subtitles, like Michel Breal's *Semantics: Studies in the Science of Meaning* (1900) or Janet Dean Fodor's

Semantics: Theories of Meaning in Generative Grammar (1977) or James R. Hurford and Brendan Heasley's *Semantics: A Coursebook* (1983) or Steinberg and Jakobovits' *Semantics: An Interdisciplinary Reader in Philosophy, Linguistics, and Psychology* (1971) or Hugh R. Walpole's *Semantics: The Nature of Words and Their Meanings* (1941) or the Georgetown University Round Table on Language and Linguistics for 1976, *Semantics: Theory and Application.* The list contains only books that share the single-word title *Semantics*— surely the most popular title the language sciences have ever seen. The list is doubtless not exhaustive. All the volumes listed here are owned by the University of California library system. The reader will notice that no less than six of them came out in the four-year period between 1974 and 1977, which was either boom time for semantics or low ebb for imaginative title construction.

1. *Semantics*, by Giulano Bonfante (1950).
2. *Semantics*, by Mario Augusto Bunge (1974).
3. *Semantics*, by F. H. George (1964).
4. *Semantics*, by Geoffery N. Leech (1974).
5. *Semantics*, by John Lyons (1977).
6. *Semantics*, by F. R. Palmer (1975).
7. *Semantics*, by Anatol Rapoport (1975).
8. *Semantics*, by Kelly Thurman (1960).
9. *Semantics*, by Stephen Ullmann (1962).
10. *Semantics*, by Stephen Walter, Michael Walrod, and Rodney A. Kinch (1977).

6 BOOKS IN ENGLISH WHOSE TITLES ARE NOT GRAMMATICAL PHRASES OR SENTENCES

Titles of books are almost universally grammatical constituents: most commonly NP (*A Christmas Carol*), but also gerund VP (*Growing Marijuana Under Lights*), PP (*Of Human Bondage*), AP (*Eyeless in Gaza*), AdvP (*Lest Darkness Fall*), S (*The President Is Missing*), occasionally N̄ (*Portrait of a Man with Red Hair*), and perhaps a few other categories. Nonconstituent titles and ungrammatical constituent titles are extremely rare, but I have been able to locate the following half-dozen.

1. *If On a Winter's Night a Traveler,* by Italo Calvino. This spectacular virtuoso display of style, very much a linguist's novel (the author invents a whole new language family, Bothno-Ugaric), breaks many molds; for one thing, the main thread of the narrative is in the

second person. The title is a nonconstituent sequence, the conditional adverbial particle *if* followed by two constituents of the clause it introduces: a fronted AdvP and the subject NP.

2. *Nuclear and Radiochemistry,* by Gerhart Friedlander et al. This startling title is a classic example of a coordination in which the conjuncts are a word and a part of a word, i.e. parallel to **surface and submariners, *Euclidean and hyperspace, *descriptive and psycholinguists,* and so on. [Hey! These are starting to sound not quite so bad!]

3. *The Fire Next Time,* by James Baldwin. Whether or not *next time* is a possible post-head modifier to a noun like *fire,* this title is taken from the lines, "God gave Noah the rainbow sign: No more water, the fire next time!", in which *next time* is an adverbial modifier to an implicit predication, making the title a nonconstituent NP-AdvP sequence.

4. *A Tad Overweight, but Violet Eyes to Die For,* by G. B. Trudeau. The title is a colloquial description of Elizabeth Taylor. Although it might pass muster colloquially, it has the form AP *but* NP. The AP and NP are not capable of being construed as predicates of the same subject (as in Sag, Gazdar, Wasow, and Weisler's *either stupid or a liar* (*NLLT* 3 (1985), p. 117). The sense is that she *is* a tad overweight but *has* violet eyes. Thus while *He is stupid but a nice guy* is fine, Trudeau's title parallels ?**He is stupid but a red beard.* The title really has no grammatical analysis, and thus does not constitute a grammatical constituent.

5. *Sometimes a Great Notion,* by Ken Kesey. A nonconstituent sequence consisting of a fronted adverb plus a subject NP.

6. *Dancer from the Dance,* by Andrew Holleran. This word sequence could be a constituent, of course, but here it isn't. It's a snatch from a very familiar epistemological line by William Butler Yeats: "How can we know the dancer from the dance?"

5 Bookstores Where You Can Find a Really Serious Stock of Linguistics Books

1. B. H. Blackwell, 48-51 Broad Street, Oxford, England.
2. Heffer's, 18 Sidney Street, Cambridge, England.
3. Dillon's, 1 Malet Street, London WC1E 7JD, England.
4. Sanseido, 1, Kanda Jimbo-cho, 1-chome, Chiyoda-ku, Tokyo 101, Japan.
5. Postma, Spuistraat 122, 1012 VA Amsterdam, Netherlands.

4 EXTRAORDINARILY IGNORANT CLAIMS ABOUT LANGUAGES IN BOOKS BY LINGUISTS

1. "Hixkaryana, a Carib language . . . whose basic word order is object-verb-subject, which they say is not known to occur in any other language, dead or alive" (David Lightfoot, *The Language Lottery,* MIT Press, Cambridge, 1982, p. 84). At least seven other OVS languages were known at the time these words were published; see *IJAL* 47, 1981, p. 193, for details. The reference appears in a list purporting to contain examples of linguists' "anecdotes about exotic phenomena they have discovered". This is in the context of a pooh-pooh passage about how unimportant facts are, naturally.

2. ". . . Quileute and two other Salishan languages" (David Lightfoot, *The Language Lottery,* MIT Press, Cambridge, 1982, p. 84). Quileute is not a Salishan language; it is in the two-member Chimakuan family, unaffiliated to Salishan and not demonstrably possessed of any phylum connection (unless you are Joseph Greenberg, in which case you are convinced that virtually all Amerindian languages are related to one another, and you are no longer invited to historical and comparative Amerindianists' parties).

3. ". . . a Bushman dialect of Wishram, called Kung and spoken by a few thousand natives of the Kalahari" (David Lightfoot, *The Language Lottery,* MIT Press, Cambridge, 1982, p. 84). Wishram is not a Bushman language and does not have a dialect called Kung (though there is a Bushman language called !Kung); Wishram is Chinookan, and the people who once spoke it lived in the American North-West, not the African South-West.

4. "The American Indian language Hopi has no words or affixes referring specifically to dimensions of time" (David Lightfoot, *The Language Lottery,* MIT Press, Cambridge, 1982, p. 84). Whorf writes: "There are three tenses: past (i.e., past up to and including present), future, and generalized (that which is generally, universally, or timelessly true), all of which are mutually exclusive. Of these, the only one to be considered here is the future (suffix -*ni*). A first approximation to its meaning is the English future". (See *Language, Thought, and Reality,* edited by John B. Carroll, MIT Press, Cambridge, 1956, p. 103.)

6 SCIENCE-FICTION NOVELS FOR LINGUISTS

1. *Babel-17,* by Samuel R. Delany (1966). A brilliant linguist heroine assigned to that ultimate linguist's nightmare, the analysis of a language from outer space that does not conform to the principles of UG; a leading character called the Butcher who has been equipped with an internalized language in which the PERSON feature has only the value 3rd, rendering him unable to distinguish between his own reactions and those of others; the fate of the solar system hanging on the solution of an analytical problem in linguistics . . . This novel won the Nebula Award for 1966, even without any linguists being asked.

2. *The Embedding,* by Ian Watson (1973). A novel about the mental organ. Experimental psycholinguistics performed on human infants without human-subject ethical controls. . . . Hallucinatory drug use by an Amazonian people with an extraordinary language called Xemahoa. . . . Interstellar travellers to earth with a scientific enthusiasm for the study of the mind/brain, who demand ". . . six brains, programmed with different languages. And instruction tapes . . .". World governments' reaction to the first contact with Beyond. . . . This first novel is somewhat unconvincing on the syntactic side (yes, the "embedding" of the title is syntactic center-embedding), but quite powerful nonetheless.

3. *The Dispossessed,* by Ursula K. Le Guin (1974). Relatively little linguistics, though there are linguistic footnotes and excursi. But what linguists will enjoy most in this novel of anarchist political structure and cross-cultural communication is the sheer intellectualism, the sense of mathematics and physics and what it is like to live the life of the mind, together with a glimpse of what academia might be like in a peaceful but thoroughly anarchist political system. The best novel in the list.

4. *Contact,* by Carl Sagan (1985). The first contact with an extraterrestrial intelligence: a message is received from outer space, and the world's intellectual community sets about the task of deciphering it. This task is, of course, essentially an instance of what learnability theorists call "language identification in the limit from text," which is unsolvable under any reasonable conditions; but somehow they figure it out, which will make the book of passing interest to those who have reflected upon learnability or language acquisition. The ending

is pretty sappy, but as light reading about interspecies linguistic communication, the book deserves a mention.

5. *The Poison Oracle*, by Peter Dickinson (1974). No spaceships; this is science-fiction only in the sense that it invents a social, geographical, and ethnolinguistic milieu, and has a scientist (a psycholinguist/zoologist) as hero. The ingredients include hijacking, murder, a linguistically competent chimpanzee witness, and the dauntingly fierce Q'Kuti marsh-dwellers, who greet our hero with the one-word formal greeting *Kt!urochaRHa'ygharalocht!in*, analyzable as follows:

Kt!u-   r-   och- aR-   Ha'y-   gharal- och-
wallow.LOC-EMPTY-POSS-1PER.PL-PERMISSIVE-buffalo-POSS-
    t!in
    2PER.SG.9th.CLAN
'Thy buffaloes may rest in my wallow.'

Kt!u is the locative of *K!tu*, the locative case being formed by consonantal metathesis, a nice little morphological touch. (If that '!' segment is a post-alveolar click, perhaps the original range of the Khoisan language family extended even further north than Hadza and Ṣandawe would suggest, because internal evidence sets this novel somewhere in the region of the Iraqi marshlands. But phonetic considerations suggest otherwise: you can't release a dental pulmonic stop and immediately embark on a velaric ingressive stop that is also coronal. Perhaps the '!' is glottal.) At one point in the book, speaking about reading Chairman Mao in the original, the hero observes, "you can understand a language without understanding what someone is saying. That's one of the things psycholinguistics is about." Quite so, and pleasant to find a novelist who knows it.

6. *The Languages of Pao*, by Jack Vance (1957). From Mao to Pao. The original language of the planet Pao had no verbs and no adjectives. How can anything be said given such a linguistic deficit? The morpheme gloss of a sentence meaning 'The farmer chops down the tree' is given as follows:

farmer-EXRT   axe-INSTR   tree-VICT

where EXRT indicates 'in a state of physical exertion', INSTR indicates 'an instrument or agency', and VICT indicates 'in a state of subjection to an attack.' A more complex example is this utterance, spoken to a representative from the planet Mercantil:

rhomel-en- shrai   bogal-mercantil- nli- en   mous- es-   nli- ro
IMPRT- RDY-two   ear- Mercantil-GEN-RDY   mouth-PROX-GEN-VOL
'There are two matters I wish to discuss with you.

Here, IMPRT is an important marker, RDY indicates being in a state of readiness, GEN is the genitive suffix, PROX indicates 'this person here', and VOL indicates 'in a state of volition': 'Two-important-things-ready Mercantil's-ear-ready this-person's-mouth-willing.' Getting the hang of it? Linguistic readers of this novel about language planning will be relieved to know that by the end of the story the hapless Paonese are being provided with a new language intended to shake them out of their political apathy, the original one having given them a bad case of Orwell's Problem.

Chapter Twenty-three

The incident of the node vortex problem

With only two TOPIC . . . COMMENT columns to go, in the summer of 1989 I decided to risk asking the editors of *NLLT* to publish a piece of pure fiction: a short story about four collaborative authors trying to finish correcting the page proofs of a complex book on grammatical theory while they are participants in a major linguistics conference. At least three friends helped me and advised me on it. They didn't like the ending I had on it at one point, so I wrote a new one (I mention this because it proves that the piece is fiction). Eventually they shrugged and agreed that if I was determined to print such crazy stuff it was up to me. I took this as approval.

This piece is probably the first short story ever published in which the central event is the discovery of a glitch in a grammatical theory. I must stress that there is no way it can be regarded as a commentary or placed in any genre other than fiction. Some have claimed to see hints of something autobiographical in it; after all, I have participated in collaborative work on grammatical theory with teams of various sizes, sometimes four. Well, it is not autobiographical, and shame on you for even thinking such a thing.

Let me say it once more: all the events in what follows are simply made up. No episode in my life corresponds to anything like the high-pressure, deadline-driven research nightmare detailed in the following pages. None of the fine scholars I have worked with will find any allusion to their lives or personal characteristics in my fictioneering. The very thought is anathema to me.

Gander looked typically impassive as Pillock came into the room and closed the door behind him. The proofs of the book were on the table in three neat stacks, the corrected text sheets face down on the left, the current page and remainder of the chapter face up in the center, and the footnotes for the current chapter and remainder of the book at the right. Gander held a red pen with a needle-fine felt tip, on which he meticulously replaced the cap as Pillock came in.

"Well?" said Pillock, "What's up?" Gander's message had said only that he had "run into a problem," and Pillock had come up immediately without asking for further details.

"Take a look at this tree," said Gander. "Run through the details, and show me how it satisfies both the Grounding Constraint and the Subscript Convention."

Pillock looked at the tree. It represented the structure of *John said to Mary that birds eat.* There were no typos in the labeling or the lettering. There seemed to be no problem.

"Well," Pillock began slowly, "the noun phrase here is licensed by rule (39), like it says just up here in the text. The index path is not colimitant with a node vortex, so you check the features here against over here and there is no interruption so you look at the VP node and there's no problem and the Grounding Constraint says that this should have this subscript and then by the Subscript Convention it's the same as on the—oh, *shit.*"

"Crudely expressed," said Gander quietly, "but I think you see the difficulty. It all works fine in anything that either has node vortices or lacks PP's, and we have been concentrating mostly on the node vortex cases since Sachs noticed the trouble with the Subscript Convention and we introduced Krane's new interpretation of indices. But there is an interaction in just this case that we didn't see, and unfortunately at this point in the exposition we chose to exhibit a tree for an example with a PP in it, and it's referred to later so we can't take it out. Strictly, we don't actually predict *any* complex sentence with a prepositional phrase in it to be grammatical, as things stand."

Pillock slumped back into his chair. "Oh, good," he said, limply, "Not now; not at the page-proof stage. Not when we've got three days to return the whole thing to the publisher."

"I'm afraid something's got to be done," said Gander, "even if it means rewriting certain parts of the page proofs, expensive though that will be."

"Does Sachs know?" asked Pillock.

"No," said Gander. "He's got a paper about this stuff to present downstairs at the conference in about an hour's time; he'll be in the bar."

This was an unnecessarily cynical comment, but Pillock didn't bother to say anything, especially since he happened to notice on his way up that Sachs was indeed in the lobby bar of the hotel, discoursing animatedly on the virtues of the Grounding Constraint to an attractive graduate student, instead of checking that his overhead transparencies were in the right order.

"Shouldn't we tell him?" Pillock suggested.

"It might be better if he didn't know just yet," said Gander. "We may be able to think of a way out of this. If we can, and someone asks a question about it, we can pop up out of the audience and supply the answer. If we can't, then we're all in trouble, and there's no point in having Sachs present his paper with that knowledge hanging over his head; if we're lucky, no one will notice the problem."

For the next hour, as the evening sessions of the conference began in the hotel ballroom five floors below, Gander and Pillock mulled over the web of implications set up by the formulations of the Grounding Constraint, the Subscript Convention, the analysis of indirect objects, the definition of "index path" and "node vortex", and the other elements of the grammatical theory they had labored over for three years. Several insights emerged as they worked, and all crumbled away within minutes, sometimes seconds.

An hour later, the problem remained much as it was when Gander had discovered it, a stark false consequence of a system of assumptions that worked with amazing subtlety on numerous complicated examples they were proud of having dealt with, and did fine on *John told Mary that birds eat*, but came to grief for suspiciously accidental-looking reasons on any clause containing both a PP and a subordinate clause, such as *John said to Mary that birds eat*. Things looked grim.

It was time for Sachs' presentation, which dealt with issues unnervingly close to the problem they had just uncovered. They left the proofs lying on the table, and went down to the floor where the meeting rooms were. The chair of the session was announcing Sachs' paper, "The Grounding Constraint as a principle of universal grammar."

"The ideas outlined in this paper," Sachs began, "derive from joint research, and many of the following ideas are drawn directly from the forthcoming book by Gander, Krane, Pillock, and myself." Gander and Pillock sank slightly lower in their seats, their pride in being associated with the conceptual edifice in question significantly diminished by their knowledge that it would come down like a dynamited smokestack if faced by any two-clause sentence with a prepositional phrase in it.

"In our forthcoming book," Sachs went on, "we show that a large proportion of the general properties of English sentences . . ."—

and he proceeded into an hors d'oeuvres of preliminary rhetoric
about explanatory power combined with responsiveness to empirical
desiderata. Gander watched as the talk continued, alert to every detail, waiting to see if Sachs' presentation was going to inadvertently
stumble on the PP unpleasantness.

Sachs talked on happily, drawing attention to important points
laser-printed in 64-point boldface italics on overhead projector transparencies, coping confidently when one or two of them turned out to
be slightly out of sequence. Pillock lost concentration, and mused on
various things, and then all at once the talk was over, and it was time
for questions.

Mercifully, no one seemed to have noticed the node vortex problem. The first question was aggressively posed but ill-informed, and
Sachs buried it nicely under a pile of confidently presented technicalities. The second was from a well-known eccentric with a methodological bee in his bonnet; people frequently groaned and slipped
out of the room when he commenced a question. Sachs persuaded
him to stop burbling in a surprisingly short time, but even so, there
was time for only one more brief question.

The last questioner presented a very perceptive remark, exposing a
subtle inelegance in the line the analysis took about relative clauses—
quite cogent, but a little bit too subtle for most of the audience, and
nothing to do with PPs. Sachs decided to settle for a friendly remark
on the "thank you for that observation" type. It was over. They had
survived.

Gander caught Sachs soon afterward, and explained that a problem
had come up with the book. He suggested that they meet the following morning to discuss it over breakfast in the Garden Terrace, a re-
pellent but convenient plastic restaurant located amid an artificial
jungle of houseplants on the second floor of the hotel. "Seven-thirty
sharp," he said crisply.

Gander arrived sixty seconds early carrying his gray leather-bound
organizer. Pillock was five minutes late, and having forgotten both
his wallet and his room key, had to request that Gander lend him a
twenty. Sachs arrived looking harried at five to eight. Gander explained the theoretical problem while Pillock and Sachs waited for
their breakfasts. Sachs saw the problem the instant Gander explained
the exact circumstances under which it arose. He looked pained, then
shocked, then thoughtful. Realizing that his performance the previ-

ous day had been an exhibition of skating on thin ice, he grumbled that Gander should have told him earlier, but Gander just shrugged.

Sachs frowned for a while, and then, leaning back into a wall of ferns and spider plants with his hands behind his head, said slowly, "You know, I've been feeling for some time that the whole business of the interaction of the Grounding Constraint with the Subscript Convention needs to be completely re-thought."

After a moment of dead silence, Gander leaned forward slightly and spoke in terms as acid as the unsweetened grapefruit juice which formed the totality of his breakfast.

"Listen, Sachs. We are not in the business of re-thinking. Those are page proofs upstairs on my table, not rough notes. We not only have to solve this problem keeping the bulk of the theory exactly the way it is now; we also have to do it in a way that changes the smallest possible number of symbols. We cannot possibly handle the ramifications of a high-level change in assumptions. It will have a ripple of implications throughout the book, and we will never finish this job."

Because two heavily loaded plates of eggs, sausage, hash browns, toast, orange slices, and sprigs of parsley were delivered at that point, Sachs' wounded reply was not. Sachs and Pillock busied themselves with making inroads into their respective mountains of starch and cholesterol, while Gander's square eyeglasses looked at them over the edge of his grapefruit juice. From time to time, Sachs essayed the beginning of one of the insights Gander and Pillock had developed the previous day, and was disappointed to find that each approach fell instantly to clear objections.

They parted without making any decisions. Gander had his own concerns that morning. He had to present to the conference a paper submitted by Krane, who at the last minute found that he would not be able to be present. Krane's paper had been express-mailed to the hotel from out of the country, and only late the previous night had the red light on the phone in Gander's room informed him that the package had arrived. Less than two hours now remained to make photocopies of the handout, and there was barely time even to skim the text. The paper dealt with a topic that was covered in the book, but it was mainly Krane who had worked that part out, and the paper provided a more extended exemplification.

Pillock paced the halls, alternately worrying about the node vortex problem, sipping sour coffee that he didn't need from a styrofoam cup that made his teeth cringe, and greeting people he still recognized but whose names he had forgotten since the last meeting. When the time for Gander's presentation of Krane's paper arrived, Pillock dutifully ensconced himself in a back-row seat in the relevant meeting room. Preoccupied with the problem, he paid little attention as Gander was introduced as proxy for Krane and commenced reading Krane's paper in his dull, bland, voice.

But after a while, a soft buzz of discontent whispering its way through the audience brought Pillock's attention back to the proceedings. Something was wrong.

"This is seen in (15)," Gander was saying. But there was no "(15)" on the handout. "In (16a)," he continued, and the puzzled murmur again passed through the room. There was a (16), but it didn't have an *a* or a *b*; there was a (17a) and a (19a), but they didn't seem to be what Gander was referring to. Pillock began to get interested, and picked up his handout. The numbering of the examples bore no relation to what Gander was saying. The imperturbable Gander was beginning to notice this, and for once, was getting just the slightest bit flustered.

"But in the case of the second reading of the first clause, on the other hand, (21c) applies to (18) to yield the . . ." Gander turned over the sheet in front of him, and Pillock saw a flicker of horror come into his eyes. It was only a tiny flicker, and in almost anyone else would have been indetectable, but Pillock knew Gander's normally ice-calm face, and he could read the beginnings of panic.

Gander turned over another sheet. He turned back two sheets to the one before the one he had stopped at. No thread of coherence was visible. Methodically, he turned forward three sheets, and then forward one more, but in vain. Krane had left out a whole page.

After a pause of what seemed like about three minutes of quiet rustling of papers, Gander murmured an apology, and proceeded as best he could. It was exquisitely painful for him. His own papers were always impeccably organized, yet here he was trapped in a nightmare of an incomplete text and a handout whose example number-sequence failed to map to a continuous subsequence of the integers. Pillock almost began to enjoy himself. This was a rare sight.

At the end of the presentation, which came quite soon amid an embarrassed silence from the baffled audience, Gander stalked away from the podium to find somewhere he could hide, but not before Pillock had got near enough to slap him on the back and say "I thought it went just fine!" The hunted look in the eyes of the unhappy Gander was something to treasure. Pillock wandered back toward the book exhibit giggling spitefully to himself.

Later, when Gander had hidden for a while, the three authors met for further discussion of the PP problem. They brainstormed; they conjectured; they backtracked; they went over and over the facts and the definitions and the details of the offending tree in the page proofs till nothing new seemed to be happening in the brains of any of them. It was like sharing a headache.

Then at some point Pillock said something about PP distributions and subscripts that he immediately realized was embarrassingly incorrect and anyway irrelevant, but he was misunderstood by Gander, who said, apparently about a different idea, "Hey, that's a thought, they only clash when . . .", and straightaway Sachs was on to something.

"But the definition of node vortex could be generalized, because PP's are never subscripted with their colimitants except in cases where there is a licensing feature for the other category," said Sachs excitedly.

Pillock didn't get it. Gander and Sachs explained to Pillock what they were thinking of doing, though this was made difficult by the fact that each had a different idea in mind. It never became fully clear who had thought of what, or whether Pillock's remark had stimulated Gander to notice something that was the germ of what Sachs had incorrectly based on what he interpreted Gander to be assuming. But as they sat and worked together, collaboration worked its odd magic, and an idea did take shape.

Sachs decided his idea would fly, and he was prepared to go with it. Pillock, when he finally grasped it, thought that at least it was sufficiently devious that very few people would be qualified to show why it was unmotivated. Gander was of the opinion that it was an ugly, ridiculous fudge: it depended on a definition designed for something completely different being "generalized" in a spurious way so that it made certain subscript assignments impossible; but since in most cases those assignments were redundantly forbidden by the Grounding Constraint anyway, its only real effect was to prevent subscript assignment in a certain specific class of cases—exactly where the Subscript Convention was going to force the undesired results in sentences with prepositional phrases. But even Gander had to agree that it worked.

The deciding factor was that it turned out to be possible to implement the solution with Gander's thin red pen by making a single change in a single line, nowhere near the page where Gander had originally noticed the problem. All that was involved was adding "or any α on the index path of β" in a definition five pages earlier.

They looked at the time. It was a quarter to five in the afternoon, and they were tired. It was nearly time for the last paper of the afternoon session to start downstairs in the ballroom, part of a syntax session they had all vaguely planned to be at. Lacking anything better to do, they went downstairs, gathered up a handout each, and sat down.

None of them felt good about the solution they had reached. Three years of toil lay in that book; it had nearly driven them out of their minds on more than one occasion, and now, at this late hour, it was clear to them although many parts of the theory worked beautifully, still they only had a solution that worked; the *answer* had eluded them.

They sat glumly, staring at the handout for the talk that was about to begin. It was by a graduate student working on a language none of them knew. In her opening remarks she explained that she would be assuming the framework that had been developed by Gander, Krane, Pillock, Sachs, and others in various articles and would be set out more fully in a forthcoming book. The authors were too dispirited even to exchange meaningful looks.

The student began to outline a thorny syntactic problem. As the details emerged it became clear that the problem was quite intricate, and looked bad for the various standard analyses she routinely tried out on it.

Then, without warning, she revealed one further fact which at first seemed unconnected, and she raised the question of what the Grounding Constraint would say about the intersection of the two sets of cases. Gander and Sachs pricked up their ears and started paying closer attention to the words as the student carefully read them off the page in front of her. Pillock was slower off the mark, but as the student explained further, he began to see it too. It actually seemed that the Grounding Constraint had a chance of explaining something here that it had not been designed to explain, in a way that didn't really interact at all with the ugly modification they had made that afternoon.

They listened intently, the shared headache forgotten. Unconsciously, they had begun to sit up straighter in their seats, as if the better to feel in their faces the fresh breeze of truth, carrying perhaps a few wind-blown particles of credit that might cling to them.

Chapter Twenty-four

Epilogue: The final curtain

With the appearance of *Natural Language and Linguistic Theory* 7.3 in the early fall of 1989, it was time for me to supply my last ever TOPIC . . . COMMENT column (the agreement having been that I would either find or write columns to complete volume 7 and then the TOPIC . . . COMMENT department would become a letters column). In the third week of October 1989 I was still thinking about what to write when my world stopped. Windows pounded their frames, steel bookcases danced, bits of concrete flew from the exterior walls of the building, trees bucked and groaned, well-trained Californians ran for desks and doorways but I couldn't get to either so I just sat on the couch in my office and juddered.

A large earthquake had destroyed the majority of the buildings in the downtown area of the town in which I live, shivered the timbers of my house till the plaster cracked and the water pipes broke, and extinguished the gas, electric power, and phones. A Walkman radio found by candlelight told parts of the story as they were phoned in to radio stations that were immediately commandeered under emergency broadcast regulations. Although the campus where I had sat through the tremors was in plain sight of the epicenter of the Santa Cruz Mountains Earthquake (now generally referred to as the Loma Prieta quake, having been named after a prominent peak that was not especially near the epicenter), my university had not been damaged much at all, and there had been no loss of life or serious injury to its students or personnel. The damage had been far more serious fifty miles north of the quake than in Santa Cruz County: a section of double-decked freeway built on soft estuarine mud in west Oakland had collapsed and a section of the Bay Bridge from San Francisco to Oakland had given way, all of this at rush hour. Many people had been killed.

It was grim. There seemed no choice for a self-respecting gadfly columnist but to write a flippant column about it, and the sooner the better; so when the power came back on and the computers booted up again (today's microcomputers can be thrown across the room by an earthquake and suffer no damage at all, I found out), I sat down and wrote the farewell piece that follows.

The quote from Mario Puzo's novel *The Godfather* was slightly wrong in the original version of this column, owing to my bad memory and the fact that it was impossible to find my copy of the book in the post-earthquake chaos of my library; the quote has been silently corrected here, and the books are now back on the shelf, with *The Godfather* nestled beside other great works that have inspired me: *Syntactic Structures, Dracula,* Coleridge's complete poems, Jespersen's *Modern English Grammar, Babel-17, The Hitchhiker's Guide to the Galaxy,* Feyerabend's *Against Method,* the *Necronomicon* of Abdul Alhazred, the complete scripts for *Monty Python's Flying Circus* . . . I don't know if I'll ever get them back in order again, actually.

The magnitude 7.1 earthquake that struck directly at the heart of the TOPIC . . . COMMENT organization at 5:04 on October 17, 1989, finally convinced me that perhaps discretion was the better part of valor, and that having inflicted my opinions and fantasies on the linguistics community for seven years, it was now time to quit. Obviously, I thought, the planet itself is offended and has begun to take its revenge. It is time for me to get out while I still can. I was prepared to stand up indefinitely to the disapproval of virtually all linguists of taste and discernment, but not to take this kind of geophysical abuse.

The TOPIC . . . COMMENT office materials and files of protest letters are being picked up off the floor and moved to Seattle immediately. There, Professor Frederick Newmeyer will be taking over.

During the time I have had the privilege of overseeing TOPIC . . . COMMENT, the only general opinion column of non-editorial commentary in any of the major refereed journals of linguistics, five other linguists[1] have contributed columns. I had hoped that they might share in the blame, but clearly they did not. The earthquake was targeted right on Santa Cruz.

It's a pity things have to end this way. It really has been fun writing for TOPIC . . . COMMENT, and I do not use that adjective lightly.

(Now don't tell me *fun* isn't an adjective. It is certainly an adjective

1. Thomas Wasow, 'The wizards of Ling', *NLLT* 3.4, 1985; Arnold M. Zwicky 'On referring', *NLLT* 4.1, 1986; David M. Perlmutter 'No nearer to the soul', *NLLT* 4.4, 1986; Paul M. Postal 'Advances in linguistic rhetoric', *NLLT* 6.1, 1988; and Ray S. Jackendoff 'Why are they saying these things about us?', *NLLT* 6.3, 1988.

in the language of my adopted home state. In the speech of younger Californians, phrases like *so fun* are now common. I have verified through informant work on the beach in Santa Cruz that speakers can describe things as *very fun*, or *funner than* something else, or as *the funnest thing* they ever did. So that is a closed issue. *Fun* has become an adjective. Linguistic change is inevitable, and if you can't accept it, then I have to say to you what Roman Jakobson is reputed to have once said to a class of students at Harvard who revealed that they couldn't read cursive Cyrillic: "You are linguist; you ought to could!")

Where was I? Ah yes, fun. Writing TOPIC . . . COMMENT columns has been funner than any other writing I have ever done. Some people (not many) have expressed sympathy for me, assuming it has been an albatross around my neck to have to produce another three thousand words of flippancy every ninety days if no one else offered anything. But they are wrong. It was always enjoyable, once the words began to flow and take on a life of their own, as they usually did after an hour or two of staring at the blank screen of my computer terminal. Many hours of effort were generally involved (I would often go through a draft column and re-edit it dozens or even scores of times), but the pleasure of creation was still there, every time.

Whether any wide cross-section of the linguistics community enjoyed my buffoonery is another matter. Some people, I know, have giggled and said they loved it and looked forward to reading more facetious nonsense in every issue. But other people were angered by what I wrote, and by the irresponsibly jocular and unseemly tone in which I persistently wrote it.

It was always my intention that the former category of people should vastly outnumber the latter, but doubtless I misjudged things and seemed simply silly or unpleasant on any number of occasions. I don't know how many such occasions there may have been, because the angriest letters complaining about TOPIC . . . COMMENT have always been sent confidentially to the editor-in-chief in Massachusetts. Although I have been told of their existence and general drift, the letters have never been shown to me, and the identities of the authors have never been revealed. They are today kept in a locked vault at Brandeis University.

What can I say to the people I have offended with my lampoons? I did take some care to avoid mentioning the name of anyone whose guts I genuinely hated, so if you were ever personally mentioned in my diatribes, it wasn't personal. But this may only remind you of

Tessio in *The Godfather,* who after being discovered in a plot to assassinate Michael Corleone, explained: "It was only business, Mike. I always liked you." I always thought that sounded a bit weak in the circumstances. And they were leading Tessio off to be executed, of course.

I attempted to respect the principle that TOPIC . . . COMMENT should not be a public forum for personal hostilities or a back door through which a pseudo-article could be snuck in without refereeing. (Some people did not understand this; the editors had to turn away a number of contributions that clearly had been refused entry to the Remarks and Replies section of another well-known journal.) My aim was to be sufficiently outrageous that at least no one could take a TOPIC . . . COMMENT column for an attempt at a serious article. I only hope that most readers were able to detect this.

Somewhat to my surprise, I came away physically unscathed from all the conferences that I risked attending between 1983 and 1989. Even after publishing the most outrageous things about some of my fellow attendees in the ceaseless quest for a cheap laugh, I checked out of the conference hotel with the same number of teeth that I had going in. Linguists are apparently not given to physical violence.

Which reminds me that Peter Salus once, long ago, briefly had sight of a most interesting document that confirmed this latter point explicitly. The document was a hotel management guide to convention crowds and their special needs and characteristics. He saw it when he was a local organizer for some meeting. Conferences are very different, it turns out, from the viewpoint of the hotels and convention centers that host them. Some groups get rowdy after an hour at the cash bar and start smashing glasses and furniture, some learned associations are a regular bonanza for the local whores, and so on; the book tells hotel managers what to expect. And the entry under linguistics conferences had simply this to say about linguists:

> Eat and drink at all hours of the day and night. Breakages few.
> Bring their own women.

We sound like a nice bunch, don't you think? The bit about bringing our own women, of course, indicates a certain unconscious sexism in hotel managers, but even more so, it is a comment on the male-dominated character of most professions and most academic disciplines in America. Linguists don't "bring their own women"; those women are linguists! They are linguists of all sorts and of every rank, and they include scholars of the greatest distinction, for example, the last two presidents of the LSA and the editors of two of the top journals in the field. One of the many things I find pleasing about the linguistics profession is that it shows so much less gender bias in its demography than do most sectors of academia.

This is true even in computational linguistics, for example, despite the traditional dearth of women in fields relating to computation. I recently did a back-of-an-envelope study on data from the participants list at the 1989 meeting of the Association for Computational Linguistics in Vancouver, which had about 300 members of the profession attending (and at which the Presidential Address was by a woman, incidentally). The registrants were 30% female; the same percentage of authors of presented papers were female; and the program committee was 45% female. These statistics are far better than one typically finds in academia (never mind in computer science and engineering); compare them with whatever you like. The percentage of women on the faculties of universities in both North America and Europe is still quite often in single digits.

Where was I? I seem to have lost track of my theme—a luxury that could not be permitted in most of the writing that appears in scholarly journals. It is permissible for the reader to get confused about where we are in the argument, but it is very bad form for the author to be lost as well, I always feel. But I have no idea what I was talking about before I went into the digression about computational linguistics that grew out of the paragraph about gender that was a digression from the bit about breakage rates after the excursus on violence . . . Perhaps the earthquake has made me slightly more scatterbrained than I was before.

Ah, well. From now on, such inability to maintain a coherent theme in my writing will have to be ameliorated, because my writing will be subject to refereeing once again. I have written my last unrefereed piece for *NLLT,* and this is it. If the previous contributions ever gave offense, I present my humble apologies, and I pledge that if similarly scurrilous material ever appears in the new letters column that TOPIC . . . COMMENT will turn into in 1990, it will not be of my doing. Seven years of acerbity, whimsy, and persiflage is enough.

Actually, it's slightly more than seven years, come to think of it. Though born in March 1983, the TOPIC . . . COMMENT column was actually conceived on December 28, 1981, when Adrian Akmajian, Frank Heny, and Joan Maling sat me down at a quiet table in the

Hyatt Regency Hotel near Grand Central Station in New York during the 1981 annual meeting of the LSA to put a proposition to me. They described to me an imaginary regular column of opinion and current commentary on the linguistics scene, and they asked me if I would consider attempting to create it. They were most persuasive. By the time they had finished talking to me about it, the twinkle in their eyes was already transferred to mine. Fertilization had taken place.

The struggle that ensued over the next six months, as I tried to write something that realized the vague notion that had caused the twinkle, amazed me. By June 1982, I had done thirty or forty re-writes of a piece about linguistics on the two sides of the Atlantic, and I felt it was good enough to publish. I chose one trusted and respected friend to read it for me and confirm my view that it was topical, interesting, and moderately witty. That friend was Gerald Gazdar, who was visiting Santa Cruz for the summer.

I printed out the results of my six months of struggle and gave it to Gazdar. He read it. He put it down, and told me simply, "I think it's all right." And from the very slight pause (I estimate about 150 ms) before the "all right", I knew immediately that it was absolute drivel ("intellectual detritus" as he would probably have put it himself, internally). I threw the printout in the trash. To this day I have never used it or reopened the file.

But for some reason a completely different idea suddenly came to me with no warning, and over the next twenty-four hours I hammered out the text of 'Watch out for the current' (chapter 2; originally *NLLT* 1.201–6), working much faster than I ever normally did after that. It was not the acme of the columnist's art, but when presented to Gazdar it caused him to say, "Now, this is better." I decided I should settle for it. The block was broken, and the seven years had begun.

I accumulated many debts over those seven years, in particular my debt to the three founding editors of *NLLT*. Adrian Akmajian, who thought of the name TOPIC . . . COMMENT, is sadly no longer with us; he died in 1983, only a few months after *NLLT* started publishing. Frank Heny left the linguistics profession in 1987, and now busies himself with photography and other nonlinguistic things that take his creative fancy. Joan Maling, with some trepidation, took over the whole burden of editing the journal in the summer of 1987 and orga-nized the present panel of associate editors; she has become just as effective an editor-in-chief as I told her she would be. (Straight after news of the Santa Cruz earthquake came in, she flashed me an electronic mail message about whether this meant there would be any delay in my getting the next column's copy to Dordrecht; I have always liked and respected fanaticism, and I found her steel-hard dedication to business very satisfying.)

None of these three fine editors ever tried to veto a column; but if they lifted an eyebrow or wrinkled a nose in a certain way, even over the phone (you can *hear* a nose wrinkle sometimes), it would always make me think again. Without their friendly oversight and advice, I would have made even more blunders than I did. They constantly encouraged and assisted me, as did other valued friends who occasionally advised me on whether some crazed rhetorical artifice or conceit worked or not (associate editor Judith Aissen is one, for example).

I thank all of them, as I thank all the readers who read what I wrote and giggled to themselves. The academic world needs to take a lot of things very seriously, even (or especially) things that other people don't take seriously; but it shouldn't always take itself seriously. So I have deliberately fooled around with our discipline, and taken the names of many worthy linguists in vain.

The way I thought I would work when I began was that I would keep my finger on the pulse of current developments in linguistics and discuss the key controversies of the day. But I soon realized that linguistics is too vast and diverse for that. So I ended up simply mixing small quantities of arguable fact and sincerely held opinion together with medium quantities of ludicrous overstatement and wicked but amusing lies, and fired the result off in random directions, in hopes of occasionally provoking new thoughts or amused reactions. This is something like what the Chinese phrase *pāo zhuān yǐn yù* must mean: 'Throw brick attract jade' is the gloss William S.- Y. Wang suggests.

Samuel Butler was not so positive about the strategy in question, but he does describe rather well why it succeeds:

> For daring nonsense seldom fails to hit,
> Like scattered shot, and pass with some for wit.[2]

Very apt, I think. Daring nonsense is what I hope TOPIC . . . COMMENT achieved at its finest. I hope it passed with some for wit. At its worst, perhaps it was too doom-and-gloomy; it seems to be far easier

---

2. Samuel Butler, 'Upon modern critics', in *Satires and Miscellaneous Poetry and Prose*, ed. by René Lamar, Cambridge: At the University Press, 1928: 93–96.

to write entertainingly about how everything is going to hell than
about how great everything is. Again, Butler had a relevant comment:

> But when all other courses fail,
> There is one easy artifice,
> That seldom has been known to miss,
> To cry all mankind down and rail . . .

It was my executive assistant, Leroy, who first pointed out this passage
to me. He remarked: "dɪsməðədəŋkæptʃəjowæ:sɪnəfolæ:nræp!"
And indeed, the passage quoted does suggest familiarity with the
general outlook I have fostered in my time at the TOPIC . . . COM-
MENT office. Our watchword has been: "If you can't think of something nice to say . . . *come on in and sit down!*"

Well, to those who enjoyed the daring nonsense, negative and de-
rogatory though it may have been, best wishes; keep your sense of
humor, because the way the 1990s are shaping up, you're going to
need it. The United States Congress has cut the budget of the National Endowment for the Arts because some members had been
shocked by iconoclastic works of art it had supported; the national
government of the United States thinks there should be a law against
expressing dissent by burning the flag but no law against expressing
right-wing sentiment by waving it; these are troubling times for those
who believe in satire and protest. But don't get me going on politics.

To those who never did enjoy my writings in this section of the
journal, rejoice, it is over. For me, this is the final curtain. I will not
keep re-surfacing to make yet one more farewell appearance, like
Garrison Keillor or the Rolling Stones. There will be no curtain
calls. I am out of the badinage business for good. I plan to devote a
few months to picking up all the books and papers that flew off my
shelves as if hurled by a poltergeist when the earthquake hit, and
then I will return to serious research. I promise. Farewell.

Appendix

Original publication details and acknowledgments

The following is a complete list of the TOPIC . . . COMMENT columns published from the foundation of *NLLT* to the end of 1989. The volume number, year, issue number, and original page numbers are given before the title; after it in parentheses is an indication of the chapter number in this book together with the original copyright details, the permission-to-reprint acknowledgment, and a note about any change of title. In the case of the columns that were not written by me, just the name of the author is given.

Volume 1, 1983
- 1.201–6: Watch out for the current (Chapter 2; © 1983 by D. Reidel Publishing Company; reprinted by permission)
- 2.311–15: Linguists and computers (Chapter 3; © 1983 by D. Reidel Publishing Company; reprinted by permission; here retitled 'The stranger in the bar')
- 3.435–40: The conduct of *Linguistic Inquiry* (Chapter 5; © 1983 by D. Reidel Publishing Company; reprinted by permission)
- 4.583–88: The revenge of the methodological moaners (Chapter 15; © 1983 by D. Reidel Publishing Company; reprinted by permission)

Volume 2, 1984
- 1.151–56: If it's Tuesday, this must be glossematics (Chapter 4; © 1984 by D. Reidel Publishing Company; reprinted by permission)
- 2.261–67: Stalking the perfect journal (Chapter 8; © 1984 by D. Reidel Publishing Company; reprinted by permission)
- 3.349–55: Chomsky on the *Enterprise* (Chapter 6; © 1984 by D. Reidel Publishing Company; reprinted by permission)
- 4.419–25: Punctuation and human freedom (Chapter 9; © 1984 by D. Reidel Publishing Company; reprinted by permission)

Volume 3, 1985

1.107–12: Memo from AVC re divisional placement of Linguistics Department. (Chapter 21; © 1985 by D. Reidel Publishing Company; reprinted by permission; here retitled 'A memo from the Vice Chancellor')

2.265–70: No trips to Stockholm (Chapter 20; © 1985 by D. Reidel Publishing Company; reprinted by permission)

3.371–77: The linguistics of defamation (Chapter 12; © 1985 by D. Reidel Publishing Company; reprinted by permission)

4.485–91: The wizards of Ling (Thomas Wasow)

Volume 4, 1986

1.121–26: On referring (Arnold M. Zwicky)

2.283–89: A guest of the State (Chapter 10; © 1986 by D. Reidel Publishing Company; reprinted by permission)

3.409–14: Footloose and context-free (Chapter 16; © 1986 by D. Reidel Publishing Company; reprinted by permission)

4.515–23: No nearer to the soul (David M. Perlmutter)

Volume 5, 1987

1.139–47: Trench-mouth comes to Trumpington Street (Chapter 13; © 1987 by D. Reidel Publishing Company; reprinted by permission)

2.303–9: Nobody goes around at LSA meetings offering odds (Chapter 17; © 1987 by D. Reidel Publishing Company; reprinted by permission)

3.453–59: Seven deadly sins in journal publishing (Chapter 11; © 1987 by D. Reidel Publishing Company; reprinted by permission)

4.603–9: Here come the linguistic fascists (Chapter 14; © 1987 by D. Reidel Publishing Company; reprinted by permission)

Volume 6, 1988

1.129–37: Advances in linguistic rhetoric (Paul M. Postal)

2.283–90: Some lists of things about books (Chapter 22; © 1988 by D. Reidel Publishing Company; reprinted by permission)

3.435–42: Why are they saying these things about us? (Ray S. Jackendoff)

4.579–88: Citation etiquette beyond Thunderdome (Chapter 18; © 1988 by D. Reidel Publishing Company; reprinted by permission)

Volume 7, 1989

1.137–43: Formal linguistics meets the Boojum (Chapter 7; © 1989 by Kluwer Academic Publishers; reprinted by permission)

2.275–81: The great Eskimo vocabulary hoax (Chapter 19; © 1989 by Kluwer Academic Publishers; reprinted by permission)

3.473–79: The incident of the node vortex problem (Chapter 23; © 1989 by Kluwer Academic Publishers; reprinted by permission)

4.605–10: The final curtain (Chapter 24; © 1989 by Kluwer Academic Publishers; reprinted by permission)

Index

1960s, 12, 23, 112, 116, 132, 156
1970s, 12–14, 34–6, 50–1, 100–1, 156
1980s, 9, 13–15, 47, 192
2001: A Space Odyssey (movie), 18

Abaza language, 178
abstractness, 10, 12–15
Academic Press publishers, 72–5, 109, 179
Academy Awards ceremony, 177ff
acceptance dates of journal articles, publication of, 34, 60, 86, 89
acoustic phonetics, 27, 187, 193
acquisition of language, 54, 85, 124
ad auctoritatem argumentation, 108
ad hominem argumentation, 44, 108
Adams, Alexander, 17
Adams, Cecil, 164
Adams, John Couch, 132
addresses of authors, publication of, 61, 86, 89
administration, 166–7, 182–9
Afrikaans language, 118
Agnew, Spiro T., 100–1, 106–9
Ahab, Captain, 178
Aissen, Judith, 215
Akmajian, Adrian, 1, 23–4, 28–9, 86, 213–4
Alabama (USA), 111
Alaska (USA), 168
Alhazred, Abdul, 210
Alien (movie), 162
Aliens (movie), 162

Allen, W. Sidney, 74, 178
Allen, W. Stannard, 74
Allerton, David, 82
allophone (origin of term), 160
alphabetical order, 63
American Anthropological Association (AAA), 162, 164
American Anthropologist (AA; journal), 160
American Indians, 176
American law, 94–9
American linguistics, 23
Amerindian languages, 176, 197
Amherst (Massachusetts), 23, 27, 100, 148
Amsterdam (Netherlands), 74, 140
Ancient Mariner, The (poem, by Samuel Taylor Coleridge), 33, 55
Anderson, James M., 74
Anderson, John M., 74
Anderson, Stephen R., 15, 76, 80
Anglo-Saxon people, 119
Animal Farm, 48
Annotated Snark, The (by Martin Gardner), 47
announcement of forthcoming journal articles, 63, 86, 88–9
anthropological linguistics, 53, 159–71
anthropology, 78, 160–1, 177, 185–6, 188
anti-intellectualism, 166, 171, 175
ape sign language, 161, 199
applied linguistics, 14, 16–17, 20–2, 29, 119

221

prizes for linguists, 131
pro, 73
PRO, 73, 81
prosodies, Firthian, 26
Proxmire, Senator William, 175–6
pseudocleft sentences, 35
psycholinguistics, 199
psychology, 36–7, 78, 165, 167, 177, 186, 189
publication lag times, 33–4
Puerto Rico, 117
Pullum, Geoffrey Keith, vii–x, 34, 45 n.1, 46 n.1, 133, 137, 151, 165
Punch (magazine), 193
punctuation, 67–75, 82, 89
pushdown storage automata, 43
Puzo, Mario, 210

Q'Kuti language, 199
Quang Phuc Dong (alias of James D. McCawley), 101 n.2
Quayle, J. Danforth ('Dan'), 115
Quebec (Canada), 114
Queensberry, Marquis of, 97
Quicoli, A. Carlos, 127–8
Quileute language, 197
Quine, Willard van Orman, 96

Rachmaninov, Sergei, ix
racism, 55, 76–7, 112, 116, 162
Rappaport, Malka, 156
rationalist philosophy of mind, 15, 79–80
Reading (Massachusetts), 72
Reagan, Ronald, 104, 107, 109
Received Pronunciation, of British English (RP), 76, 79
recursive enumerability (of languages), 51
recursiveness (of languages), 51
reduplication, phrasal, 43, 135–6
Reed, John Shelton, 159
refereeing, 31–7, 64–6, 84, 162
reference of noun phrases, 94, 96–7, 108–9
reflexives, 149–50, 152, 155
Reidel, D. (now Kluwer Academic; publishers), 88

Reighard, John, 75
relational grammar (RG), 9–10, 14, 148–56
relative clauses, 22
religion, x, 81
Republican Party (USA), 103
research assistants, 64 n.2, 86
Research Laboratory of Electronics (MIT), 187
revolutions, scientific, 10, 41
Richard III, King (play, by William Shakespeare), 67, 70
Riemsdijk, Henk van, 38, 40, 42, 135, 179
Ringen, Catherine, 67, 74
Ritchie, Robert W., 51
Robocop (movie), 17
robotics, 17
Rêgo, Eduardo, 139, 142–6
Rolling Stones, The, 2, 216
Romance languages, 184
Romance linguistics, 25
Romance Philology (journal), 88, 90–1
Rome (Italy), 71
Ronat, Mitsou, 39
Röntgen, Wilhelm, 176
Rosen, Carol, 155
Rosetta Stone, 171
Ross, John Robert 'Haj', 12, 193
Rostow, Walter W. and Eugene V., 107–8
Rourke, Colin, 139, 142–6
Royal Society, The, 39
Royko, Mike, viii
RP, *see* Received Pronunciation
Ruby, Jack, 104–5
rule ordering, 13–15
Rules and Representations (by Noam Chomsky), 51
Russian language, 85, 176
Rutgers University, 144
Ruwet, Nicolas, 150

Sabra (Lebanon), 93
Sachs, Ian Anthony, 201–8
Sadock, Jerry, 74–5
Safire, William, 68
Sag, Ivan A., 19, 34, 135, 196
Sagan, Carl, 198–9

Straight, Stephen, 75
Strategic Computing Initiative, 16
stratificational grammar, 180
strong equivalence, 43
structural representations, 49
Studies in Language (journal), 89,
    90–1
style sheets, 63, 67, 79, 85–6, 88–9
stylistics, 54
subject (in grammar), 73, 147–58
SUBJECT (in grammar), 73, 81
Subscript Convention, the, 202–7
such that clauses, 136
Sunday Times, The (London, England;
    newspaper), 107
survey-oriented teaching, 25
Sussex (England), 39
Swiss German language, 134–5, 140–2
Switzerland, 135–6
Syntactic Structures (by Noam
    Chomsky), 50, 55
syntactic theory, x, 12–14, 28, 85,
    201–8
Syntax and Semantics (book series), 75
System Development Corporation, 182
System Development Foundation, 21,
    182

tape recorders, 39
Tasmania, 178
Taylor, Elizabeth, 104, 109
Tbilisi (Georgia, USSR), 118
teaching, 23–9
Technology Review (magazine), 163
Teeter, Karl v., 179
Tennessee (USA), 111
tense, 197
TESOL (Teaching English to Speakers
    of Other Languages), 54
Tetons, Grand (mountains; Wyoming),
    67, 72
Texas (USA), 111
Thatcher, Margaret, the Right Honor-
    able, 25
theta-roles (= θ-roles), 55
Thompson, Hunter S., viii
Thompson language, 179

Thompson, Laurence Cassius, 179
Thompson, M. Terry, 179
Thompson, Sandra Annear, 179
Thurber, James, 4
Thurston, William P., 143
Tiersma, Peter Meijes, 93
Timbuktu (Mali), 135
Time (magazine), 93
time reference in languages, 197
*Times Higher Education Supplement,
    The* (magazine), 24–5
Times Roman (font), 165
Times, The (newspaper, London), 97
Tinbergen, Jan, 176
Tlingit language, 153
Tokyo (Japan), 39, 118
TOPIC . . . COMMENT column,
    vii–x, 1–5, 9, 23–4, 39, 47, 59, 64
    n.1, 72, 76, 78, 82–3, 111, 131,
    201, 209–19
TOPIC . . . COMMENT office, 77–8,
    85, 87
Tough Movement, 151
toxicology, 27, 138
Toyota, 72, 77, 123
Tranel, Bernard, 183
transformations, 44, 155
transitive verbs, 150–2
transparencies, overhead projector, 20,
    203–4
trenchmouth, 107, 110
trilateral string-length equivalence
    ($a^nb^nc^n$), 43
Trillin, Calvin, 4
Trommelen, Mieke, 140
Trudeau, Gary B., 59, 196
Trudeau, Pierre, 114
Trumpington Street (Cambridge, En-
    gland), 102
Tucson (Arizona), 24
Twain, Mark, 4
Twilight Zone, The (TV series), 84
type 2 rewriting systems, *see* context-
    free grammars
typesetting, 63
typographical errors, 3, 201
Tzotzil language, 176